PARADISE FOUND

PARADISE FOUND

by

ARTHUR R. CHARLESWORTH

PHILOSOPHICAL LIBRARY

NEW YORK

UXORI MEAE ....

J. H. C.

CONTENTS

PART III

THE AFFIRMATION OF ORTHODOXY

PART IV

THE LURE OF THE IDYLLIC

INTRODUCTION

Utopia means "nowhere." In the Greek the word is of three syllables. The first is "ou" which means "not." The second and third syllables are in the word "topos" which means "place."

From this literal definition, utopia moved into the imaginary. For a time the imaginary has a great content of myth. Under adverse political and social conditions, the imaginary moves beyond myth and becomes real. What begins as "nowhere" has a development toward the ideal commonwealth.

Perhaps this contrast is best seen in the *Utopia* of Sir Thomas More (1478-1535). Against the adverse and hostile political and religious circumstances of his time, More placed, in *Utopia*, favorable human developments. His selection included the conviction that

> No one could gain wealth at the expense of others.
> Everyone may worship as he chose.
> All men are equal.
> Property is the common possession of all.
> All must work equally hard.

For More, there was anarchy on the island where he lived, England; and in response to it he placed social and religious principles, very real to him. His *Utopia*, then, was no island but the great ideal that has inspired men through the ages.

From the title of More's book, we have drawn the adjective, "utopian." The adjective still carries the visionary and imaginary aspects of the improvement of society.

With Sir Thomas More there was an advance from the imaginary to the inspired. He moved from *Utopia* as a claim of a commonwealth to be, and made it a contrast, involving his life.

"More's Utopia begins with a satire on the chaos of sixteenth-century life in England and presents the *Utopia* itself as a contrast to it."[1]

So deep was the commitment of Sir Thomas More to the reality of his commonwealth, he resigned the position of Chancellor, under Henry the Eighth.

Holding to these convictions, More was committed by Henry VIII to The Tower of London, on the charge of treason. On July 6, 1535, Sir Thomas More was beheaded on Tower Hill.

Four hundred years later, July the sixth was made his festival day, when he was canonized by Pope Pius XI.

His fame continues not so much for his statesmanship, or even his martyrdom, but as the author of *Utopia*. From the myth of "nowhere," utopia became for Thomas More, a cause worthy of life dedication; July 6, 1935, is a testament to this.

There is universal appeal in a happy society, free from misery, anxiety, and cares. All the principles on which *Utopia* is structured may not stand. The principle of the perfect society remains. This principle tantalizes every generation for fulfilment.

To get beyond repeated disappointment and know hope fulfilled is real, in every age. This is the true meaning of Eden. There is in the heart of every man an Eden. The purpose of his life is to fill this Eden with his own structured principles. *This, John Milton did.*

Atlantis

The Atlantic Ocean secured its name, not from Mount Atlas, but in all probability from the fabled island, "Atlantis" described by Plato (428-348).

"And Poseidon, receiving for his lot the island of Atlantis, begat children by a mortal woman, and settled them in a part of the island, which I will describe."[2]

The description that follows in *Critias* is that of Paradise. Paradise was an island, with a plain at the very center,

"fairest of all plains and very fertile."[3]

Romance enters the account of this Paradise, by name Atlantis. Near the plain there was a mountain,

"not very high on any side"[4]

In the mountain lived one of the earth-born primeval men, by name, Evenor, whose wife was Leucippe. They had,

"an only daughter who was called Cleito."[5]

At the time of her parent's death, Cleito had reached womanhood. Poseidon fell in love with her. He surrounded the hill where she lived with zones of sea and land, alternating in such a way,

"So no man could get to the island, for ships and voyages were not as yet."[6]

Being a god, Poseidon made special appointments for comfort and living ease. He brought up,

"Two springs of water from beneath the earth, one of warm water and the other of cold, making every variety of food to spring up abundantly from the soil."[7]

He had children of Cleito,

"Five pairs of twin male children."[8]

He divided the island of Atlantis,

"Into ten portions, he gave to the first-born of the eldest pair his mother's dwelling and the surrounding allotment, which was the largest and best, and made him king over the rest; the others he made princes, and gave them rule over many men, and a large territory. And he named them all; the eldest, who was the first king, he named Atlas, and after him the whole island and the ocean were called Atlantic."[9]

The description of Atlantis continues with vast wealth, both in city and country. Atlantis contained animals tame and wild, fruits and flowers, a royal palace, a great canal, with harbour, with the holy temple,

"dedicated to Cleito and Poseidon."[10]

In this temple the ten kings did obeisance to Poseidon from whom they received the law, and the order of their precedence. When each king gave judgment, they

"put on most beautiful azure robes . . . . and wrote down their sentences on a golden tablet."[11]

Over the vast population the kings exercised their power to rule, with the people on 60,000 lots with 60,000 officers. While rules governed the people, the nature of Atlantis can readily be seen in the laws affecting the kings.

"They were not to take up arms against one another, and they were all to come to the rescue if any one in any of their cities attempted to overthrow the royal house. Like their ancestors, they were to deliberate in common about war and other matters, giving supremacy to the descendants of Atlas. And the king was not to have the power of life and death over any of his kinsmen unless he had the assent of the majority of the ten."[12]

The virtues of the people of Atlantis united "gentleness with wisdom."[13] They had little regard for the present state of life, but lived for virtue. They had self-control. They were sober, and ascertained that these excellent qualities increased, with the increase of the divine nature within them. In time,

"The divine portion began to fade away, and became diluted too often and too much with the mortal . . ."[14]

The Critias is an unfinished dialogue. In fact the dialogue breaks off in the middle of a sentence. The dialogue closes with reference to,

"the lost island of Atlantis."[15]

The demise came when the divine portion phased out to the mortal. In their mortality, at the very time when true happiness appeared glorious and blessed; they had lost the distinction between good and evil, between the divine and the human.

"To those who had no eye to see the true happiness they appeared glorious and blessed at the very time when they were full of avarice and unrighteous power."[16]

The god of gods, Zeus himself, saw that this

"honourable race was in a woeful plight."[17]

and placed them in the center of the world, and

"spake as follows"[18]

With this, the dialogue ends.

The dialogue ends with reference to

"the lost island of Atlantis"[19]

Tradition has it that the island was swallowed up by the sea.

New Atlantis

Lord Francis Bacon (1561-1626) who is considered second only to Shakespeare, as the most talented intellectual and literary artist in the Elizabethan Age of England, wrote prolifically. Among his noteworthy writings are, "Essays" (1597); "The Advancement of Learning" (1605); "Novum Organum" (1620) which affirms his philosophy, and "History of the Reign of Henry VII".

In the year of his death, 1626, he wrote the "New Atlantis," setting forth the principles of an ideal state, or Utopia.

Writing this "New Atlantis" at the very close of his life, in the year he died, may serve as the basis of a double observation. The *first*, already noted, is that in the heart of every man there is an Eden, an Atlantis, or as with Bacon, "New Atlantis."

The Atlantis, presumably swallowed up by the sea, brings to an end Atlantis, but does not bring to an end the happy, hopeful improvement of society toward Utopia, also called Paradise.

The *second*, is the dream of Paradise that does not get beyond the reach of man. In the year Sir Francis Bacon died the "New Atlantis" was born. It was a literary achievement that holds status with the other principal writings of Bacon. It was, lamentably, written at a time when Bacon could not add years to his life to assure that the dream of an ideal state did not elude man.

"Most utopia-writers follow either More (and Plato) in stressing the legal structure of their societies, or Bacon in stressing its technological power. The former type of utopia

xiv

is closer to actual social and political theory; the latter overlaps with what is now called science fiction. Naturally, since the Industrial Revolution a serious utopia can hardly avoid introducing technological themes. And because technology is progressive, getting to the utopia has tended increasingly to be a journey in time rather than space, a vision of the future . . ."[20]

Sir Francis Bacon had a "vision of the future," but he did not have length of life here to move it into practical reality. The "vision of the future" was the ideal state, set forth in the "New Atlantis." The death of Bacon brought an end to both his practical reality, and the "New Atlantis".

Paradise Found

John Milton avoided this pitfall, not because he knew the time of his death. It was because, as he wrote the epic of the English language, he wrote into it the structural principles of Paradise. Because Milton did so, the title of the epic of the English Language is a misnomer. Instead of "Paradise Lost" the correct title is "Paradise Found."

The purpose, then, of this writing is to furnish material to show that while, presumably, John Milton (1608-1674) was writing about "Paradise Lost," he was setting forth, for him, the basic principle of *Paradise Found.*

Furthermore, this writing provides material to demonstrate the traditional Eden was too small for the emancipated couple, known as Adam and Eve. The smallness of Eden did not in any way endanger the Paradise Found of Adam and Eve, as they left it. The larger Paradise to which, as Milton claims, they went also did not endanger the Utopia to which they were introduced, as they departed traditional Eden.

This is not a challenge to the integrity of John Milton, in the epic. There is *honesty* of mind and purpose throughout this writing. In fact, the honesty shows a mind at its best, and the determination not to stoop below his best. This enhances the stature of the epic, as well as of Milton.

There is *courage* in this writing of Milton. In it Milton holds a religious position, all his own. The fact that his religious position was separate from the orthodoxy of his day, does not diminish Milton. No one need endorse his religious position; however, once understood, all stand in admiration of his courage.

There is *involvement* with great events, and with themes of great literature, in this writing. Unlike Henry Thoreau (1817-1862) who wrote of the ideal state of life, as he lived apart from others at Walden Pond, near Concord, Massachusetts, Milton plunged into the vortex of life: social, political, literary, and religious.

There is nothing to be found of the life of the time in "Walden, or Life In The Woods,"[21] by Thoreau, other than the aesthetic woodsman in his own Eden, called by him, Walden. The central theme is of one who voluntarily makes a break with society in order to discover his true self. He felt he could do this best in solitude, and in kinship with nature.

"What makes him (Thoreau) relevant to a paper on utopias is the social criticism implied in his book. He sets out to show how little a man actually needs for the best life, . . ."[22]

In his "Walden . . .," Thoreau separates the essence from the non-essentials of life. For this separation Thoreau needed something more than a sabbatical from society, but a complete separation. Waldon Pond provided this, for him.

It was so very different with John Milton. There is so much to be found of the life and times of John Milton. David Masson wrote six volumes with the title, "The Life of John Milton Narrated in Connexion With The Political, Ecclesiastical, and Literary History of His Time."[23]

Socrates places his utopia in the agora, which is the market-place of Athens. This is where people congregate. While the utopia of Socrates, commonly known as *Plato's Republic*, opens in the house of Polemarchus; the material is of the city, and of people. In fact, the father of Polemarchus, Cephalus, said to Socrates,

"You do not come to see me, Socrates, as often as you ought: if I were still able to go and see you I would not ask you to come to me. But at my age I can hardly get to the city. . . ."[24]

The climax of the ten books of The Republic, comes in the ninth, where it is affirmed the Republic exists in the present, not in the future. It is not the imagination, or the imaginings of the mind, but the informing power of the mind.

"I understand; you mean that he will be a ruler in the city of which we are the founders, and which exists in idea only; for I do not believe that there is such an one anywhere on earth.
In heaven, I replied, there is laid up a pattern of such a city, and he who desires may behold this, and beholding, govern himself accordingly. But whether there really is or ever will be such an one is of no importance to him; for he will act according to the laws of that city and of no other."[25]

There is here creation, and joined with it as the fulfilment of purpose, consummation. The consummation is in *Paradise Found;* and for this we are in deep debt to John Milton.

What St. Augustine (354-430) set forth as a utopian metaphor, namely the *City of God,* is the ideal community where individuals, in selected fashion, go *at the end of time.* While much of the material in the Paradise of Dante comes from *The Summa Theologia* of Thomas Aquinas; Dante's treatment of utopia is more fictional than factual. It is dated by Scholasticism, and mediaevalism.

In Christianity, the conception of the Messianic kingdom, is of the very nature of utopia: past, present, and for all time to come. It is with this that Milton deals in *Paradise Found*; and deals significantly in his own Miltonic thought and style. This is of epic proportions, not only as literature but as thought itself. Perhaps Milton's thought went too far beyond the accepted configuration of his day.

ACKNOWLEDGMENTS

The author wishes to thank the following for use of material
from the cited works:

The Abingdon Press, New York, New York. Lewis, Edwin, *A
Christian Manifesto*, pp. 14, 15, 137, 154.

———, McConnell, Francis J. *John Wesley*, p. 205.

G. S. Appleton, Philadelphia, Pennsylvania. Brydges, Sir Egerton,
Paradise Lost By John Milton, p. xv.

G. Bell and Sons, London, England. Elton, Oliver, *The English
Muse*, p. 238.

A. L. Burt Company, New York, New York. Green, John Richard,
A Short History of the English People, p. 186.

Cambridge University Press, Cambridge, England. Tatham, G.
B., *The Puritans In Power*, p. 2.

The Century Company, New York, New York. Tieghem, Paul
Van, *Outline Of The Literary History of Europe Since The
Renaissance*, p. 79.

Chatto and Windus, London, England. Tillyard, E. M. W.,
Milton, pp. 90, 213, 237, 297, 323.

Columbia University Press, New York, New York. Milton,
John, *The Works Of John Milton*, Vol. I Part I, pp. 19, 21,
25, 60, 71, 211-213, 293. Vol. I Part II, pp. 339, 340, 350,
Vol. II Part I, pp. 8, 50, 51, 53, 80-89, 91, 100-102, 106,
114, 117, 121, 123-125, 129, 132, 133, 152, 155, 160, 161,
165, 167-168, 172-173, 179, 202-204, 209, 217-218, 230,
233-234, 243, 245-246, 248, 253, 257-258, 346-347. Vol. II
Part II, pp. 9, 217, 271-272, 280, 294-298, 308, 311-312,
332-335, 337-339, 341-347, 351, 356, 358, 363-364, 370-

371, 375-377, 381-383, 388-389, 390-401, 411, 477. Vol. III Part I, pp. 5, 79, 232, 235, 237, 239, 242, 300, 303-304. Vol. V, p. 25. Vol. VI, p. 120. Vol. VII, p, 551. Vol. VIII, pp. 61, 119, 121, 129. Vol. XII, p. 27. Vol. XIV, pp. 5-7, 16-17, 25, 403, 427. Vol. XV, pp. 2, 409. Vol. XVI, pp. 3, 381. Vol. XVII, pp. 2, 421. Vol. XVIII, p. 270.

F. S. Crofts, New York, New York. Hanford, James Holly, *A Milton Handbook*, pp. 106, 243.

Dodd, Mead, and Company, New York, New York. Saintsbury, George, *A History of English Criticism*, p. 91.

E. P. Dutton and Company, New York, New York. Augustine, *The Confessions Of . . .*, pp. 138, 144.

Gould and Lincoln, Boston, Massachusetts. Mansel, Henry L., *The Limits Of Religious Thought*, pp. 220, 221.

Harper and Brothers, New York, New York. Campbell, Douglas, *The Puritan In Holland, England and America*, Vol. II, p. 127.

————. Lewis, Edwin, *A Philosophy Of The Christian Revelation*, pp. 178, 287.

————. Pattison, Mark, *Milton*, pp. 13, 56, 57, 69, 103.

————. Schaff, Philip, *The Creeds Of Christendom*, Vol. II, p. 66.

Harvard University Press, Cambridge, Massachusetts. Thaler, Alwin, *Shakspere's Silences*, p. 210.

Henry Holt and Company, New York, New York. Larson, Laurence M., *History of England And The British Commonwealth*, p. 373.

Houghton Mifflin Company, New York, New York. Allen, Alexander, V. G., *The Continuity of Christian Thought*, pp. 1-438.

————. Manuel, Frank E., *Utopias and Utopian Thought*, pp. 27, 28, 47, 262, 264, 296-298, 308.

————. More, Paul Elmer, *Shelburne Essays*, pp. 239, 243.

Hurd and Houghton, New York, New York. Bacon, Sir Francis, *The Works Of . . .* p. 438.

J. B. Lippincott Company, Philadelphia, Pennsylvania. Belloc, Hilaire, *Milton*, pp. 16, 242, 260, 307.

Longman's Green and Company, London, England. Gardiner, Samuel R., *History of The Commonwealth and Protectorate,* Vol. II, 17.

Longman's Green and Company, New York, New York. Macaulay, Thomas B., *The Works Of . . .,* Vol. V, pp. 22, 23.

The Macmillan Company, New York, New York. Brunner, Emil, *The Mediator,* pp. 214, 273, 274, 281, 490, 491.

The Macmillan Company, London, England. Keats, John, *Letters,* p. 314.

The Macmillan Company, New York, New York. Legouis, Emile, *A History Of English Literature,* p. 280.

The Macmillan Company, London, England. Masson, David, *The Life Of John Milton,* Six Volumes: Vol. I, pp. 50-54, 341, 355-366, 395-407, 424. Vol. II, pp. 336-345, 506. Vol. III, Part One, pp. 300, 305, 718. Vol IV, p. 77. Vol. V, pp. 25, 581-587, 658-659. Vol. VI, pp. 664, 670, 682.

Thomas Nelson and Sons, New York, New York. Wolfe, Don M., *Milton In The Puritan Revolution,* pp. 242, 273.

Oxford University Press, Oxford, England. Highet, Gilbert, *The Classical Tradition,* p. 393.

Presbyterian Board Of Christian Education, Philadelphia, Pennsylvania. Calvin, John, *Institutes Of The Christian Religion,* Book One, and Book Two: Book I, Chapter XIII, Sections 1, and 5. Book I, Chapter XV, Sections, 2, and 3. Book II, Chapter I, Section 8.

Presbyterian Board Of Publication, Philadelphia, Pennsylvania. Hodge, Archibald A., *A Commentary On The Confession of Faith,* pp. 70, 83, 147-161, 190, 515.

Princeton University Press, Princeton, New Jersey. Elliott, G. R., *The Cycle Of Modern Poetry,* p. 182.

Random House, New York, New York. Plato, *The Dialogues Of . . .* (Two Volumes), *The Critias,* Paragraphs 114-121. *The Republic,* Book I, Paragraph 328, and Book IX, Paragraph 592.

Charles Scribner's Sons, New York, New York. Fisher, George P., *The Reformation,* p. 460.

————. Fisher, George P., *History Of Christian Doctrine*, p. 366. Student Christian Movement Press, London, England. Mackintosh, H. R., *The Christian Apprehension Of God*, pp. 204, 205. John C. Winston Company, Philadelphia, Pennsylvania., *The Holy Bible* (King James Version), Genesis 2: 7; 3: 15. Isaiah 45: 6, 7. Matthew 10: 28; 20: 26, 27; 25: 34, 41; Mark 4: 8; John 6:56. John 14: 10; 17: 21; Romans 7: 19-24; 12: 33; Philippians 2: 5, 6; I John 3: 8.

DR. ARTHUR R. CHARLESWORTH

PART I

MILTON THE WRITER

CHAPTER ONE

MILTON'S PERIOD

POLITICAL AND RELIGIOUS

The involvement of John Milton poetically is a study all its own. His involvement polemically is a study also all its own. However, the poetical and the polemical are inseparable.

Milton's power of writing poetry, developed early in life, was applied to the political and religious life of his day. It was Milton's ability to put words together effectively and persuasively, in both the poetical and polemical, that made him the commanding literary leader of his day.

The writings of Milton, poetical, political, and religious all combined as preparation for the great epic of the English language. A study of these writings makes it evident that a Biblical theme increasingly commands the mind of Milton.

This surrender to the Bible as the theme of his central writing, the epic, is evident in his increasing passion for liberty. Milton brought this deep concern for liberty to bear upon the life of his time, in personal, national, and religious aspects. In the *personal* realm, it is expressed in his writings on divorce. In the *national* realm, it is expressed in the twenty years devoted to political freedom of his beloved England. In the *religious* realm, it is expressed in the comprehensive theological treatise, *De Doctrina Christiana*. These three areas are explored in that spirit of complete independence which had come to be characteristic of Milton.

In the treatise, *De Doctrina Christiana,* there are boldly stated affirmations which carry the full force of his independent mind.

1

The same affirmations, boldly and independently stated in the treatise, are artfully concealed in the epic, *"Paradise Lost."* These bold and radical affirmations are not there in incidental fashion. They are structural to Milton's theology. What makes it the more significant is the fact that the two writings — the treatise and the epic — were in process at the same time, but that *the treatise was never published during Milton's lifetime.* He was clearly aware of its implications. He did arrange for its posthumous publication, but it was not until 1823 that it actually appeared.

*Life of Milton**

The life of John Milton is interwoven with the development of personal, political, and religious events of his day. Apart from these events, one cannot see the emerging literary, political, and religious development of Milton.

The year of Milton's birth, 1608, was the same year in which the Puritan congregation of Scrooby in Nottinghamshire left England for Holland to sail thence, twelve years later, to New England, in America.

The reason for their migration was the religious oppression brought upon them by James I. The feeling for religious toleration in England had become crystallized into action. These Puritans were a group of men and women who stood for a serious thoughtfulness in religion and for strict purity in church life. They gave themselves to a complete reformation in religion.

"Primarily the Puritans stood for purity in church life . . . Their demand was for a complete reformation, for the abolition, in matters of religious worship and ecclesiastical government, of all that had been superimposed upon primitive forms."[26]

When James I came to the throne of England, the Puritans hoped to find in him an advocate for their position. Even

(*) See Bibliography: Masson, David for an outline of Milton's life.

though his mother espoused the Catholic faith, they had reason to believe that the King's training in Presbyterianism would align him with the Puritan cause. The King, they soon learned, did not favor the republican government of the Scottish church. Such a government did not suit his ideas of monarchy.[27] The manner in which the King handled the first problem of his reign filled the Puritans with dismay.

A few hundred Anglican priests requested major changes in the Prayer Book as well as modifications in the service away from the priestly form of worship. To bring about these changes would be a victory for the Puritans.

King James called together some of the high divines to meet with these advocates of Puritanism, at Hampton Court. The King presided at this assembly, and took an unequivocal position with the Anglicans, that without Bishops there could be no Church. This was a major defeat for the Puritans. This policy of absolutism in Church and State directed itself against Parliament and occasioned the Parliamentary conflict throughout the entire reign of James I.

The distance between the King and Parliament was further widened in the King's foreign policy. In 1619 the Bohemian nobility called to their throne Frederick, the son-in-law of the King of England. Frederick was the leader of a Protestant German Union, organized against an expected war with the Catholic states in the Empire.

The sympathy of the people of England with Frederick placed James I in an awkward position. Frederick had accepted the throne after King Ferdinand had been dethroned. Even though Frederick was the son-in-law of England's King, James I could not endorse such an outrage against his conviction of the divine right of kings. The English people endorsed Frederick's defense of Protestantism. When Parliament met in 1621, Frederick had been overwhelmed in the battle of White Mountain. Parliament favored English support against the enemies of German Protestantism, and was eager to take up the war along with Frederick. The King relied upon negotiations. Frederick failed and ended his career as King.

The estrangement between King and Parliament was increased when the King attempted to join his son in marriage to a princess of Spain. The princess was a Catholic, and the English people could not look with favor upon a future Catholic queen. Parliament requested the King to find a Protestant bride for his son. This infuriated the King who thereupon lectured Parliament for an interference in foreign affairs concerning a subject that had not been referred to them. The "Great Protestation" was drawn up, stating the right of Parliament to consider and discuss any matter involving the welfare of the State. James sent for the journal and tore from its pages the "Great Protestation". James dismissed Parliament, and the breech became complete. All through the reign of King James, Puritanism grew as the political force, in opposition to his autocratic policy in both Church and State.

With the death of the King and the ascent to the throne of his son, Charles I (1625), every effort was made by the new King to change the limited monarchy into an absolute one. Although a Protestant in position, the King followed a lenient policy toward the Catholic influence within the Anglican church.[28]

This policy, along with his attempt to govern England as if there were no Parliament at all, finally issued in organized opposition within Parliament. The leadership of this opposition was directed by John Pym, John Eliot, John Selden, Thomas Wentworth, and Oliver Cromwell.

In 1633 Laud became Archbishop of Canterbury.[29] He joined with the political tyranny of the country in his efforts to persecute the Puritans and to prevent the preaching of Calvinism. He attempted to enforce uniformity in the worship and law of the Church. Through the Star-Chamber, Laud controlled the propaganda of the Puritan cause. All this repression only increased the growing enmity and power of the Puritans against both the Church and the State.

The attempt to unify the form of worship in Scotland by means of the English Prayer Book proved disastrous to England. In Scotland there was a solid front of religious conviction in Presbyterian Calvinism. The people there determined to resist these plans of Laud and Charles. They refused any modification in the government and law of the Church apart from the General Assembly of the Scottish Church. The King agreed to such an assembly, but the outcome disfavored Laud, the King, and England itself. The result was the Solemn League and Covenant of the Scots for the defense of Presbyterianism. Against this solid Scottish front Charles brought an English army of some 10,000 men in what is called the First Bishop's War (1638). No battle followed, but a treaty was signed in which Charles agreed to the settlement of the affairs of the northern kingdom by means of Parliament and Assembly.

In 1640 The Second Bishop's War issued in the treaty of Ripon in which the Scots made secure their position. The total result of this Scottish opposition and of the rising tide of rebellion against the crown of England, marked the close of absolute monarchy for the Stuarts. Charles found himself at the head of a kingdom bankrupt financially, and confronted on all sides by opposition. There was one and only one thing to do and that was to open the way for a new Parliament.

This became famous as the well-known Long Parliament. Chief among the many reforms instituted by the Long Parliament was the block of strength in the republican form of government, made possible by some new legislation. This legislation provided that Parliament could not be adjourned without its consent, and that Parliament must meet every three years. This restricted both the position and power of the King, and prevented the return of a personal monarchy.

"The effort of Charles I and the Stuart partisans to establish a form of absolute monarchy in England and the English dominions beyond the seas ultimately failed. It is not to be forgotten that this effort was not an isolated instance of royal ambition along absolutistic lines; it was part of a great movement in that direction which covered the entire continent. When the seventeenth century closed, absolutism had conquered in nearly all the more important states in Europe, the notable exceptions being the Dutch republic and the British kingdom. The failure of the Stuart experiment in Great Britain, is, therefore, a matter of European importance."[30]

In 1642 Charles went to the House of Commons with several hundred armed partisans to arrest John Pym and his Puritan associates. He had received information that they had invited the invasion of England by Scotland, in the interest of religious liberty. The attempted arrest failed.[31]

In the eyes of Parliament Charles had not only disregarded the privileges of Parliament, but this was the climax of a series of events that broadened the rift between Parliament and the King. Civil War followed, between the King and his follow ers, and the Parliamentarians. Oliver Cromwell commanded the forces of the Parliamentarians, and brought them to success.

Along with Cromwell, John Milton's interest in liberty was more religious than political. In January 1643 Parliament abolished the episcopacy. In July of the same year Parliament called the Assembly to meet in Westminster to formulate a creed as well as a government of the Church. This Assembly presented to Parliament a *Directory of Worship* which was substituted for the *Prayer Book,* in 1645. The next year Parliament adopted the Presbyterian form of government as recommended by the Westminster Assembly, but the rigid Presbyterianism was as distasteful to the army as the previous rule of Bishops. This prevented the complete establishment of Presbyterianism in England.[32] For a time Milton joined his efforts with the Presbyterians, but came to the conclusion: "New Presbyter is but old Priest writ large."[33]

Many held this same conviction about Presbyterianism. They organized into a party known as the Independents, of whom

Cromwell was leader. Milton joined his efforts for religious liberty with the Independents. In opposition to the King there were essentially two religious factions, the Presbyterians and the Independents. The Presbyterians sought to attain their system of government through Parliament. The Independents were bent upon achieving full religious toleration under Cromwell, by war if necessary. The King stirred up a Scottish invasion. This embittered Cromwell who stationed Colonel Thomas Pride at the House of Commons, preventing the entrance of 143 members favorable to the King. This took place December 6, 1648, and is known as Pride's Purge. The Independents now were in control of Parliament. This Rump Parliament, so called because it was the "sitting part" of Parliament, came under the full control of the army. The King was declared a traitor, and was executed January 30, 1649.

Milton, The Pamphleteer of England

As the pamphleteer of England, Milton approved the execution of the King in, *The Tenure of Kings and Magistrates.* This position placed Milton foremost in the radicalism of his day.[34] It resulted in his appointment as Secretary for Foreign Tongues to Council of State.

Cromwell, eager to form a new Parliament, suggested that new elections be held. The members of Parliament refused, and with this the soldiers of Cromwell drove the members of Parliament from the House. This was the end of the Long Parliament.

Cromwell and a provisional Council of State secured the election of a new Parliament. This was virtually a Parliament appointed by Cromwell. Five months after its organization this Parliament was dissolved, in December 1653. Cromwell and the army were once again in sole authority. Cromwell received from General John Lambert a written constitution, the "Instrument of Government", recommending a single Commonwealth of England, Scotland, and Ireland.

7

This document placed the sovereign power in a House of Commons, along with the President of the Commonwealth, called the Protector. Cromwell accepted this, and held the position of Protector for the rest of his life. In January 1655, Cromwell dissolved Parliament and was in complete authority with the army, until 1657 when a new Parliament was created. This Parliament formulated a new constitution strikingly similar to the traditional government of England. There was an upper house as well as a House of Commons, and a Council of State with a Protector who had the privilege to select his successor.

The first constitution was amended by the "Humble Petition and Advice." This new government allowed freedom of worship to the Puritans, but not the Anglicans and Catholics. Within the English Church, Cromwell set up a "Board of Triers" to examine candidates. This board was composed mainly of Independent ministers who saw that candidates for the ministry were of the Puritan type. With all this power in both secular and religious affairs the Protector lost the strength of his position. The royalists considered him a novel expedient in a sham commonwealth. Those of the Commonwealth looked upon him as one who had sacrificed the principles of Puritanism for the monarchy. On February 4, 1658 Cromwell dismissed Parliament, and a few months later died. With his death the Puritan Revolution came to an end. For Milton the fall of the Commonwealth was itself the defeat of Christianity.[35]

The total outcome of the English Reformation, though religious in origin and impetus, proceeded along political and social lines.[36] The outstanding contribution of Milton to the political life of England was his Christian concept of government. Milton implicitly believed in a Commonwealth in which the right of franchise belonged only to those of a life of discipline, the result of one's free will choosing good and not evil. Theocrat that he was, Milton exemplified Puritanism in his conviction that only the spiritually superior should hold positions of leadership in the Commonwealth. He interpreted the precept of Christ in the Scripture passage, ". . . he that is greatest among you let him be as the younger, and he that is chief, as he that serveth."[37]

"And what government coms nearer to this precept of Christ than a free Commonwealth; wherin they who are greatest, are perpetual servants and drudges to the public at thir own cost and charges, neglect thir own affairs; yet are not elevated above thir brethren; live soberly in thir families, walk the streets as other men, may be spoken to freely, familiarly, friendly, without adoration."[38]

This political philosophy of Milton was of large influence in the next century, in the departure from kingship in America, and in the abolition of kingly eminence throughout Europe.[39]

After the death of Milton, Puritanism accomplished in the Revolution of 1688 what it failed to accomplish previously.

"In the Revolution of 1688 Puritanism did the work of civil liberty which it had failed to do in that of 1642. It wrought out through Wesley and the revival of the eighteenth century the work of religious reform which its earlier efforts had thrown back for a hundred years. Slowly but steadily it introduced its own seriousness and purity into English society, English literature, English politics. The whole history of English progress since the Restoration, on its moral and spiritual sides, has been the history of Puritanism."[40]

The life of John Wesley (1703-1791), mentioned in the quote above, embraces almost the whole of the eighteenth century. It follows the century dominated by John Milton, the seventeenth. However, Milton and Wesley belong together in more than this sequence of one century following another.

Both Milton and Wesley were men of discipline, and even asceticism. Some of the asceticism, if it can rightly be called

9

such, of Milton was imposed from without. Blindness, financial bankruptcy, domestic rupture, failure in the cause of the commonwealth, were not chosen experiences for Milton. There was, however, about Milton an inner austerity of discipline that was academic.

John Wesley viewed the Christian life as disciplined by the ordinary lot of people in that day: with little of this world's goods. If not the main, this was one of the motivating forces in Wesley's drive toward perfection.

Puritanism had common cause in the academic discipline of John Milton and in the stride toward perfection of John Wesley. The Puritan ideal is a part of the background from which came into being, *Paradise Found*.[41] *Paradise Found* moves from the Puritan ideal to the consummation of the ideal in the real. For Milton this achievement is by academic discipline. What saves Paradise from being lost and makes it found, is for Milton, the full flowering of this academic discipline. This enlightenment moves the reading and interpretation of the epic from the simple and superficial acceptance of what appears to be, on to what constitutes Milton's basic affirmations of *Paradise Found*. An essential part of this motion is Milton's writing in the cause of the commonwealth, and the literary accomplishments in multiple fields, especially the theological. We shall first consider the literary. We affirm here that John Milton was a man of the Enlightenment, in advance of his day, before the Age of Enlightenment in the eighteenth century.

CHAPTER TWO

THE LITERARY

Milton followed the illustrious Elizabethan period in English
literature. Edmund Spenser (1552-1599) had proved himself
a master with the English language in the unfinished epic, *The
Fairie Queene* (1589-1596).

"Although we cannot turn to the *Fairie Queen* any more
than to *Paradise Lost* to study the life of the time, we find
in each something of its spirit. Spenser and Milton were
both Puritans, but standing three-quarters of a century apart.
Each represented what Puritanism might have become under national conditions favorable for its development. Each
was a scholar; but the one had studied only the classics,
the other had added the Bible, theology, and politics. In
one of his earlier poems, the *Shepherd's Calendar,* published in 1579, when he was at Penshurst with Philip Sid-
ney, Spenser had come out on the side of the Reformers.
As his model for a Christian pastor he had taken Archbishop Grindal, then suspended from office for his lax en-
forcement of the Church's discipline, and he had boldly attacked the vices of the higher clergy. In the *Fairie Queene*
he struck the key-note of the broad Puritanism of the
future, which made duty the chief concern of life."[42]

William Shakespeare (1564-1616) was the foremost dramatist
as well as the unexcelled poet of his day. He had the power
to delineate individual character in such a way that the words
not only brought to life the individual, but awakened all humanity to the new character portrayed. He had the incredible power

11

to focus attention from one moving scene to the next until the action was completed. His sonnets declare him the master of the English language.

"His dramatic gift alone would have secured his immediate popularity, but would hardly have ensured his glory. The first dramatist was also the first poet of his day and one of the first of all time. The poet is not only revealed by the hundred exquisite songs with which the plays are strewn. The ardent passion for beauty which is the distinction of the sonnets, and causes the best of them to reach the high-water mark of beauty in English poetry, attains in the plays to results as fine . . .[43]

Ben Jonson (1573-1637) was a contemporary of Shakespeare. He had a moral earnestness about the Elizabethan stage. Shakespeare accepted the stage of his time, recognizing its imperfection and limitations. Jonson directed his combative spirit against the tendencies of the popular taste. He berated romanticism. He admonished against the liberty in Elizabethan writing, urging reality and literalness. He criticized the use of variety just for the sake of difference.

"Ben's theory (if not entirely his practice, especially his exquisite lyrics and almost equally exquisite masques) constrained him to be severe to those contemporaries, from Spenser, Shakespeare, and Donne downwards. The mission of the generation may be summed up in three words, Liberty, Variety, Romance. Jonson's tastes were for Order, Uniformity, Classicism."[44]

In comedy, tragedy, and poem Jonson advocated a unity in time, and action. There was a logic about his construction combined with truism in local color. He was a satirist in his own right. Even though Milton followed such great men of letters as

12

these, a native power and independence characterized his literary genius.

"The style, the picturesqueness of language, the character of the imagery, which Milton adopted from the first, was peculiar to himself. I do not say that many of the words, and even images, might not be found scattered in preceding poets, as Spenser, Shakespeare, Ben Jonson, Beaumont and Fletcher, and Joshua Sylvester's DuBartas; but they could not be found combined into a uniform and unbroken texture, nor with the same uniformity of elevated and spiritual thought. In almost all preceding poets they are patches. That Milton was minutely familiar with the poems of all his celebrated predecessors is sufficiently evident: but so far as he used them, he only used them as ingredient particles. Spenser is rich and Picturesque, but Milton has a character distinct from him. Milton's texture is more massy: the gold is weightier: he has a haughtier solemnity."[45]

Milton did not hold the narrow attitude toward the stage the Puritan did.

". . . the corrupting influences of the theatre ought to be eliminated . . . it is not necessary to abolish altogether the performance of plays. This on the contrary would be quite senseless; for what in the whole philosophy is more impressive, purer, or more uplifting than a noble tragedy, what more helpful to a survey at a single glance of the hazards and changes of human life?"[46]

Milton's works renewed not only individual reading and attention, but were the source of both dramatic and musical entertainments. *Comus, Arcades,* and *Paradise Lost* we expect to be presented on the stage. It is a matter of surprise to learn that *L'Allegro, Il Penseroso, On The Morning Of Christ's Nativity, Samson Agonistes,* and even the epigram, *On Shakespear,*

13

received dramatic production. Milton did not write these with the specific intention that they be given dramatic presentation.[47] He did have the didactic intention of writing a true poem for the improvement of youth, as well as the evils of the time.

"And what a benefit this would be to our youth and gentry, may be soon guest by what we know of the corruption and bane which they suck in dayly from the writings and interludes of libidinous and ignorant Poetasters, who having scars ever heard of that which is the main consistence of a true poem, the choys of such persons as they ought to introduce, and what is moral and decent to each one, doe for the most part lap up vitious principles in sweet pils to be swallow'd down, and make the tast of vertuous documents harsh and sowr."[48]

Milton did not give himself to any practical plan for the improvement of the theatre. He did set forth such principles of beauty and purity in his poems and in the epic that would refine and elevate the desires of the audience. Milton, therefore, did not write down to an audience, but called his auditors up to the beauty and purity of his stately poetic passion. At one and the same time this was the Puritan in Milton, and the Milton who in his classic achievement *went beyond Puritanism.* Though he enjoyed the theatre he had a revulsion against any personal contact with the stage.

". . . when in the Colleges so many young Divines . . . have bin seene so oft upon the Stage writhing and unboning their Clergie limmes to all antick and dishonest gestures of Trinculo's Buffone, and Bawds; prostituting the shame of that ministry which either they had, or were nigh having, to the eyes of Courtiers and Court-Ladies, with their Groomes and Madmoisellaes. There while they acted, and overacted, among other young scholars, I was a spectator;

14

they thought themselves gallant men, and I thought them fools."[49]

We can honestly say that Milton had a constructive attitude toward the theatre. He did not condemn the theatre for the nature of the productions but elevated the character of the productions in the works he himself produced.

CHAPTER THREE

THE BIBLICAL THEME

The translations of the Bible of this period, coming to their climax in the King James version three years after the birth of Milton, comprise the basis and subject matter of literary effort.[50] The reading of the Bible by the masses not only produced social and religious impulses throughout England, but had a definite influence upon the literature and style of the English language. It is important to note the flowering of the Elizabethan age in literature followed the wide circulation and extensive assimilation the Bible received by the masses. Whereas the new learning, held by the few, occasioned the translation of the Bible, the circulation of the Bible occasioned the increase in learning and the enthusiam for reform among the people. This enthusiasm for reform overflowed in the religious and political events of the sixteenth century, and came to its climax in the Puritan Revolution of the seventeenth.

The reformers within the Church were essentially men of action, and not men of literary excellence.[51] They gave an impetus to literature in the dominant place the English Bible held in their efforts, and on the tongues of the people. Such men as Spenser, Shakespeare, Jonson, Fletcher, Sylvester fashioned the literature of the day into an easy flow and elegant grace of language. Especially was this the case in Spenser's *Fairie Queene,* and Shakespeare's dramatic productions. Chief among these literary men was John Milton, who found in the English Bible the setting as well as the inspirational source for the great epic of the English language, *Paradise Lost.*

The Humanism of John Milton

Humanism is reflected dominantly in the literature of the English Renaissance. This is seen in the works of Colet, More, Erasmus, and especially in John Milton. They were essentially Platonists, for they reasoned from God manward. This Platonism travelled northward to England from Italy, in Colet and Erasmus. During the sixteenth century it found lodgement in England. In the next century it came to expression in a learned Puritanism in the Cambridge Platonists. Under the severity of Puritan life, Platonism gave a reasoned interpretation for exalted virtue and piety. Platonism gave as well an idealistic cast to poetic efforts, as seen in *The Fairie Queene.* This stands in marked contrast to the rejection of the principles of knowledge already attained, and the devotion to a scientific analysis of things to which Francis Bacon gave himself. Bacon placed men under the sovereignty of nature. Beyond this position of subservience to nature man could not go, either by his powers of interpretation or his knowledge.

"Man, being the servant and interpreter of Nature, can do and understand so much and so much only as he has observed in fact or in thought of the course of nature: beyond this he neither knows anything nor can do anything.

. . . .

Human knowledge and human power meet in one: for where the cause is not known the effect cannot be produced. Nature to be commanded must be obeyed."[52]

On the one hand you find in England the growing conviction of the sovereignty of God in Calvinistic Puritanism. In contrast one finds the sovereignty of man burying its true essence beneath the scientific and methodical search of Francis Bacon, for material progress. No greater contrast could be made than that between Bacon and Milton. As Bacon gave himself to a scientific analysis of things in pursuit of knowledge, Milton's study took him back into the Greek beginnings of Classical thought. Both Milton and Bacon began on the same expansive theme of investigation. Their destinations were radically different. Milton was for the classical and religious. He combined them both in a pattern of interpretation for life. Bacon proceeded along a scientific materialism. The outcome was that Bacon did not rise above the human. Milton raised the human in a sense of Puritan responsibility to God that is personal. He began with God, and by his majesty of thought drew others before "Jehovah's aweful throne." In the combined majesty of thought and religious discipline, Milton belongs to the great literary tradition with Dante, and *The Divine Comedy.*

In theology Milton moved from Anglicanism to Presbyterianism, and then to the Independents. He belonged to the Independents as one of his own class and creed. Milton followed this course as he advocated freedom of an ever wider sort. His position of individualism lay in his classical humanism, namely, that *freedom resided in man's disciplined reason in control.* This is applied in *Paradise Found.*

Classic humanist that he was, Milton brought to the interpretation of the Bible his literary genius as well as a disciplined mind. The result was the great Christian epic. The religious epic had many examples in previous literary productions. Those who believe Milton borrowed from other works have not measured the lofty and noble poetic stature of the man. They do not know his genius for creative art, or his mastery of a lofty and majestic style.

"The source hunters have spent immense pains . . . to show that Milton imitated, borrowed from, or, in this way and that, followed, the *Adamo* of the Italian dramatist Giambattista Andreim (1613), the *Lucifer* also a drama, of the Dutch poet Vondel (1654), the *Adamus Exul* of Grotius (1601) and even Caedmon, whose Genesis was published

18

by Milton's friend Junius, in 1655. . . . Supposing Milton to have read all these books, *Paradise Lost* remains Milton's; and it is perfectly certain, not merely that nobody else could have constructed it out of them, but that a syndicate composed of their authors, each in his happiest vein and working together as never collaborators worked, could not have come within measurable distance of it, or of him."[53]

John Milton was the first to combine a Biblical theme with the stately proportions of the epic. Dante had used a religious theme and employed the mediaeval theology of Aquinas in the *Divine Comedy.* Coming four centuries later, Milton inherited both the Reformation principle of individual thought and judgment. He put the two virtues together in the unexcelled epic of the English language, *Paradise Lost.*

With the Reformation principle of the sixteenth century, of individual thought and judgment in religion, Milton moved beyond his own seventeenth century, and became the first great interpreter of the eighteenth century Enlightenment. This emancipation from the interpretative principles of his own century is important for an understanding of the epic.

One cannot read *Paradise Lost* with *De Doctrina Christiana* at hand, without the insight that John Milton was not writing *Paradise Lost,* but *Paradise Found.* The Milton who was writing the epic, we will see, was not so interested in either what Adam and Eve had *lost.* He was interested in what Adam and Eve, and all humanity had *found.* Humanist that he was, Milton was interested in a freedom larger than the configuration of traditional Eden. The independent stature and strategic importance of Milton's mind is in *Paradise Found.*

That the epic of the English language does not emphasize what man has lost; but, agreeing with Milton, what man has found, may be revolutionary to both Protestantism and Catholicism alike.

19

CHAPTER FOUR

MILTON'S POLEMICAL PROSE

Interlaced with the events of Milton's personal life are national events so radical, they develop and constantly stimulate his thinking, beyond his own age and time. It was this quality of Milton's mind to bring to events of his day an interpretation, considered radical, that engages our attention now, in Milton's Polemical Prose.

John Milton was born of prosperous parentage, in London, on the ninth of December, 1608. His father was a scrivener. His ancestors had been farmers, one of whom, his grandfather, Richard, was a yeoman. By that is meant he held land under his own name and would be considered prosperous. Richard's son, the father of the poet, was John Milton Sr., who came to London about the year 1585. His departure from home and journey to London was due to the fact that his father had closed the family door upon him because he became a Protestant. The poet's father was a man of considerable culture with a special devotion to music.[54] He was more than generous with the educational opportunities he made available for his son whom he was eager to see enter the Church. John Milton the future poet, responded with enthusiasm to the education offered him, but he never entered the Church.

Milton entered Christ's College, Cambridge, April 9, 1625, where he pursued his studies until he received the Master of Arts degree in 1632. The time of his departure from Cambridge was an ominous one within the life of State and Church. Rather than take up a formal life of service within the Church with its restrictions upon freedom of thought and preaching, Milton preferred the retirement of his father's house at Horton in Buckinghamshire, and the opportunity for study and the further exercise of his powers within the literary field. Of this period in his life, Milton wrote:

"At my father's country house. . . I gave myself up entirely to reading Greek and Latin writers; exchanging, however, sometimes, the country for the town, either for the purchase of books, or to learn something new in mathematics, or in music, which at that time furnished sources of my amusement."[55]

This is not to suggest that Milton prior to this time had failed to apply himself diligently to the opportunities afforded him. Rather was it the case that Milton had given himself to diligent and lengthy hours of study from his boyhood onward; and it was possibly due to this early strain upon his eyes that blindness came at the age of forty-two.[56]

During the Horton period, Milton applied himself to the attainment of scholarship within the general field of learning. In a letter to his Protestant Italian friend, Charles Diodati, London, September 23, 1637, we have a picture of Milton's eager scholastic pursuits, and of his passion to write in such a way that his name will have immortality.

"Hearken, Theodotus, but let it be in your private ear, lest I blush; and allow me for a little to use big language with you. You ask what I am thinking of? So may the good Deity help me, of immortality. And what am I doing? Growing wings and meditating flight; but as yet our Pegasus raises himself on very tender pinions. . . . I will now tell you seriously what I am thinking of. I am thinking of migrating into some Inn of the Lawyers where I can find a pleasant and shady walking-ground, because there I shall have both a more convenient habitation among a number of companions if I wish to remain at home, and more suitable headquarters if I choose excursions in any directions.

. . You shall also have information respecting my studies. I have by continuous reading brought down the affairs of the Greeks as far as to the time when they ceased to be Greeks. I have been long engaged in the obscure business of the state of Italians under the Longobards, the Franks and the Germans, down to the time when liberty was granted them by Rodolph, King of Germany: from that period it will be better to read separately what each City did by its own wars. . . . Meanwhile, if it can be done without trouble to you, I get you to send me Justiniani, the historian of the Venetians."[57]

In 1638 Milton began a journey to Italy which took him through Paris, Nice, Genoa, Pisa, and Florence, where he tarried for a period of about two months. Here he met persons of distinction, especially men of letters and learning, among them Galileo. Milton then went on to Rome, where he remained two months. He contemplated an extended journey through Sicily and Greece, when the patriotic zeal for his native country, and the out-break of the Civil War brought him back to England. Upon his arrival in London, he became involved in a succession of events which mark the beginning of a new period in his life.

Milton found growing upon him the ambition to write something that would have within it the quality of endurance. The series of events which followed his arrival in England would have postponed the application of the mind of an ordinary man to such a subject, but not so Milton. Upon his arrival in England, he received news that Charles Diodati had died. He was soon occupied with the management of the Horton household, which was finally broken up by the death of his mother. Milton took residence in London. Here he wrote:

". . . in the privat Academies of Italy, whither I was favor'd to resort, perceiving that some trifles which I had in memory, compos'd at under twenty or thereabout (for the manner is that every one must give some proof of his wit and reading there) met with acceptance above what was lookt for, and other things which I had shifted in scarsity of books and conveniences to patch up amongst them, were receiv'd with written Encomiums, which the Italian is not forward to bestow on men of this side the Alps, I began thus farre to assent both to them and divers of my friends here at home, and not lesse to an inward prompting which now grew daily upon me, that by labour and intent study (which I take to be my portion in this life) joyn'd with the strong propensity of nature, I might perhaps leave something so written to aftertimes, as they should not willingly let it die."[58]

While in London, Milton assumed the responsibility of the education of his nephews, John and Edward Phillips. He found he had a natural enthusiasm for tutoring and soon added other pupils, some of his friends.

In the summer of 1643 Milton suddenly married. His hasty choice of a life-mate brought him no end of sadness. He had left London for a journey into the country, going to the house of Richard Powell of Forest Hill, Oxford County. Mr. Powell had been debtor for some time to Milton's father. The obligations of the debt out-ran the ability of the estate to pay. The eye of Milton fell upon Mary, the eldest daughter of Richard Powell. When he left the Powell household, he took Mary as his wife. Along with them went a whole retinue of the bride's relations to celebrate the nuptial event in the house on Alder-stage Street.[59]

Milton anticipated too much, and laid too great emphasis upon his powers to take an uncultured girl of seventeen, and mould her life into his living. She had been accustomed to the freedom of a Cavalier house. The reaction to Milton's recluse way of living with his books and thoughts was too solemn and sombre a change for the young girl. It was Mary who took the initiative. After a month she wrote her parents, who in turn entreated Milton for the privilege of their young married daughter's company for the remainder of the summer. Milton, seeing that the bride's mother would have more influence upon her, consented to the arrangement. The outcome of it was that Mary Milton did not return to her husband until two years later, when the pressure of political events, and the pinch of poverty brought her, and finally the whole family, as dependents upon Milton's gratuitous nature.

During this two year period, when the absence of his young wife suggested to the whole of England, estrangement and indifference, the pride of the Puritan minded Milton along with his austere mode of life was under great strain. He must justify himself and his pride before the esteemed mind of England. Rather than direct the controversy to the individual who inflicted the wound, for it was Mary who arranged the plan of separation, Milton lifted into critical examination the institution of marriage. It was a most unfortunate thing for Milton to do, for he published in two separate printings his radical reactions against the institution of marriage. The first edition was sent forth anonymously, but the second edition of *The Doctrine and Discipline of Divorce,* in much enlarged form, carried his name. The whole work may be read in the light of a compensation on the part of Milton for the lack of the companionship he so definitely pictured as part of domestic happiness.

At the time Milton suffered this indignity, England was in the crisis of the Civil War. The national and personal cessation of serenity and peace changed the course of Milton's literary efforts for a period covering twenty years. In the same manner in which he had turned his back upon the extended trip through Greece and the East, and turned homeward in the cause of liberty and freedom of his country, Milton turned his literary attention away from his solemn avowal and dedication of his life to poetry. His pen did not cease its polemic activity until the overthrow of the cause he served.

"Milton's pen accompanied the whole of the Puritan revolution from the modest constitutional opposition in which it commenced, through its unexpected triumph, to its crushing overthrow by the royalist and clerical reaction."[60]

Prior to his marriage, Milton had entered the controversy in the publication of his first pamphlet entitled, *Of Reformation Touching Church-Discipline in England* (1641). As one might expect, the position of his Protestant minded parents became reflected in the position Milton so ardently advocated. It must be remembered that his brother, Christopher, reverted to the Papist position of his grandparents. This caused Milton much concern, and inflamed his already combative nature against Popery. However, Milton had an independence of spirit and a sense of divine election concerning himself that makes it rather difficult to classify him as an exemplary Puritan. He was a Puritan, it is true; but he was a Puritan of his own special Miltonic kind. As the champion of the Puritan cause, which he was, we must remember that he was also a student of the Greek and Roman humanities, which a strict Puritan ignored and rebuked. In the treatise, *Of Reformation . . . in England,* Milton does not hesitate to give his candid opinion of the Catholic Church, and to elucidate with unusual clarity and vigor his convictions concerning the Reformation.

". . . when I recall to mind at last, after so many darke Ages, wherein the huge overshadowing traine of Error had almost swept all the Starres out of the Firmament of the Church; how the bright and blissful Reformation (by Divine Power) strook through the black and settled Night of Ignorance and Antichristian Tyranny, me thinks a soveraigne and reviving joy must needs rush into the bosome of him that reads or heares; and the sweet Odour of the returning Gospell imbath his Soule with the fragrancy of Heaven. Then was the sacred BIBLE sought out of the dusty corners where prophane Falshood and Neglect had throwne it, the Schooles opened, Divine and Humane Learn-

25

ing rak't out of forgotten Tongues, the Princes and Cities trooping apace to the new erected banner of Salvation; the Martyrs, with the unresistable might of Weaknesse, shaking the Powers of Darknesse, and scorning the fiery rage of the old red Dragon."[61]

With fiery words and lofty contempt Milton turned his polemical powers against the Bishops. This appears in the closing part of, *Of Reformation . . . In England* and is more fully treated in *Of Prelaticall Episcopacy* (1641). Milton castigates the authority of the prelates.

"But they . . . after a shamefull end in this life . . . shall be thrown downe eternally into the darkest and deepest Gulfe of HELL, where under the despightfull controule, the trample and spurne of all the other Damned, that in the anguish of their Torture shall have no other ease then to exercise a Raving and Bestiall Tyranny over them as their Slaves and Negro's, they shall remaine in that plight for ever, the basest, the lowermost, the most dejected, more underfoot and down-trodden Vassals of Perdition."[62]

The reason for this eventful attack upon the bishops was due not only to the carnal state to which the Church had fallen, but to the alliance between Charles I and the Prelates. King and Bishops carried the war on the Puritans. Charles directed his attack against the power of Parliament. The Bishops worked with the obstinate clergy. Both of them attacked a common enemy, and in this they upheld each other. Throughout all of this controversy we cannot lose sight of Milton and of his religious background, especially the revolt of his father against the Catholicism of his parents. We cannot forget that Milton had been the recipient of all that education could give, and that all of this was proffered to him by his father, who had turned his son hopefully toward the Protestant Church. We cannot forget that Milton postponed his entrance into the Protestant Church mainly because of the restrictions upon freedom of thought and preaching which such a step involved. In the name of religious freedom, under the conviction to fight for civil liberty, he exerted himself with unreserved passion.

Milton's burning desire for freedom manifested itself in three areas of life where the function of freedom was challenged. *In the Church,* freedom was challenged at the seat of authority. Should that authority be recognized as invested in Popery, or should the rising tide of conviction concerning the Bible, with the privilege of individual interpretation, become pre-eminent?

In the State, freedom was likewise challenged at the seat of authority. Should the voice of the people have recognition and hold sway by means of the Parliament, or was the King to be the unchallenged and final voice upon all public and private affairs?

Milton's passion for liberty and freedom was flagrantly challenged, *in his own domestic life,* in the effrontery of his wife. In asserting his personal liberty in the domestic sphere, he found a spearhead of power and conviction in controversial matters that penetrated deeply as well in the life of Church and State.

Year after year we find the voice of this man growing into national importance as the Protestant voice of England, as the voice of eloquence, as the voice of expression for the convictions of the people concerning Protestantism in the Church and Parliamentarianism in the State. With due deliberation and the firmness of conviction of one who dedicates his powers to the righteous cause, Milton began that pamphleteering career which carried him so deeply into the national and religious events of his day. All of this he makes clear in the following lines:

"As the parliament acted with great vigour, the pride of the bishops began to lose its swell. No sooner did liberty of speech begin to be allowed, than every mouth was open against the bishops. Some complained of their personal

vices, others of the vice of the order itself. It was wrong, they said, that they alone should differ from all other reformed churches; that it was expedient the church should be governed by the example of the brethren, and above all by the word of God. I became perfectly awake to these things; and perceiving that men were in the right way to liberty; that, if discipline originating in religion continued its course to the morals and institutions of the commonwealth, they were proceeding in a direct line from such beginnings, from such steps, to the deliverance of the whole life of mortal man from slavery. . . . Moreover . . . as I had considered, whether I could ever be of use, should I now be wanting to my country, to the church, and to such multitudes of the brethren who were exposing themselves to danger for the gospel's sake — I resolved, though my thoughts were then employed upon other subjects, to transfer to these the whole force of my mind and industry."[63]
". . . it were sad for me if I should draw back, for me especially, now when all men offer their aid to help ease and lighten the difficult labours of the Church, to whose service by the intentions of my parents and friends I was destin'd of a child, and in my own resolutions, till coming to some maturity of years and perceaving what tyranny had invaded the Church, that he who would take Orders must subscribe slave, and take oath withall, which unlesse he took with a conscience that would retch, he must either strait perjure, or split his faith. I thought it better to preferre a blamelesse silence before the sacred office of speaking bought, and begun with servitude and forswearing. Howsoever thus Church-outed by the Prelats, hence may appear the right I have to meddle in these matters, as before, the necessity and constraint appear'd."[64]

Milton's use of the Bible in these controversial matters was of unequaled importance, and it was of far-reaching influence as the basis of authority for what he declared. Merely to open

Milton's, *The Doctrine and Discipline of Divorce* is to be confronted with a wide and extensive use of Scripture. Upon closer reading, however, one cannot fail to be impressed with the dexterous manner in which he twists Scripture to justify divorce as a means of freedom from his deeply wounded heart. The amazing fact is that the freedom Milton has thus "scripturally" justified for himself, he promises to all men as their Christian prerogative.

Milton's extravagance in the cause of domestic liberty in *The Doctrine and Discipline of Divorce,* brought him disfavor. The Parliament to whom he directed the enlarged second edition with his name attached, considered it ephemeral and unworthy of their deliberation, when the demands of the State so definitely occupied their minds. Milton continued with two other tracts on divorce, *Tetrachordon,* and *Colasterion,* each of which is an elaborated restatement of the thesis essential to the first publications on divorce. That thesis was that Marriage has for its sole purpose the establishment of quiescent happiness for each man. Any union, therefore, which did not have this beatific result, gave the man just cause to put away his wife. Of course, Milton failed utterly in the public eye with such a thin, ineffective conception and slanderous assault upon the vow which men hold sacred. He was attacked sternly by the clergy, and became the object of much ridicule by the Episcopalians and was disowned by the Presbyterians.[65]

Mention should be made here of the fact that in the same year he wrote his tracts on divorce, Milton entered into the composition of a work that has particular significance in the light of his total personal career. That work is entitled, *Areopagitica: for the Liberty of Unlicenc'd Printing.* He completed this work along with his treatises on divorce within the same year (1644) which marked the year as one of the most productive of his entire effort. When his plea for domestic liberty fell upon ears unresponsive to his contention, he shifted his plea to that of freedom of speech.

29

The *Areopagitica* marks for Milton a departure from the theological and religious controversy into the rising tide of secular and political freedom. There continued ever on his part that religious passion for freedom and liberty; however, the development of events within the nation nurtured and deepened his consuming interest in political freedom. More and more he was drawn away from those offices which mark a man as a minister of religion, to those forensic duties associated with public and political activities. Of all things Milton most cherished his own personal brief about life. He would not fit that brief into any existing order or system, but would order the developing systems about him in such a way that they would bear the imprint of his name and character.

In the field of national freedom the *Areopagitica* was the first evidence of this secular, political, national concern. The immediate occasion for the writing of this treatise was an act of Parliament passed June 14, 1643, which required that all books before publication must be licensed by an officially recognized censor. The independent spirit of Milton revolted against this added tyranny to the extent that he published both editions of *The Doctrine and Discipline of Divorce,* and the *Areopagitica* without recognition of this new act of Parliament concerning licensing. Milton wrote: "I have determin'd to lay up as the best treasure, and solace of a good old age, if God voutsafe it me, the honest liberty of free speech from my youth."[66]

There is the definitely personal factor in these writings. Milton wrote no word of slander against marriage until he had domestic difficulties.[67] Then his pen broke loose in a torrent of slanderous ink. Similarly, there is no evidence of incitation against licensing in printing until Milton felt those restrictions personally. In an unmistakable measure, Milton's pride of England was an extension of his own self-esteem. His passion for liberty was a liberty which had an intensely personal basis. It was to this arrogant pride that Milton's wife, who had arranged her own estrangement, now herself under the pressure of national events, bowed in contrition and obedience. The decisive victory of Cromwell over the Royalists in June 1645 pressed hard upon the Powell family, leaving them financially bankrupt. This victory of the Independents made Milton a man of consequence. For the Powells, Milton was useful as a covert for his wife as well as for the entire destitute family.

By this turn of events in which the Powells lost their national security, they were willing to concede the domestic liberty which they had paraded for their daughter in times of peace, in order to have security and even sustenance. The following plan of reconciliation was adopted by the family and executed by Mary. Friends of both sides concurred for different reasons in the procedure. Milton often visited the house of a friend in the lane of St. Martin's-le-Grand. Near this house he had a relative living by the name of Blackborough who helped to perfect the plan. At the time when Milton was known to be coming for a visit, Mary was placed secretly in an adjoining room. Upon his entrance she burst forth with arms outstretched, and cast herself at his feet imploring forgiveness. Milton repulsed her at first, but under the earnest supplication of Mary and the circle of friends, he accepted her entreaty for reconciliation. Mary would stay at the home of Mrs. Webber, in St. Clement's Church-yard, until Milton had things in order at his new house at Barbican. Milton had found his house in Aldersgate Street too small for the greater number of pupils which were brought under his training. It was therefore at the larger house in Barbican that the arrangement was made for their reunion. Within the year after the reconciliation Oxford fell, the house of the Powells was sequestered, and the entire Powell household came to live with the son-in-law. At the end of the same month, July 1646, there was born to the Miltons the first of their four children.

Twenty years later when Milton was writing *Paradise Lost,* the events of Mary's reconciliation still had clear delineation in his mind, and found a place in that epic.

                                          . . . but Eve
. . . with Tears that ceas'd not flowing,
And tresses all disorderd, at his feet
Fell humble, and imbracing them, besaught
His peace . . .[68]

. . . . . . .her lowlie plight,
Immoveable till peace obtain'd from fault
Acknowledg'd and deplor'd, in Adam wraught
Commiseration; soon his heart relented
Towards her, his life so late and sole delight,
Now at his feet submissive in distress,
Creature so faire his reconcilement seeking,
His counsel whom she had displeas'd, his aide;
As one disarm'd, his anger all he lost,
And thus with peaceful words uprais'd her soon."[69]

Consonant with the events which were developing against
King Charles I, Milton was engaged in a task which would
have its repercussions throughout Europe as well as England.
During the uncertain days of the Civil War, when the men
under Cromwell began to direct their efforts against the King's
life, Milton secretly threw in his meditative powers for the
execution, in *The Tenure of Kings and Magistrates*.[70]

When the King was executed, January 30, 1649, the manuscript was already completed, which indicates that Milton was
at least a mental accomplice in the regicide. With the King
dead, Milton published the treatise, and in that act he entered
the official ranks of the victorious minority who would control
England for eleven years.

The literary daring of Milton in this publication is apparent
in the fact that all of English as well as European opinion was
directed against the act. Milton had become the apologist for
regicide. He declared: "Our ancestors who were not ignorant
with what rights either Nature or ancient Constitution had endowed them when Oaths both at Coronation, and renewed in

Parliament would not serve, thought it no way illegal to depose and put to death thir tyrannous Kings."[71] All Christendom had been profoundly shaken in the regicide; yet Milton with unequivocating directness stepped into the center of the ominous circle as the apologist of the act.

The immediate outcome of this daring position which Milton took was his appointment as Secretary For Foreign Tongues to Council of State. The appointment involved the responsibility of writing letters to foreign courts, and of handing the correspondence in the accepted language of the court, which was Latin. To Milton, as a part of the work of the appointment, there came the responsibility to answer a book whose increasing popularity constituted a great danger to the authority of the Council of State. The book entitled, *Eikon Basilike — the True Portraiture of His Sacred Majesty in his Solitudes and Sufferings,* described the sufferings of the King and exalted the superior quality of his piety during the last eight years of his life. It was a dark and difficult day for the new revolutionary government, and especially for Milton. Before taking the position as secretary, Milton had been cautioned by the physicians to use his eyes with the utmost economy. During the period when he was writing *Areopagitica* he noticed that his eyes had developed an unprecedented weakness. Already the duties of his appointment exceeded his ability to execute them with zealous concern. By government command, Milton was under the necessity to write a reply to this amazingly successful book, *Eikon Basilike* . . . , a book that had captured the emotions of the people, a book that demanded forty-seven editions to supply the desires of the people, a book that turned the impassioned desires of the people against the new government. In his reply, Milton made an analysis of each argument within the book, and met each argument with a counter-argument, often with a decided lack of diplomacy. As a piece of work *Eikonoklastes* (1649) has very little literary value. From the viewpoint of historians of a later date, the work reveals the hold the injustice

33

of the crime had upon English feeling, and the influence of that feeling upon the usually persuasive powers of Milton.

Another indictment of the regicide government of England, as well as a memorial to Charles I, was prepared by Claude de Saumaise, better known as Salmasius, Latin professor of eminence. The book was written and published under the commission of Charles II, who was living at the Hague. The title of the book was an appropriate one, *Defence of Kings*. The purpose was to stimulate the already stirred-up feelings of the English people against the government, because of the injustice done to Charles. Milton's task was to make reply; and his reply was all the more difficult because of the critical state of his eyes. He was inattentive to the warnings of his physicians, and gave himself with unreserved passion to the cause of liberty. He labored long and ceaselessly in the reply, which became in his mind a *Defence of the People of England*, and bore that title. The effort left him hopelessly blind.

The Loss of Milton's Eyesight

The loss of Milton's eyesight demonstrates the increasing dedication, as well as the caliber of his determination, in the pursuit of the cause of liberty.

This determination, and this quality of dedication is incorporated in the very structure of *Paradise Found*. The outcome of freedom is necessary not only for Adam and Eve, but for all males who follow successively upon Adam, and all females who follow Eve.

Both of these works that left John Milton hopelessly blind, namely: the reading of the work of Salmasius and the writing of *Defence of the People of England*, were in Latin. In addition, each of them employed to capacity the invectives possible with that language. For Milton, there was not only the psychological strain of an adequate answer to England and all the world, but the extended use of his eyes. Mark Pattison says,

34

"The contending interests of the two great English parties, the wider issue between republic and absolutism, the speculative inquiry into the right of resistance, were lost sight of by the spectators of the literary duel. The only question was whether Salmasius could beat the new champion, or the new man beat Salmasius, at a match of vituperation."[72]

The use of invectives against personalities is unfortunate, for Milton had ample opportunity to relieve the charges of rebellion and regicide in the eyes of the whole of Europe.

"Milton's name, long familiar to Englishmen, was now spread abroad in Europe to be mentioned with admiration for the purity of his Latin style and the vigor of his strokes, with horror for the opinions he entertained. A later generation, caring for none of these things, may pause over the heroism of the man who, with eyesight already failing, knowingly courted blindness rather than spare a line in defence of that Commonwealth which, imperfect as he acknowledged it to be, was to him the only road leading to that ideal government by a sage and noble people which formed the object of his dreams."[73]

It is worthwhile noting that John Milton "courted blindness" as he moved to the "only road leading to the ideal government" (cf. 73 above). Such was the increasing motivation, now politically deferred, that led to the writing of *Paradise Found*.

In the *Defence of the People of England*, Milton gave evidence of a more comprehensive conception of kingship. He was not so pointed in his attack against kingship in general; but modified his attack and directed it to tyrants. At the end of this treatise, Milton wrote:

"And now I think, through God's help, I have finished the work I undertook at the beginning, namely to defend both at home and abroad the noble actions of my countrymen against the brainsick envious rage of this mad sophist, and to assert the people's common rights against the unrighteous despotism of kings, — and this not out of any hatred of kings, but of tyrants."[74]

Milton pleaded for democracy as the basis for social action. The point and plan of the *Defence . . .* was to gain the approval of the people and their representatives for the regicide. He went further. As the title implies, Milton defended the English people for their execution of Charles I.

Between the first and second editions of *Defence . . .* certain significant events took place which influenced Milton concerning kingship and democracy. The first had little or no relation to national affairs, but nevertheless affected Milton. That was the death in childbirth of Mary Powell Milton, in 1652. His second wife, Catharine Woodcock also died, in childbirth, within the first year of their marriage (1658). His little son died also. With these misfortunes went the affliction of the blindness of Milton. All of this was more than enough to break a strong man. Milton withstood it. Noteworthy among all these ominous events was the manner in which he faced and answered the attack of his enemies, based on his personal misfortunes. The enemies of Milton took these misfortunes as a signal opportunity to point out that they were the visitations of Heaven. Milton was receiving the due and just reward for his sins, chief among which they said were his attacks against the right and authority of kings. The intense life which Milton lived brought him constantly in touch with people. This redeemed him from the loneliness of his misfortunes. Contrary to what most men would do under these misfortunes, Milton refused to be mastered by affliction. The loss of eyesight became the occasion for an increased and vital illumination from within. Far from being the source of disillusionment, despair, disgrace, or defeat, Milton saw in his blindness a divine seal in which he was set apart by God for a particular service worthy of reverence. That this conviction was deeply felt by him became clear in his later works.

36

The greatest of his works was not yet begun. It is noteworthy that these polemic writings of Milton have enduring value not so much because of their intrinsic worth, as because they were written by the same pen that wrote *Paradise Lost.*

In the *Second Defence of the People of England,* Milton used his blindness as an illustration of genuine relation to the cause of the English people, and commended himself to his enemies by saying that his eyes:

". . . to external appearance . . . clear and bright, without the semblance of a cloud, as the eyes of those whose sight is the most perfect. In this respect only am I a dissembler; and here it is against my will."[75]

In the *Second Defence* . . . Milton was forced by the book he was answering, to bring up for review the events that followed one another in Charles I's escape and execution. That book came from the continent in Latin form, and bore the English title, *The Cry of the Royal Blood to Heaven, Against The English Parricides.* Milton was deeply concerned to answer this attack against his beloved England. In the effort his domestic difficulties became lost in the cause of the Commonwealth.

The Cry of the Royal . . . was brought to publication by a French minister, Alexander Morus. Morus was not the author of the work. He received it at the hand of Salmasius to whom the work had been bequeathed by a canon of Canterbury. It was Alexander Morus, however, who was the object of the caustic invectives Milton hurled. Apparently the French minister had become involved in moral acts which defame the character of any minister or laymen. Milton became aware of these moral lapses, and directed the most turgid of literary invectives toward his enemy. For Milton the national cause of England became a matter of personal combat with words as weapons. In the light of literary ethics the procedure was most petty and provincial. In all of these torrents of literary abuse Milton declared himself victor, but he was a vagabond to the higher and nobler art that same pen later achieved.

With the publication of the *Second Defence* . . . the literary efforts of Milton against the king came to an end. This, however, did not mark the end of his public career as a polemic; although only four years elapsed before the death of Cromwell, and less than six remained before the fall of the republican cause.

During this period Milton directed his active pen to ecclesiastical matters, writing, *A Treatise of Civil Power in Ecclesiastical Causes.* This pamphlet was a rebuke of the interposition of civil authority into matters of religous belief. He attacked the subsidy of the clergy by the civil authorities. The argument was largely a Scriptural presentation.[76] Milton continued with his convictions concerning ecclesiastical matters in another pamphlet, *Considerations touching the likeliest means to remove Hirelings out of the church.* The brief which Milton presented in this pamphlet was against the mercenary spirit among the clergy. He fought the legal system of taxation for the support of the clergy, and declared that in that procedure men unworthy of the calling were drawn into the Church. Milton would withdraw all laws of this kind and any kind of support from the clergy other than that which was purely voluntary. In this way, he held ministers will preach and serve for the glory and satisfaction of preaching the Word.

In the same year (1659) in which Milton produced these ecclesiastical pamphlets, Richard Cromwell abdicated the throne, and the original Rump Parliament was restored. Milton was engaged in the writing of *The Readie and Easie Way To Establish A Free Commonwealth.* He would not let himself be persuaded that the Stuarts would come back to power. Intense discussion centered around the best way to establish a republican form of government, and that under the menace of the people who clamored for the restoration of the monarchy. The political direction of this pamphlet followed a course between monarchy on the one hand, and true democracy. In his departure from the true democracy, Milton gave evidence of a growing distrust in the ability of the common people to manage their own government.

> "Tracing the record of these twenty years of Milton's association with Parliament, I have found one conviction inescapable: Milton cared not one jot whether the Parliament which he lauded or condemned was representative, whether it was appointed or elected, whether it was legal or illegal. What concerned him was whether or not, in his opinion, the Parliament which had assumed power was acting for the public welfare, was securing the liberties which he held so dear. Thus Parliament was to him any group strong enough to maintain order and courageous enough to legislate fearlessly. Once this point of view is understood, one may read the record of Milton's relations to Parliament with some understanding of his apparent loss of faith in republican government."[77]

Milton was outspoken in presenting the evils that would attend the restoration of Charles's son. While he wrote, he was continually forced to modify and rewrite sections of the pamphlet, due to the rapid flow and change of events. *The Readie and Easie Way* . . . found circulation and eager readers. The cause, however, was lost. The Republic for which Milton had given so much of himself, had come to an end. The Restoration of the monarchy with Charles II silenced Milton's political writings.

The Loss of the Commonwealth

The loss of the Commonwealth was an occasion and particularly a challenge for John Milton, to write of a commonwealth that could not be lost. His defeats in many areas were but challenges for Milton to overcome defeat, with the victory of freedom.

When one reviews the events of Milton, at this time, and

particularly Milton's reaction to them; he is deeply impressed with the quality of character of the man who resolved to bring greatness out of defeat. This is another facet of understanding, that when John Milton was writing the epic, *Paradise Lost,* he was not writing about the loss of Paradise, but *Paradise Found.*

Let the ominous events pass in review. Milton suffered in the defeat of the Republic. He lost considerable money which he had placed in government securities. He lost his Latin secretaryship. Although some say he was continued in this office, the nature of Milton's character as well as the circumstances point definitely to the contrary. With the Restoration of the monarchy, Milton lost the cause for which he had given his life for a period of twenty years, and he had nothing to show for it. In fear of his life, he fled to the house of a friend. As a partisan in the ruined party, he expected the scaffold. The virile attack he had made against Charles I, and his sanction of the execution, placed him in a very dangerous position. He was put in the custody of the Sergeant at Arms. Two of his regicide pamphlets were publicly burned by the hangman.

> "The Attorney General had expressed the opinion (but not as a public pronouncement) that he deserved hanging."[78]

Milton escaped this ignominy, as well as the suffering of the scaffold.[79] The peril passed with Milton safe, but he was broken in wealth and in reputation. He was broken in everything but the quality of being indomitable.

The death of Mary Powell, his first wife in 1652, occurred almost simultaneously with his total blindness. With three small children, all girls (the eldest six and the youngest just a baby) Milton faced life and responsibility. With increasing vigor, he became the center of political attack because of his position in the Republic. Four years after the death of Mary, he married Catharine Woodcock, a woman who understood him and made possible a brief return of happiness. For fifteen months he enjoyed the companionship for which he longed. The happiness and companionship were cut short with Catharine's death. in childbirth. Face to face with this unprecedented series of tragedies and disappointments, Milton confronted the challenge in the beginning of his epic, *Paradise Lost*. How true it is that profound and relentless tragedy will either leave a man's potentialities wanting in dignity and true development, or will turn them to their majestic fulfillment. In this sense, *Paradise Lost* was born out of personal darkness and tragedy. From these events onward to the end of his life Milton was occupied with the writing of *Paradise Lost*, followed by *Paradise Regain'd*, and *Samson Agonistes*.

In the following lines Milton became almost autobiographical concerning this period:

"Servant of God, well done! Well hast thou fought
The better fight, who single has maintained
Against revolted multitudes the Cause
Of Truth, in word mightier than they in Armes;
And for the testimonie of Truth hast born
Universal reproach, far worse to beare
Then violence: for this was all thy care
To stand approv'd in sight of God, though Worlds
Judg'd thee perverse . . ."[80]

CHAPTER FIVE

MILTON'S POETRY

The earliest evidence of Milton's poetic tendencies in the English paraphrases of Psalms 114 and 136 reveals also the serious nature of his mind. Written when he was fifteen, the paraphrases remind us of the industry with which Milton gave himself to the literary field, and which characterized his efforts to the close of his life. The serious nature of Milton's mind and its ceaseless industry brought to full use the genius of his literary endowment. Little of the ability of Milton was seen or could be seen in these paraphrases; however, in them he gave evidence of his early and diligent passion for learning, and singularly enough, his choice of religious themes.

Milton's Early Choice Of Religious Themes

At sixteen years of age Milton entered Christ's College, Cambridge. In the begining of this period of his education, he had at his command a readiness and ease of speech in both the Latin and English languages. Later he added, by his study and travel in Italy, a fluency in the use of the Italian language. During the seven years at Cambridge the genius of Milton was unrecognized; although in the very middle of this period he produced a high piece of lyrical verse, *On the Morning of Christ's Nativity.*

The first poem written during his Cambridge career, as well as the first to follow the paraphrases on the two Psalms was entitled, *On the Death of a Fair Infant Dying of a Cough.* The infant was the daughter of the poet's sister. The opening mood

42

deals with grief and then progresses to the lofty elevation of the theme of immortality.

While at Cambridge Milton wrote a considerable amount of Latin poetry. When seventeen years of age he wrote: *Elegy the First, To Charles Diodate; Elegy the Second, on the death of the Beadle of the University of Cambridge; Elegy the Third, On the Death of the Bishop of Winchester; On the Fifth of November,* and *On the Death, of the Bishop of Ely.* During his nineteenth year he continued his Latin efforts, as well as writing, *At a Vacation Exercise in the College.* This poem was part Latin and part English. This division suggests Milton was making a choice of language for the expression of his thoughts. His choice was for his native tongue:

"Here I salute thee and thy pardon ask,
That now I use thee in my latter task:
Small loss it is that thence can come unto thee,
I know my tongue but little Grace can do thee:
Thou needst not be ambitious to be first
Believe me I have thither packt the worst:
And if it happen as I did forecast,
The daintiest dishes shall be serv'd up last.
I pray thee then deny me not thy aide. . . .[81]

. . . .

Hail native Language, that by sinews weak
Didst move my first endeavouring tongue to speak,
And mad'st imperfect words with childish tripps,
Half unpronounc't, slide through my infant-lipps. . . ."[82]

With the exception of several sonnets in the Italian tongue, Milton kept his resolve to invest his poetic powers within the English language. He resolved furthermore that his use of the English tongue should find worthy expression in some enduring theme.

"I have some naked thoughts that rove about
And loudly knock to have their passage out;

43

And wearie of their place do only stay
Till thou hast deck't them in thy best array;
That so they may without suspect or fears
Fly swiftly to this fair Assembly's ears;
Yet I had rather, if I were to chuse,
Thy service in some graver subject use. . . ."[83]

The serious and religious nature of Milton directed his efforts away from subjects of little value. *Elegy the Sixth, to Charles Diodati,* written a few days after the *Nativity* ode, gives a picture of Milton in contemplation of the high task of Heroic poetry.

"But if a poet sings of wars, of Heaven controlled by a Jove full grown, of duty-doing heroes, of captains that are half gods, if he sings now the holy counsels of the gods above, now the realms deep below wherein howl a savage hound, let him live a simple, frugal life, after the fashion of the teacher who came from Samos, let herbs offer him food that works no harm, let pellucid water stand near him, in a tiny cup of beechen wood, and let him drink only sober draughts from a pure spring. On such a poet are imposed, too, a youth free of crime, pure and chaster, and a character unyielding, and a name without taint. . . . For the bard is sacred to the gods, he is priest of the gods; the secret deeps of his soul, and his very lips alike breathe forth Jove."[84]

Later in life, when he was deeply involved in the polemic of his day, Milton wrote in *An Apology . . . of the Remonstrant Against Smectymnuus:*

"And long it was not after, when I was confirm'd in this opinion, that he who would not frustrate of his hope to write well hereafter in laudable things, ought himselfe to bee a true Poem, that is, a composition, and patterne of the best and honourablest things; not presuming to sing high praises of heroick men, or famous Cities, unlesse he have himselfe the experience and the practice of all that which is praiseworthy."[85]

As a sequel to the ode *On The Morning of Christ's Nativity,* he wrote, *The Passion.* Milton was disappointed with himself in this work. In a footnote at the end of this attempt he placed the comment,

"This subject the Author finding to be above the years he had, when he wrote it, and nothing satisfi'd with what was begun, left it unfinisht."[86]

With this failure he turned for a period to lighter themes, to the *Song On May Morning,* the sonnet, *O Nightingale,* the epigram, *On Shakespear.* On the occasion of his twenty-third birthday he wrote a sonnet in which he voiced his decision to invest his efforts outside the Church. This sonnet, *How Soon Hath Time* was written at the close of his Cambridge career. The last lines of the sonnet reveal his continued dedication to give his powers in the service of God.

"Toward which Time leads me, and the will of Heav'n;
All is, if I have grace to use it so,
As ever in my great task Masters eye."[87]

Milton went to live with his father at Horton. Here he joined the leisure of the lovely setting with his indomitable energy and passion for great poetic achievement.

Arcades, On Time, Upon the Circumcision, At a Solemn Music, Il Penseroso, Comus, and *Lycidas* were kritten during the Horton period. Mark Pattison gives a brief and lucid digest of the poet's life which is included here for its special reference to the Horton period and to the writing of *L'Allegro, Il Penseroso,* and *Lycidas.*

45

"Milton's life is a drama in three acts. The first discovers him in the calm and peaceful retirement of Horton, of which *L'Allegro, Il Penseroso,* and *Lycidas* are the expression. In the second act he is breathing the foul and heated atmosphere of party passion and religious hate, generating the lurid fires which glare in the battailous canticles of his prose pamphlets. The three great poems, *Paradise Lost, Paradise Regain'd,* and *Samson Agonistes,* are the utterance of his final period of solitary and Promethean grandeur, when, blind, destitute, friendless, he testified of righteousness, temperance, and judgment to come, alone before a fallen world."[88]

From the productive solitude of Horton, Milton answered the urgent call for his leadership in the cause of national liberty. The Milton who responded to this great challenge was already Milton the poet.

The Sonnets

Before Milton entered the field of sonnet writing, sonnets had the singular theme of Love, with an occasional sonnet on another subject. From this limitation Milton emancipated the sonnet, and wrote of many and divergent subjects. This wide range of subjects is what we should expect in Milton, due to the scope of his literary interests and reading, as well as to his activity in the political, social, literary, and religious life of his day.

"A victory, an expected attack upon the city, a momentary fit of depression or exultation, a jest thrown out against one of his books, a dream which for a short time restored to him that beautiful face over which the grave had closed forever, led him to musings which, without effort, shaped themselves into verse. The unity of sentiment and severity of style which characterize these little pieces remind us of

46

the Greek Anthology, or perhaps still more of the Collects of the English Liturgy: the noble poem on the Massacres of Piedmont is strictly a collect in verse.

The sonnets are more or less striking, according as the occasions which gave birth to them are more or less interesting. But they are, almost without exception, dignified by a sobriety and greatness of mind to which we know not where to look for a parallel."[89]

An example of this wide range of subjects is in the sonnet, *Cromwell, Our Chief of Men.* The occasion of this sonnet was the necessity of defending religious toleration at a time when the Church was in a state of confusion. Parliament had appointed a committee for the Propagation of the Gospel to examine and study the situation, and to arrange for some acceptable understanding as a basis for action and procedure for the Church. The most knotty problem concerned the spread of the Gospel by means other than the recognized clergy. A group of fifteen Puritan ministers had submitted to the Committee a plan which involved, among other things, the power of unrestricted censorship—the right to determine what was orthodox and what was not — and the placing of this function with unlimited power in the hands of the clergy. Milton's sonnet to Cromwell was a vehement protest against the adoption of such an ecclesiastical policy.

The Sonnet, *To the Lord Generall Cromwell, May* 1652, bears below this title the phrase, "On the proposalls of certaine ministers at the Committee for Propagation of the Gospell". As a challenge to religious, secular, and political freedom, Milton wrote as follows, in the sonnet to Cromwell. The first eight lines of the sonnet are words of praise to Cromwell. The last six lines that complete the sonnet, are an admonition and challenge to Cromwell to defeat this restriction to liberty.

"Cromwell, our chief of men, who through a cloud
   Not of warr onely, but detractions rude,

47

Guided by faith and matchless Fortitude
To peace and truth thy glorious way hast plough'd,
And on the neck of crowned Fortune proud
Hast reard Gods Trophies, and his work pursu'd,
While Darwen stream with blood of Scotts imbru'd,
And Dunbarr feiled resounds thy praises loud,
And Worsters laureat wreath; yet much remaines
To conquer still; peace hath her victories
No less renownd then warr, new foes aries
Threatning to bind our soules with secular chaines;
Helpe us to save free Conscience from the paw
Of hireling wolves whose Gospell is their maw."

At this time, not only Royalists but also members of Parliament did not have the worthy picture of Cromwell. This misjudgment has its expression in line two of this sonnet, in the phrase "but detractions rude." In the phrase, "peace hath her victories no less renownd then warr," Milton was calling upon Cromwell to meet the new foes, within the Church, who would "bind our soules with secular chaines."

There is here further development of the role of freedom that had singular development with John Milton, as he now moves from twenty years' involvement with the cause of the Commonwealth: to the cause of freedom for a Paradise that is not lost, but for *Paradise Found*. Milton's early choice of religious themes, postponed for the cause of the Commonwealth, under Cromwell, now comes to developed expression in the epic of the English language. What was *lost* in the Commonwealth is now *found* in the epic!

The Great Epic, *Paradise Lost*

The evidence, over the course of his lengthy period of preparation, is unmistakable that Milton's desire to write the English epic was first of all literary, and then theological.

48

His entrance into the deeper study of the literary classics during the Horton period is a part of the evidence. The fact that his first plan for the epic had a non-religious theme, carries with it the importance which the purely literary had for him. It was after the Horton period, in fact during the sojourn in Italy, that at Naples Milton penned some lines to his friend Mansus. These lines give us a true insight into his first choice for a theme.

"O, may my lot vouchsafe to me a friend so fine, one who knows so well how to honor the men of Phoebus, true men, if ever I shall bring back to my songs the kings of my native land, and Arthur, who set wars in train even 'neath the earth (i.e., in Fairyland), or shall tell of the high-hearted heroes bound together as comrades at that peerless table, and — O, may the spirit come to my aid — I shall break to pieces Saxon phalanxes under the might of Britons' warring."[90]

The letter reveals the eager desire to write for his own country, and in his own language, that which would be a literary monument. In this letter Milton also stated his desire to write an epic about King Arthur. The final selection of the theme for the epic was the desire of the writer for enduring greatness. That enduring greatness was not only in the cause of the English language, but of the Milton who adopted the English rather than the Latin as the literary medium of the epic. Tillyard, in comment upon the letter to Mansus says:

"No wonder if after such . . . Milton again considered the question of writing his great works in Latin. Certainly the way in which he here writes — with complete grasp of his medium and with hardly a falter from beginning to end — is quite astonishing."[91]

Hilaire Belloc pictures the centuries of literary influence which had their effect upon Milton and the theme of the epic.

"Now Milton was built up on the Greek and Roman classics: Scripture was in the making of him, and he was of those who took all the inspired Hebrew folklore literally in every detail of its text, but the Hebraic never ousted in him the Greek and the Latin classics. He drew not from the Levant, but from Athens and Rome. Joy in its more solemn form he would not abandon: and as for beauty, beauty, was for him all his life an appetite, an object and a guide. Of all the English poets he is the one for whom sudden beauty in diction seems most inevitable, in whom you never know under what incongruous conditions beauty at white-heat will not appear, shining through an immortal line. He knew that he was the vehicle, and, after a fashion, the priest of beauty; and he worshipped at that shrine all his life — to our immense advantage."[92]

The important contribution of the Greek and Roman classics found its way into the total mind and temper of Milton. However, the century before the advent of Milton into this life had been the century of the Reformation, with its singular emphasis upon the importance of the Bible, and the centrality of its message for life.

Within England the movement for reform and the emphasis upon the Bible ante-dated the Reformation on the Continent, and especially in Germany. The Bible became the unquestioned authority for life and thought. It was the English John Wyclif (? -1384) who first presented the Bible to the world as an open book for all to read. It was the English Milton who presented to the world the great epic, *Paradise Lost,* on a theme chosen from the Bible.

Paul Elmer More has an illuminating essay entitled, "The Theme of Paradise Lost," in which he states:

". . . two distinct elements must enter into the constitution of an epic: it must be built upon a theme deeply rooted in national belief, and, further, the development of this theme must express, more or less symbolically, some universal truth of human nature. The first requisite is indeed a truism of the critics, who find it fully satisfied in the Trojan war of Homer, in the wandering of Aeneas and the founding of Rome, in the political allegory of Dante."[93]

The selection of the story in Genesis as the theme of *Paradise Lost* carried with it the great national loyalty of England's Protestant faith. This national loyalty to the theme found a kindred loyalty among the other countries of the Protestant Reformation; and in this sense the theme would have an international appeal. The second essential element of the theme of an epic was likewise true of *Paradise Lost* in that the epic embodies a universal truth of human nature. What that universal truth of human nature was, the authorities do not agree. Oliver Elton presents the question:

"What is made of the central myth? Does it in Milton's hands, embody some enduring truth that speaks to the imagination? I doubt it. It is of no consequence that we do not accept it as a fact; but what of it as a symbol? The topic is the irruption of evil through the misuse of man's freewill."[94]

In contradiction to this Paul Elmer More writes:

"Sin is not the innermost subject of Milton's epic, nor man's disobedience and fall; these are but the tragic shadows cast about the central light. Justification of the ways of God to man is not the true moral of the plot: this and the whole divine drama are merely the poet's means of raising his conception to the highest generalisation. The true theme is Paradise itself; not Paradise Lost, but the reality of that 'happy rural seat' where the errant tempter beheld

'To all delight of human sense exposed

51

In narrow room nature's whole wealth, yea more,
A heaven on earth.'

This truth, indeed, we might have learned from Tennyson
who, with a fellow-craftsman's sympathetic insight, discerned what gave the poem its profound value and interest.
Not that Titan angels or the roar of angel onset was to Tennyson the significant matter. 'Me rather,' he sings in his
musical Alcaics,

'Me rather all that bowery loneliness,
The brooks of Eden mazily murmuring,
    And bloom profuse and cedar arches
        Charm, as a wanderer out in ocean,
Where some refulgent sunset of India
Streams o'er a rich ambrosial ocean isle.'

There lies, you may know the veritable matter of *Paradise
Lost*.[95]

In agreement with Paul Elmer More is G. R. Elliott who,
not only makes a similar statement, but goes on to point out
the universal appeal of the theme as the favorite story of humankind. His emphasis upon real happiness has a true foundation
with illustrations within the field of literature: witness for example the beautiful relationship of Robert and Elizabeth Brown-
ing.

"The myth of a human paradise is European and indeed
universal rather than Greek or Christian. In one form or
another it always has been and always will be the favorite
human story — whether the paradise is supposed to reside
in the Hesperian Isles, or the Garden of Eden, or the 'intense inane' of Shelley, or the 'one far-off divine event' of
Tennyson, or the state of the aesthetic caveman which is
popular just now. It images that quest of happiness which

52

is the main theme of human life and therefore of poetry. But the myth itself, like the human quest of happiness, is predominantly idyllic. It means a withdrawal, in one way or another, from the real conditions of Personality. Milton preserved its idyllic quality in the 'bowery loneliness' that so enchanted Tennyson, 'the brooks of Eden mazily murmuring.' But at the same time he tried to make his paradise emblematic of the real happiness that men have found, by experiment, to be achievable though precarious: a rational, temperate fullness of life sustained always by an abnegation that is clearly and cheerfully undertaken. The dominant tone of *Paradise Lost* is one of healthy cheerfulness, in the best sense of this bitterly abused word."[96]

Happiness Is One

In the development of the epic there is more than a Platonic similarity between the nature of heaven and the earthly paradise. The happiness is one, whether in the paradise of time or the eternity of heaven.[97] As the epic progresses, Milton makes the actual scenery of paradise recede into the distance. This departure from the actual scene of paradise itself is more than physical. It has a metaphysical significance in the complete development of the theme. The Garden of Eden as a real place in the world loses its preference to an inward Paradise which he affirms is "happier far." With growing importance throughout the epic this truth develops until the climax is reached near the end of the poem. Milton puts into the mouth of the Archangel Michael important words when Adam and Eve were to be escorted by him from the Garden of Eden.

The importance of these words cannot be over-rated in an understanding of the epic.

"...................... onely add
Deeds to thy knowledge answerable, add Faith,
Add Vertue, Patience, Temperance, add Love,

By name to come call'd Charitie, the soul
Of all the rest: then wilt thou not be loath
To leave this Paradise, but shalt possess
A Paradise within thee, happier farr."[98]

After one has read the entire epic, and then gives oneself to its interpretation, it is most profitable to review the scenes and the whole development with the above lines as the key. The development of the theme is subtle, with an interpretation of paradise unique with Milton in the early history of Protestant Biblical interpretation.

Some would call the interpretation too general. Others would label it mythical. Some would even dare to call it heretical. This subtleness has a more evident counterpart in a literary effort of wide theological importance, a work for which Milton began to collect material as early as 1645. That was ten or a dozen years before he began to plan *Paradise Lost.* The great epic was planned in 1655, and finished in 1663. In fact, close examination will reveal that the same year Milton began to plan the writing of *Paradise Lost,* he was actually in the composition of another document of far-reaching significance with almost unbelievable theological implications. The name of that document was *De Doctrina Christiana.* We shall consider later the importance of *Paradise Lost* and *De Doctrina Christiana,* and the relatedness of their theological positions. At this time, however, it is important to state that their relatedness necessarily writes into Paradise, not a condition of being *lost,* but of *Paradise Found.*

In the concluding part of his treatment of *Paradise Lost* Hilaire Belloc declares:

"It has produced an exaltation. Will that exaltation be maintained? Will *Paradise Lost* stand on the same level of fame, enduring unshaken through the coming generations? Many would say not, and for this reason: the English Bible is

54

read more and more rarely, and even less believed than read."[99]

He gives reasons for this startling statement; and they have the quality of good judgment for one who is an ardent advocate for Catholicism. He affirms that the cosmogony which Protestant English-speaking folk possessed, has faded. Modern education has given a new mythology, known as scientific, to the origin of man. In this new conception there is no tragedy, no Fall, and therefore no redemption. There is no Paradise, no Eden, no Hell. With all of this considered, however, one need not join with the pessimism of Belloc.

This new and scientific interpretation, with all its admittedly good elements, has an element of transcience which time would serve to bring to light. At first this new and scientific view directly opposed the Biblical account. The latest achievements in the scientific realm have brought us closer to the place where we can see the scientific conception of man's origin and the religious conception, join hands in a friendly Biblical record. In fact science has thrown helpful light upon some difficult Biblical passages. The rapid advance in archaeological investigation in Biblical lands has affirmed the growing harmony between these two approaches to truth. We may therefore believe, Belloc not-withstanding, that the Bible will continue to have earnest and believing readers.

Likewise, but for a different reason, *Paradise Lost* will continue to have diligent and earnest readers. Indeed Tillyard, writing in 1930, suggested that *Paradise Lost* in the matter of interpretation had really come into its own within the last ten years:

"It is not surprising, then, that in the last ten years or so there has been more discussion of the subject than in all the rest of the time during which *Paradise Lost* has been in print. From the differences of opinion it may be judged that the question has by no means been settled, and another attempt to answer it may well be pardoned."[100]

For Tillyard *Paradise Lost* is a living book and the subject of much discussion among literary critics.[101] The epic of John Milton is a living book for Tillyard because he, with others, penetrates the surface of easily accepted religious language of Milton's time, and gets to the real meaning of *Paradise Lost*.

"It is strange how little, till quite recently critics have concerned themselves with the meaning of *Paradise Lost*. . . . Perhaps to those of earlier generations the meaning appeared too simple to need discussion. . . . But such simplemindedness can ill satisfy a generation which is sceptical of professed motives and which suspects the presence of others, either concealed or not realised by the author."[102]

We are moved onward by John Milton himself in the epic, for Milton does not consider the state of Adam and Eve entirely happy before the lapse. This is further motivation for the proper meaning of the epic to be, not *Paradise Lost,* but *Paradise Found.*

"Milton does not . . . . convince us that the prelapsarian life of Adam and Eve in the "happy Garden" was genuinely happy."[103]

In Book Five of the epic, line 513, The "Patriarch of mankind," Adam, puts his finger upon the unhappy nature of Eden, in the words:

"What meant that caution joind, if ye be found
Obedient? can wee want obedience then. . . .?"

The apparent lack of perfection in the Paradise of Eden, due to the necessity of both Eve and Adam to prove their obedience, is basic to the continued motivation of Milton: in moving the development of the epic from what is, for him, essentially Paradise Lost, on to *Paradise Found.*

The Epic Will Continue To Live

By whatever title, preferably that of *Paradise Found,* the epic will continue to live because it unfolds with matchless poetic imagery and beauty of expression that which is native and vital to the religious faith of the entire world. The epic will live by reason of the universal appeal to human nature of its account of the "bowery loneliness" of Paradise that so enchanted Tennyson. The epic will live by reason of its inseparable connection with Biblical truth. The epic will live by reason of its sheer artistry as an intellectual and emotional achievement. As long as the English language endures, the epic will hold its place in the reverent regard of understanding men.

PARADISE REGAIN'D

A study of both epics in terms of their contents and development will make clear the desire of Milton to relate at length and with great emphasis "the paradise within." This becomes the material of the second epic.

"The paradise within" is the climax of *Paradise Lost,* and it is handled too briefly in comparison with the weight and emphasis given the earlier development of the epic. This criticism does not at all affect the synthesis and completeness of *Paradise Lost,* nor does it mean that *Paradise Regain'd* was needed to round out the full development of the theme of *Paradise Lost,* which stands by itself, complete and final with no need of any sequel. *Paradise Lost* is a literary monument, self-contained, symmetrical, wanting nothing. Tillyard renounces any incompleteness within *Paradise Lost* in the following words:

"The mistaken idea that *Paradise Regain'd* is a sequel to *Paradise Lost* rests partly on the titles of the two poems and the opening lines of *Paradise Regain'd*, partly on the statement of Thomas Ellwood. When Milton writes

'I who E're while the happy Garden sung,
By one mans disobedience lost, now sing
Recover'd Paradise to all mankind'

he might appear to mean that he will now complete *Paradise Lost* by a supplementary poem. But he cannot really mean this, because the recovery of Paradise is an essential part of *Paradise Lost*."[104]

Hanford maintains the same position but believes that there are two separate epics:

"In spite of Ellwood's statement it seems likely that both (epics) had been in Milton's mind for some time. In *Reason of Church Government* he had expressed an equal interest in three literary forms, the long epic like the Aeneid, the short epic like the Book of Job, and tragedy on classical lines. *Paradise Lost, Paradise Regain'd,* and *Samson Agonistes* perfectly answer to the descriptions."[105]

In turning to Milton for the authentic picture from his pen, we find in *The Reason of Church Government* the plan projected in such a way that would suggest *Paradise Lost, Paradise Regain'd,* and *Samson Agonistes* to be the complete fulfillment of his plans.

"Time servs not now, and perhaps I might seem too profuse to give any certain account of what the mind at home in the spacious circuits of her musing hath liberty to propose to her self, though of highest hope, and hardest attempting, whether that Epick form whereof the two poems of Homer, and those other two of Virgil and Tasso are a diffuse, and the book of Job a brief model: or whether the rules of Aristotle herein are strictly to be kept, or nature to be follow'd, which in them that know art, and use Judgement is no transgression, but an inriching of art. And lastly what King or Knight before the conquest might be chosen in whom to lay the pattern of a Christian Heroe."[106]

The movement of *Paradise Regain'd* has a dominant appeal for the reader. The introduction links the writer with the former epic as the Book of Acts has an attachment to the writer of the Third Gospel. There is a common authorship in both cases. In the writing of the epics, Milton lifts one phase of the former epic to become the principal theme of the second. We dare not press the analogy too far; however, just as the Book of Acts was an out-growth of the Gospel of Luke, so *Paradise Regain'd* was an out-growth of *Paradise Lost*. The theme of the second epic presents the manner in which Christ, as the representative of man, confronts with overwhelming victory the temptation experiences, in contrast to the failure of Adam.

The epic opens with a statement of its relation to the former and much greater work, and presents the theme of the work at hand, *Paradise Regain'd*. The introduction likewise includes a reference to the One who will, by his victory "raise Eden in the wast Wilderness," and to the method by which the victory will be accomplished.

"I Who e're while the happy Garden sung,
　By one mans disobedience lost, now sing
　Recover'd Paradise to all mankind,
By one mans firm obedience fully tri'd
Through all temptation, and the Tempter foil'd
In all his wiles, defeated and repuls't,
And Eden rais'd in the wast Wilderness."[107]

The action proceeds from the baptism of Jesus and the divine pronouncement, to the preparation on the part of Satan and Christ for the conflict. This follows the invocation for help in the great task. The invocation in *Paradise Regain'd* is not to a Muse, as in *Paradise Lost,* but directly to the divine Spirit.

"Thou Spirit who ledst this glorious Eremite
Into the Desert, his Victorious Field
Against the Spiritual Foe, and broughtst him thence
By proof the undoubted Son of God, inspire,
As thou art wont, my prompted Song else mute. . ."[108]

The construction of *Paradise Regain'd* has a similarity to that of the Book of Job. The narrative of both works links together a series of dialogues. The division of the epic into four books, follows closely the Lukan account of the temptation experiences of Jesus in the wilderness. However the three distinct temptations as taken over from Luke into the body of the epic do not receive the same proportion of emphasis. The first temptation "to turn stones into bread" constitutes the prelude of the epic, and summons into action the challenge between the two main characters of the epic, Christ and Satan. The second temptation, "the kingdoms of the world," occupies the main body of the epic and stresses the predominance of this temptation over the other two. The important and significant place which the second temptation holds in the epic may be due to the personal experience of Milton. No doubt he associated with "the kingdoms of the world" his activity in the cause of England over a period of twenty years, which came to naught. The third and final temptation closes the challenge with the victory of Christ over Satan, a victory followed by the sudden exit of the vanquished Satan. Tillyard gives a clear picture of the construction of the epic.

"In structure the poem might be likened to an imaginary church. The preludes would correspond to an elaborate doorway at the west end leading to an ante-chapel (the first temptation). A second doorway (the prelude to the second temptation) leads from the ante-chapel to the body of the church. This, opening into transepts, corresponds to the second temptation with its visions expanding to Parthia and Rome. The chancel is the third temptation and the apse the epilogues."[109]

All men are Sons of God

There is a theological reference in *Paradise Regain'd* which has importance for the later consideration of this work. It is in regard to the words of Satan. We must remember it is Milton who places those words in the mouth of Satan. It is Milton who raises the question. It is Milton who presents at this point the character of Christ, and his relation to the Father. With the lines of the epic stating this, we will leave *Paradise Regain'd* with the bare statement of the relevant lines, to return to the importance of what these lines reply, in later consideration.

> "Thenceforth I thought thee worth my nearer view
> And narrower Scrutine, that I might learn
> In what degree or meaning thou art call'd
> The Son of God, which bears no single sence;
> The Son of God I also am, or was,
>
> . . . .
>
> All men are Sons of God."[110]

SAMSON AGONISTES

A good portion of the greatness of *Samson Agonistes* is due to the familiarity of Milton with the Greek Classics, as well as the Bible. In this regard we cannot overlook the parallel between the development of the theme and certain significant events within the life of Milton.

61

The poem is a tragedy, and Milton's life was full of the tragic. It is

"in effect a metaphor of the tragedy of his own life."[111]

Milton experienced with full public effect the meaning of desertion by the one in whom he had so definitely anticipated all that domestic happiness could mean for a man. He knew the grim effects of defeat in the national cause to which he gave so great a portion of his life. There is a parallel of emotion and tragedy mixed together in their separate lives, drawing them together in a unity of experience that made Milton the unexampled narrator and poet of this experience of Samson.

"Nothing put forth by Milton in verse in his whole life is so vehement an exhibition of his personality, such a proclamation of his own thoughts about himself and about the world around him, as is *Samson Agonistes*. . . . The Hebrew Samson among the Philistines and the English Milton among the Londoners of the reign of Charles the Second were, to all poetic intents, one and the same person. They were one and the same not only by the similarity of their final circumstances, but also by the reminiscences of their previous lives."[112]

It certainly takes a depth of emotional sensitivity and feeling to put into the beauty of poetic language the experience of another; and nothing is greater preparation for this than a kindred experience. Milton had that; and it is one reason for the great poetic monument, *Samson Agonistes*. Milton was able, to a large extent, to put himself in the place of Samson. With Samson he knew the utter loneliness of isolation and the bitter experience of blindness. Only one who knew the personal loss of eyesight could write with such emotional power and feeling, Samson's soliloquy on his blindness.

"O loss of sight, of thee I most complain!
Blind among enemies, O worse then chains,

Dungeon, or beggery, or decrepit age!
Light the prime work of God to me is extinct,
And all her various objects of delight
Annull'd, which might in part my grief have eas'd,
Inferior to the vilest now become
Of man or worm; the vilest here excell me,
They creep, yet see, I dark in light expos'd
To daily fraud, contempt, abuse and wrong,
Within doors, or without, still as a fool,
In power of others, never in my own;
Scarce half I seem to live, dead more then half.
O dark, dark, dark, amid the blaze of noon,
Irrecoverably dark, total Eclipse
Without all hope of day!
O first created Beam, and thou great Word,
Let there be light, and light was over all;
Why am I thus bereav'd thy prime decree?
The Sun to me is dark
And silent as the Moon,
When she deserts the night
Hid in her vacant interlunar cave.
Since light so necessary is to life,
And almost life it self, if it be true
That light is in the Soul,
She all in every part; why was the sight
To such a tender ball as th' eye confin'd?
So obvious and so easie to be quench't,
And not as feeling through all parts diffus'd,
That she might look at will through every pore?
Then had I not been thus exil'd from light;
As in the land of darkness yet in light,
To live a life half dead, a living death,
And buried; but O yet more miserable!
My self, my Sepulcher, a moving Grave,
Buried, yet not exempt
By priviledge of death and burial

From worst of other evils, pains and wrongs,
But made hereby obnoxious more
To all the miseries of life,
Life in captivity
Among inhuman foes.
But who are these? for with joint pace I hear
The tread of many feet stearing this way;
Perhaps my enemies who come to stare
At my affliction, and perhaps to insult,
Thir daily practice to afflict me more."[113]

Where Samson and Milton Part Company

There is the singularly autobiographical for Milton. He is "blind among enemies" in a commonwealth defuncted, which he so definitely wished to see well defined in England and the world. The light of the lost commonwealth was for Milton like the light entrusted to "such a tender ball as the eye." Why was sight not like feeling, entrusted throughout the body in "every pore"? In point of time, of course, *Samson Agonistes* was written after *Paradise Lost*. At the time *Paradise Lost* was written, however, John Milton had the same blindness, and consequently the same conviction. In the epic of the English language, Milton was not writing about the loss of anything worthwhile. Though "dark, dark, dark amid the blaze of noon" in the loss of physical eyesight, John Milton had the insight to write singularly about *Paradise Found*.

There is obvious danger in pressing too far this identity between Samson and Milton. One evident exception is the high sense of pride Milton almost invariably maintained. Unlike Samson, he had no fault which he was ready to confess. Samson confesses his fault in the following lines:

"Nothing of all these evils hath befall'n me
But justly; I myself have brought them on,
Sole Author I, sole cause."[114]

Here Milton and Samson part company, in a profound sense, even though Milton is the author of the lines. Perhaps this is one, if not the main reason, for the writing of *Samson Agonistes*. The full sense of the tragic comes when Samson, under the complete sense of guilt, gains victory over the personal isolation which temptation brought. The means by which that victory is achieved breathes the distinctly Greek spirit. The victory comes in the noble and magnificent sacrifice of self to bring defeat to the enemy and declare the righteous justice of God. For Milton, omit the sense of guilt, be sure to include the Greek spirit, join the classic with the Bible, and you have at least some of the metaphysical metaphors and material that constitute, *Paradise Found.*

PART II

MILTON THE THEOLOGIAN

CHAPTER SIX

A THEOLOGICAL COMMENTARY FOR PARADISE LOST

We have followed Milton in his poetic growth, from the ode, *On The Morning Of Christ's Nativity,* where we found first declared his genius, through the Sonnets to the great epic, *Paradise Lost,* and its lesser successor, *Paradise Regain'd.*

Each accomplishment placed a new gem in the literary crown of Milton. With one exception we gloried in his strength to write in such a way that those who read would "not willingly let it die." That one exception was the writings on divorce. Apart from his eagerness for the beautiful in life as well as literature, Milton had the esteem of Puritan England. He was the national Poet. By his poetic accomplishment, he held a commanding religious position in the orthodox Protestantism of England. He was indeed its voice — "its mighty voice."

The Liberal Tendency In Milton

The radical departure of Milton from the customary position concerning marriage and divorce suggests a tendency within his mental temperament. That tendency was to explore with the full spirit of independence and with complete freedom of mind the most conservative and established positions of life and thought. The full force of this spirit of individualism was turned by Milton upon the orthodoxy of the Christian Faith.

He was urged to this task by more than a mere desire for personal theological satisfaction. He undertook the work during the religious tolerance under Cromwell, and continued it during the Commonwealth period, at a time when the flexibility of religious faith allowed him unusual freedom in religious mat-

69

ters. During this time it was his ambition to write a handbook on theology with a distinctly Biblical basis, a handbook which would serve to unite Protestant Christianity, both in England and abroad. The ambition was realized in a work written in Latin, *De Doctrina Christiana.*

The work falls into its own historical setting, although there is considerable difficulty in determining the exact date of the completion. This is due to the fact that the work was not discovered until 1823. It was Milton's desire not to have the manuscript published until after his death, and this for political as well as for personal reasons. With the Restoration in England all hope for the plan of Protestant unity, as far as England was concerned, vanished. From the personal viewpoint, the material of *De Doctrina Christiana* was of such a nature that Milton's religious freedom as well as personal safety would have been endangered.

The manuscript has a romantic history. From the hands of Daniel Skinner, the last of Milton's secretaries, it was sent to Amsterdam, Holland, to the publisher Elzevir, to be printed. Skinner was warned of the political risk he incurred in the publication.[115] The manuscript was therefore returned, and found its way, along with the State letters Milton had written for Cromwell, into the Public Records office for safe keeping. There it lay buried until it was discovered by Robert Lemon, in 1823. King George IV placed the responsibility of translation and editing the work in the hands of Bishop Charles Sumner, who by 1825, completed the task and the book was published.

The nature of the *De Doctrina Christiana*, with its many references to Scripture, and the detailed construction on the basis of collated material, involved a lengthy period of preparation. In the preface Milton refers to the beginning of the work in his youth, and to the meticulous way he classified passages of Scripture.[116] The work was early started and long continued. Like *Paradise Lost*, it occupied Milton's thoughts over a lengthy course of his life. The time of its final completion is uncertain; however, evidence points to the fact that *De Doctrina Christiana* was in complete form about or shortly after the year 1661. Tillyard says:

"There is good evidence for dating *De Doctrina Christiana* from 1655 to 1660."[117]

J. H. Hanford writes:

"The details of the composition of Milton's great theological work . . . are not so clear. . . . The statement of Phillips indicates that he returned to it in 1655. There is evidence in the preserved manuscript that the work stood complete by about 1661."[118]

Hilaire Belloc says:

"Milton's mind began to turn against the body of orthodox tradition (in so far as this remained with the Protestant side of Europe at that time) after the violent shock of his ruined marriage in 1642.
During the seven years that followed, when he was unoccupied by any public duty, was in full possession of his sight, and at the height of his energy, with his books all round him for consultation at any moment, he collected his material, increasingly confirming the doubts that had arisen in him. He probably also actually composed the greater part of the text of the book in those years. But when with the year 1649 he had become plunged in heavy public work he could not continue it or complete it . . . .

. . . .
Thus we should have for the *De Doctrina* three main periods — no doubt joined up by notes and jottings. First, the collection of the material and probably much of the actual writing, between 1642 and 1649. Second, perhaps the last two years of the Commonwealth — 1658-1660, though he had already begun *Paradise Lost*. Third, for the

71

interpolation of special passages and the rounding up of the whole, the last years after the completion of the *Samson Agonistes* — 1667-1674."[119]

The date of *De Doctrina Christiana* has been given a place of literary and theological importance, in order that we might come to this statement in which all the authorities agree concerning at least the substance of the work. *De Doctrina Christiana* was in process at the same time Milton undertook the task of his great epic, *Paradise Lost. De Doctrina* . . . with its sober and closely reasoned development of the sincere thought of Milton, becomes a splendid theological commentary on both *Paradise Lost* and *Paradise Regain'd*. What, therefore, may have been ascribed to poetic license in the two epics, may in the light of the serious prose work of *De Doctrina* . . . be set forth as the true theological position of Milton. This is the case when we find agreement between the prose work and either or both of the epics. To ascertain the measure of this agreement becomes the adventure into the real theme of *Paradise Lost,* and the true outcome of the epic, in *Paradise Found.*

Before we enter directly into this, a consideration of Milton's philosophical procedure as he brought into question Protestant orthodoxy, will be helpful. Evident in the Preface, is the primacy of the Word of God. Milton intends to give himself to the compilation of an original treatise on Christian doctrine "derived solely from the word of God itself."[120] Even a cursory glance at *De Doctrina* . . . reveals with what faithfulness Milton studied Scriptural reference and cross-reference, until a conclusion was reached. The procedure is excellent, but we cannot overlook the nature and spirit of the mind that was brought to that inquiry. Milton brought to that significant and serious inquiry the *a priori* right of his own mind to judge every question, and the decision reached became determinative for his own life and thought (and for others who will accept that judgment) regardless of conclusions reached by the Church or State. In this procedure, if carried to its full implications, as Milton does, the spirit of the Reformation under Luther takes on radical proportions.

CHAPTER SEVEN

THEISM AND CHRISTOLOGY:
Comprising the following six sections

Section 1. The Theistic View
Section 2. The Divine Decrees
Section 3. Predestination
Section 4. The Son of God
Section 5. The Holy Spirit
Section 6. The Creation

Agreement Between Treatise and Epic

The format and structure, section by section of the treatise, *De Doctrina Christiana,* with parallel affirmations in the epic, *Paradise Lost,* serve our purpose. We, therefore, use the development of each point and section, in the order given in the treatise. Then we draw the parallel in the epic.

The adventure to find agreement between the treatise and the epic, or epics, reveals the true theological position of Milton. The measure of this agreement leads into the real theme of *Paradise Lost,* and the true outcome of the epic, in *Paradise Found.*

The first chapter of the treatise contains, after the introduction, a statement of what Milton understands as Christian doctrine, which he defines as:

". . . that Divine Revelation disclosed in various ages by Christ (though he was not known under that name in the beginning) concerning the nature and worship of the Deity,

73

for the promotion of the glory of God, and the salvation of mankind."[121]

Milton conceives the nature of faith, as "not the habit of believing, but the things to be habitually believed."[122] We proceed with these things, section by section, that for Milton are the objects of faith.

Section 1. *The Theistic View,* being a synopsis of the treatise(*)

The first important thing to be believed is that with reference to the nature and the character of God.

Every individual is so surrounded with the traces of God apparent throughout the whole of nature, that no one in his senses can remain ignorant of their meaning. Evidences of God are also imprinted upon the human mind. The beauty of the order and uniformity in the world bespeaks a beneficial purpose, as well as testifies some supreme efficient pre-existent Power ordained the world.

What we term conscience, or the ability of right reason to distinguish between right and wrong, requires the existence of God, the Lord and ruler of all things, to whom we must give an account of our actions, whether good or bad.

To know God completely is beyond the comprehension of the human mind; however, God has offered Himself to our contemplation both in Scripture and through His works. In this He has condescended to accommodate Himself to our capacities, as He desires we should conceive Him. We should not seek to go beyond the extent of this knowledge which God allows.

Within the Scriptures God has set forth His nature as spirit,

(*) *Ibid.,* Vol. XIV, pp. 25-61. This synopsis, and those that follow, are a summation of the essential points, in my own words. Direct quotations are so indicated from the treatise, with specifically located footnotes.

74

with the attributes of immensity, infinity, eternity, immutability, incorruptibility, omnipresence, and omnipotence, and with a unity of character that neither allows nor involves a contradiction.

The power of God, the wisdom of God, the will of God — all these have in a measure been made known to us. God is "the living God": His power is in sheer vitality of His being. God is wise: He is not only omniscient respecting the past and the present, but He is also prescient, knowing before-hand the thoughts and actions of free agents as yet unborn, and many ages before those thoughts or actions have their origin. The will of God is directed to man's good. It is a will infinitely pure and holy, most gracious, being abundant in goodness, in long-suffering and in mercy. In a word, just as God is true in respect of His nature, so He is true, faithful and just in respect of His will. To all of this Scripture bears witness; and in all of this man confronts God both as wonderful and beyond His comprehension.

The Character of God

In the treatise, Milton confronts the concept of fate, in more than one of its aspects.

". . . fate can be nothing but a divine decree emanating from some almighty power."[123]

In the epic,

"Though I uncircumscrib'd my self retire
And put not forth my goodness, which is free
To act or not, Necessitie and Chance
Approach not mee, and what I will is Fate."[124]

Treatise,

"Further, those who attribute the creation of every thing

75

to nature, must necessarily associate chance with nature as a joint divinity; so that they gain nothing by this theory, except that in the place of that one God, whom they cannot tolerate, they are obliged, however, reluctantly, to substitute two sovereign rulers of affairs, who must almost always be in opposition to each other.

In short, many visible proofs, the verification of numberless predictions, a multitude of wonderful works have compelled all nations to believe, either that God, or that some evil power whose name was unknown, presided over the affairs of the world. Now that evil should prevail over good, and be the true supreme power, is as unmeet as it is incredible."[125]

Epic,

"O Adam one Almightie is, from whom
All things proceed, and up to him return.
If not deprav'd from good, created all
Such to perfection, one first matter all
Indu'd with various forms, various degrees
Of substance, and in things that live, of life;
But more refin'd, more spiritous, and pure
As neerer to him plac't or neerer tending
Each in thir several active Sphears assignd,
Till body up to spirit work, in bounds
Proportiond to each kind. So from the root
Springs lighter the green stalk, from thence the leaves
More aerie, last the bright consummate floure
Spirits odorous breathes: flours and thir fruit
Mans nourishment, by gradual scale sublim'd
To vital Spirits aspire, to animal,
To intellectual, give both life and sense,
Fansie and understanding, whence the Soule

76

Reason receives, and reason is her being,
Discursive, or Intuitive; discourse
Is oftest yours, the latter most is ours,
Differing but in degree, of kind the same."[126]

In these passages in *Paradise Lost,* Milton affirms the unrivaled supremacy of God in nature, power and action. The parallelism with the treatise is at once evident. The place which Milton gives to Fate and Chance in these references immediately undermines the contention of the devils that Fate or Chance has proved their undoing. Our first Parents had another kind of freedom.

"As if predestination over-rul'd
Thir will, dispos'd by absolute Decree
Or high foreknowledge; they themselves decreed
Thir own revolt, not I: if I foreknew,
Foreknowledge had no influence in thir fault,
Which had no less prov'd certain unforeknown.
So without least impulse or shadow of Fate,
Or aught by me immutable foreseen,
They trespass, Authors to themselves in all
Both what they judge and what they choose; for so
I formd them free, and free they must remain
Till they enthrall themselves."[127]

Moral consciousness operates only when there is a distinction between what one should do from what one must do. This fact of moral consciousness is evident in the epic, in the following lines, so significant:

"Freely they stood who stood, and fell who fell.
Not free, what proof could they have givn sincere
Of true allegiance, constant Faith or Love,
Where onely what they needs must do, appeard,
Not what they would? what praise could they receive?

What pleasure I from such obedience paid,
When Will and Reason (Reason also is choice)
Useless and vain, of freedom both despoild,
Made passive both, had servd necessitie,
Not mee."[128]

Treatise and Epics

The conditions for obedience were prescribed. Deeper, these conditions were written into the very structure of the traditional acceptance of the prelapsarian state of Eve and Adam. That Milton does not accept these conditions for obedience can be seen only as one discerns the irony beneath and between the lines. Milton here plays philosophically with the conditions for obedience.

Can Eden, or Paradise, be considered altogether good if obedience is conditional? Can Eden, or Paradise be considered altogether good if, in revolt to these conditions; Milton, after the Fall, invests Eve and Adam with something higher than obedience?

We repeat Book Five, line 513 of the epic, where Adam expresses the unhappy nature of Eden, in the words:

"What meant that caution joind, if ye be found
Obedient? can wee want obedience then. . . .?"[129]

For Milton the tree of knowledge, representing reason, is metaphysically real! The development later in *Paradise Lost,* and the structural development throughout *Paradise Regain'd* affirm the power in man, by unaided reason, to work out his own salvation.

At this place in the epic the reduction of Reason to servitude, and loss of freedom, is expressed by Milton for acceptance by the orthodoxy of his day. As the epic develops later, it is but an interlude for the later introduction of the supremacy of Man, like Christ in *Paradise Regain'd* to achieve true freedom.

"Since thy original lapse, true Libertie
Is lost, which alwayes with right Reason dwells
Twinn'd, and from her hath no dividual being:
Reason in man obscur'd, or not obeyd,
Immediately inordinate desires
And upstart Passions catch the Government
From Reason, and to servitude reduce
Man till then free."[130]

Milton will not accept the conditions for obedience, as prescribed, with their limitation upon freedom and their reduction of Reason to a condition of servitude, respecting salvation. Read again the line above,

"Reason in man obscur'd, or not obeyd,"

and you have another key to the displeasure of more than Eve and Adam in Paradise. It is supremely the displeasure of John Milton. This displeasure leads, later, to material where with the aid of *De Doctrina Christiana* there is openly declared the supremacy of reason in, *Paradise Found*. This becomes somewhat evident in the Divine Decrees, now to be considered.

Section 2. *The Divine Decrees,* being a synopsis
of the treatise(*)

The efficiency of God is either internal or external. The internal efficiency of God is that which is independent of all extraneous agency. Such are the decrees of God.

These decrees are general or special. God's general decree is that decree from all eternity which establishes His own most free and holy and wise purpose, whatever He himself willed, or whatever was about to do.

(*) *Ibid,* Vol. XIV, pp. 61-89.

God makes a reservation in the fact that He decreed nothing absolutely, which He left in the power of free agents. These decrees that are not absolute, Milton calls contingent decrees. He relates them to man, who is endowed by God with freedom of the will. This places man's actions on a basis independent of divine compulsion.

The success or failure of man under temptation depends entirely upon His free will, and does not come under the divine necessity or the prescience of God. It is therefore clear that Man's liberty of action was not subject to an absolute decree, nor the result of his actions the consequence of God's foreknowledge of the Fall.

Of the special decrees, the first and most important is that which regards the Son of God. It is from this decree that God derives His name of Father. Both the decrees and the will of God must neither be separated from his counsel and foreknowledge, nor given priority of order. The foreknowledge of God is the idea of everything God wanted to do before He actually made the decrees. Thus past, present, future are for God but one view.

Treatise,

"For the foreknowledge of God is nothing but the wisdom of God, under another name, or that idea of everything, which he had in his mind, to use the language of men, before he decreed anything."[131]

Epic,

"Him God beholding from his prospect high,
Wherein past, present future he beholds,
Thus to his onely Son foreseeing spake."[132]

80

Even though God foreknows all future events, His decrees do not cover all absolutely. This avoids any imputation of sin to God, and allows for the free agency of man and natural cause. Thus God's prescience means that He sees events will happen, and certifies their taking place, but His prescience is intransitive to the actual cause of the events.

> ". . . They therefore as to right belongd,
> So were created, nor can justly accuse
> thir maker, or thir making, or thir Fate;
> As if Predestination over-rul'd
> Thir will, dispos'd by absolute Decree
> Or high foreknowledge; they themselves decreed
> Thir own revolt, not I; if I foreknew
> Foreknowledge had no influence on their fault,
> Which had no less prov'd certain unforeknown.
> So without least impulse or shadow of Fate
> Or aught by me immutablie foreseen,
> They trespass, Authors to themselves in all
> Both what they judge and what they choose; for so
> I formd them free, and free they must remain,
> Till they enthrall themselves: I else must change
> Thir nature, and revoke the high Decree
> Unchangeable, Eternal, which ordain'd
> Thir freedom, they themselves ordain'd thir fall."[133]

Milton notes a difference between man made perfect and being immutable. The burden of man's freedom then is to persevere in his perfection, rendering unto God a service, voluntary as well as obedient. Again there comes into focus the conditional aspect of Paradise being perfect, and perfectly acceptable to Adam, Eve, and especially Milton. In the lines above, Milton discerns in the treatise, as indicated in the foregoing synopsis, and now localized in the epic, a strategic tension between the perfect being of God, and the imperfectness of man, by way of the divine decrees.

81

"I formd them free, and free they must remain,
Till thy enthrall themselves."

We cannot dismiss from the mind of Milton the unhappy nature
of Eden, as a real Paradise, and God's prescience to the actual
fall of "our first Parents," though God claims being intransitive
to this Fall.

If God, who established the conditions of the first Paradise
of Eden, knew that Eve and then Adam, in that order, would
"enthrall themselves"; then the central question is: What kind
of Paradise is this Eden?

Accepting all the structured relationships that constituted
Eden, could Eden have been a real Paradise for God, let alone
for Eve and Adam, if beforehand there was known by God
the enthrallment of the First Pair? Milton never leaves this
condition of enthrallment, and places the responsibility for this
imperfection of Eden, as a Paradise, not in the lap of Fate,
but in that of God. To avoid a dichotomy, a division in the
Godhead, John Milton has the total adventure of Eve and Adam
issue, not in enthrallment of *Paradise Lost*, but in *Paradise
Found*.

The irony, for Milton, is more than subtle. It is direct. With
God all powerful, all-knowing, and prescient of the result; He
yet did not hinder Satan. He yet did not prevent the separation,
commonly known as the Fall. The responsibility for this separation presses back, for Milton, beyond Eve and Adam, and finds
central and ominous location in God.

"Meanwhile the hainous and despightfull act
Of Satan done in Paradise, and how
Hee in the Serpent had perverted Eve,
Her Husband shee, to taste the fatall fruit,
Was known in Heav'n; for what can scape the Eye

82

Of God All-seing, or deceave his Heart
Omniscient, who in all things wise and just,
Hinder'd not Satan to attempt the minde
Of Man, with strength entire, and free Will arm'd,
Complete to have discover'd and repulst
Whatever wiles of Foe or seeming Friend."[134]

How could the Paradise of Eden be perfect, for Milton or anyone else, when in it there was to be found, "wiles of Foe or
seeming Friend?" There is more than an uneasiness about the
foreknowledge of God concerning future events, and the certainty with which these events are held to follow. It is a very
thin line which Milton purposely draws between the certainty
and the necessity of these actions which are God's knowledge
of future events.

"They will happen certainly, because the divine prescience
cannot be deceived, but they will not happen necessarily,
because prescience can have no influence on the object
foreknown, inasmuch as it is only an intransitive action.
What therefore is to happen according to contingency and
the free will of man, is not the effect of God's prescience,
but is produced by the free agency of its own natural causes,
the future spontaneous inclination of which is perfectly
known to God."[135]

Milton insists that the occurrence is certain of the events
which God forsees. This is so in order to substantiate the
divine prescience. It is man's will that produces the certainty
of these events.

In the depths of this situation one is forced to ask how man
can execute these events other than in keeping with the divine
prescience. Man's viewpoint, being temporal, he does not know
what the future events are, even though he is in the position
of the creator in respect of them. He cannot view them ob-

jectively or give them final evaluation, until they are consummated.

God's viewpoint being eternal, His omniscience holds in full and perfect survey the events in their consummation. When this is contemplated with the full emphasis placed upon the prescience of God, we must affirm that before the act of creation itself God knew of the Fall. This Milton affirms. Before creation, God knew that the Fall would involve Him and His holy nature in a process of Redemption.

When God pronounced the creation *good,* that evaluation, in the light of the divine prescience, would include all that is involved in the total process of creation, both present and future. This includes, sin, salvation, all of life. To assert otherwise would seem, as we view the divine prescience in the light of the total organism of truth, to involve God in contradiction. For John Milton, the only way to avoid this contradiction in the being of God, is to accept the unhappy state of the Paradise Eden, and move as he does to *Paradise Found.*

Section 3. *Predestination,* being a synopsis
of the treatise(*)

The principal special decree of God relating to man is termed Predestination, whereby God in pity for mankind, though foreseeing that they would fall of their own accord, predestinated to eternal salvation before the foundation of the world those who should believe and continue in the faith, and this for a manifestation of the glory of His mercy, grace, and wisdom, according to His purpose in Christ. Predestination, according to Milton, includes election alone, and does not refer to reprobation. The ultimate purpose of predestination is salvation of believers, a thing in itself desirable, whereas the object which reprobation has in view is the destruction of unbelievers, a thing

(*) *Ibid.,* Vol. XIV, pp. 91-175.

in itself ungrateful and odious; whence it is clear that God could never have predestinated reprobation, or proposed it to himself as an end.

There is no particular predestination, with Peter elected because he is Peter or John because he is John. The election is general, including Peter and John because they are believers. The privilege of election belongs to all who heartily believe and continue in their belief.

Predestination was not an absolute decree before the fall of man, but was contingent upon the fall of man. True, the apostasy of the first man was foreknown by the infinite wisdom of God; however, predestination ought always to be considered and defined as arising, not so much from a decree itself, as from the immutable condition of a decree.

Predestination is the effect of God's mercy, love, and grace, and wisdom in Christ: and it is to these qualities that we ought to attribute it, and not to His absolute and secret will, even in those passages of Scripture where mention is made of His will only.

Only on the condition of faith in Christ, has God predestinated us. This faith must be exercised by the will of man; therefore there is no inconsistence here with justice, or with grace. This is not to be construed as making God dependent upon the human will. The human will is to be seen as made free by God for the purpose that man, of his own volition, may express love, and worship, and devotion to God, and thus, by such an exercise of faith and devotion, receive from God predestination to eternal salvation.

Those who do not believe or continue in the faith, come under reprobation; and this reprobation is a consequence of their lack of faith, not a decree. There can be no reprobation of individuals from all eternity. Within man some remnants of the divine image remain, which enable him to choose the grace of God which is sufficient for salvation. Just as election is established and confirmed by faith, so reprobation is rescinded by repentance. From all this it follows that God excludes no one from the pale of repentance and eternal salvation, till he has despised and rejected the propositions of sufficient grace offered even to a late hour.

In predestination God's mercy, grace and wisdom are seen as they unfold in Christ Jesus. Those who believe and continue steadfast in faith become predestined to eternal salvation. This becomes effectual in the might and power of the Son, and in keeping with the eternal purpose.

"O Son, in whom my Soul hath delight,
Son of my bosom, Son who art alone
My word, my wisdom, and effectual might,
All hast thou spok'n as my thoughts are, all
As my Eternal purpose hath decreed:
Men shall not quite be lost, but sav'd who will,
Yet not of will in him, but grace in me
Freely voutsaft; once more I will renew
His lapsed powers, though forfeit and enthrall'd
By sin to foul exorbitant desires;
Upheld by me, yet once more he shall stand
On even ground against his mortal foe.
By me upheld, that he may know how frail
His fall'n condition is, and to me ow
All his deliv'rence, and to none but me."[136]

Milton uses believers in the same category as the elect.

Treatise,
". . . whence I infer that believers are the same as the elect, and that the terms are used indiscriminately."[137]

Epic,
"The Spirit of God, promis'd alike and giv'n
To all Believers. . . ."[138]

Treatise,

"In this was manifested the love of God towards us, because that God sent his only begotten Son into the world." &c. Hence there was no grace decreed for man who was to fall, no mode of reconciliation with God. Independently of the foreknown sacrifice of Christ; and since God has so plainly declared that predestination is the effect of his mercy, and love, and grace, and wisdom in Christ. . . ."139

Epic,

"And now without redemption all mankind
Must have bin lost, adjudg'd to Death and Hell
By doom severe, had not the Son of God,
In whom the fulness dwels of love divine,
His dearest mediation thus renewd.
Father, thy word is past, man shall find grace;
And shall grace not find means, that finds her way,
The speediest of thy winged messengers,
To visit all thy creatures, and to all
Comes unprevented, unimplor'd, unsought,
Happie for man, so coming.............."140

Treatise,

"When, however, God determined to restore mankind, he also without doubt decreed that the liberty of will which they had lost should be at least partially regained, which was but reasonable. Whomsoever therefore in the exercise of that degree of freedom which their will had acquired either previously to their call, or by reason of the call itself, God had seen in any respect willing or running (who it is probable are here meant by the ordained), to them he gave greater power of willing and running, that is of believing."141

87

Treatise,

"For **God** has predestinated to salvation, on the proviso of a general condition, all who enjoy freedom of will."[142]

Treatise and Epic

These last two extracts are exceedingly important, especially for the later development, that Milton was not writing about the loss of Paradise. He was affirming *Paradise Found.*

The focus is not upon the external state of man, but the internal. It is what essentially is *within man* that concerns John Milton in *Paradise Found.* This is, in the epic, a parallel to the last two quotations from the treatise, *De Doctrina Christiana.* Milton affirms the freedom of the Reason, and the fact that **God** made Reason right.

Epic,

"To whom thus Adam fervently repli'd.
O Woman, best are all things as the will
Of God ordaind them, his creating hand
Nothing imperfect or deficient left
Of all that he Created, much less Man,
Or ought that might his happie State secure,
Secure from outward force; within himself
The danger lies, yet lies within his power:
Against his will he can receave no harme.
But God left free the Will, for what obeyes
Reason, is free, and Reason he made right,
But bid her well beware, and still erect,
Least by some faire appearing good surpris'd
She dictate false, and missinforme the Will
To do what God expresly hath forbid."[143]

Section 4. *The Son of God,* being a synopsis
of the treatise(*)

(*) *Ibid.,* Vol. XIV, pp. 177-357.

The external efficiency of God, or the execution of His decrees, whereby He carries into effect by external agency whatever decrees He has purposed within Himself is comprised under heads of Generation, Creation, and the Government of the Universe.

Under the first of these heads, namely Generation, falls the fact that God has begotten His only Son; and from this God has derived His appellation of Father. In Scripture there is a double sense in which the Father is said to have begotten the Son, the one literal, with reference to the production of the Son, the other metaphorical, with reference to His exaltation. The passages which refer to the exaltation and mediatorial functions of Christ must not be used as proof of His generation from all eternity. In Scripture it is impossible to find a single text to prove the eternal generation of the Son. There are various passages which prove the existence of the Son before the world was made, but they conclude nothing respecting His generation from all eternity.

Of His own free will God begot the Son, not out of necessity, but in consequence of His own decree. The decree, therefore existed before its operation and fulfillment in the generation of the Son; and this places the Son within the limits of time. *The Son is not eternal,* as the Father; but is the first born, and the beginning of the creation of God. When it is said that "all things were made by Him" (the Son), it must be understood of a *secondary* and *delegated* power.

Neither from reason nor from Scripture can it be maintained that the Son and the Father and the Spirit are one in essence. There is one indivisible God. The Son declares that He is one with the Father, *not in essence, but in unanimity of action, or in intimacy of communion.* (*) The Son declares that He is one with the Father in the same manner we are one with Him:

(*) The italics above are entirely my own: to give importance to these statements of John Milton, in the treatise, *De Doctrina Christiana.*

89

that is, not in essence, but in love, in communion, in agreement, in charity, in spirit, in glory. This — the purest Arianism — is the interpretation Milton gives of the passages in John:

"Believest thou not that I am in the Father, and the Father in me? the words that I speak unto you, I speak not of myself, but the Father that dwelleth in me, He doeth the works."[144]

". . . that they all may be one, as thou, Father, art in me, and I in thee; that they also may be one in us."[145]

Treatise and Epic

From the standpoint of reason, Milton guards well the indivisible unity of God, as the Father. Whenever the name, attributes, and works of God are ascribed to the Son, they belong in their original and proper sense to the Father alone. *The Son possesses whatever share of Deity is assigned to Him by the peculiar gift and kindness of the Father.*

In this view, the Father is greater than the Son in all things; both the Son and the apostles bear witness to the truth of this. This external efficiency of God by the execution of His decrees places the day of the Son's generation within the events of creation.

These facts, drawn from the treatise, *De Doctrina Christiana,* have prominent parallels in the epic, *Paradise Lost.*

"Hear all ye Angels, Progenia of Light,
Thrones, Dominations, Princedoms, Vertues, Powers,
Hear my Decree, which unrevok't shall stand.
This day I have begot whom I declare
My onely Son, and on this holy Hill
Him have annointed, whom ye now behold
At my right hand."[146]

The regal power of the Father invested in the Son is a security against the designs and tumults of His foes.

"To whom the Son with calm aspect and cleer
Light'ning Divine, ineffable, serene,
Made answer. Mightie Father, thou thy foes
Justly hast in derision, and secure
Laugh'st at thir vain designes and tumults vain,
Matter to me of Glory, whom thir hate
Illustrates, when they see all Regal Power
Giv'n me to quell thir pride, and in event
Know whether I be dextrous to subdue
Thy Rebels, or be found the worst in Heav'n."[147]

The Regal Scepter in the Son is the occasion for spiritual obeisance.

"Canst thou with impious obloquie condemne
The just Decree of God, pronounc't and sworn,
That to his only Son by right endu'd
With Regal Scepter, every Soule in Heav'n
Shall bend the knee, and in that honour due
Confess him rightful King?"[148]

Both the power and the glory of the Father are conferred on the Son.

"To honour his Anointed Son aveng'd
Upon his enemies, and to declare
All power on him transferr'd: whence to his Son
Th' Assessor of his Throne he thus began.
Effulgence of my Glorie, Son belov'd,
Son in whose face invisible is beheld
Visibly, what by Deitie I am,
And in whose hand what by Decree I doe,
Second Omnipotence."[149]

Through his victory the Son has proved himself worthy to reign,

91

and is thus received by the Father seated at the right hand of God.

> ". . . each order bright
> Sung Triumph, and him sung Victorious King,
> Son, Heire, and Lord, to him Dominion giv'n,
> Worthiest to Reign: he celebrated rode
> Triumphant through mid Heav'n, into the Courts
> And Temple of his mightie Father Thron'd
> On high; who into Glorie him receav'd,
> Where now he sits at the right hand of bliss."[150]

Prior to all other acts of Creation the Son existed as the Logos. Through him all other things were made both in heaven and earth.

Treatise,
> "Certain, however, it is, whatever some of the moderns may allege to the contrary, that the Son existed in the beginning, under the name of the Logos or word, and was the first of the whole creation, by whom afterwards all other things were made both in heaven and earth."[151]

In the Son the effulgence of the Father's glory shines and has its temporal abode.

Epic,
> "Thee next they sang of all Creation first
> Begotten Son, Divine Similitude,
> In whose conspicuous cont'nance, without cloud
> Made visible, th' Almighty Father shines,
> Whom else no Creature can behold; on thee
> Impreast the effulgence of his Glorie abides,
> Transfus'd on thee his ample Spirit rests.

Hee Heav'n of Heavens and all the Powers therein
By thee created. . . ."[152]

There is no necessity encumbent upon God in the generation
of his Son, and no inhibition to the free execution of his works.

Treatise,
". . . particularly since the Father is God, all whose works,
and consequently the works of generation, are executed
freely according to his own good pleasure, as has been already proved from Scripture."[153]

Treatise,
". . . That however the generation of the Son may have
taken place, it arose from no natural necessity, as is generally contended, but was no less owing to the decree and
will of the Father than his priesthood or kingly power, or
his resuscitation from the dead."[154]

Epic,
". . . Necessitie and Chance
Approach not mee."[155]

Epic,
". . . No need that thou
Shouldst propagat, already infinite."[156]

The relationship between the Father and the Son is not one
of essence. The Son attributes to the Father that which is greater than all else, and therefore essentially different from him.
*It is a relationship in which Father and Son are one, not in
essence but in speaking and acting with unanimity.* The Son
is also one with the Father in the same way we are one with
Christ, in love and communion, in spirit and glory.

Treatise,

> "In the first place, they are one, inasmuch as they speak and act with unanimity."[157]

Treatise,

> "Secondly, he declares himself to be one with the Father in the same manner as we are one with him; that is not in essence, but in love, in communion, in agreement, in charity, in spirit, in glory."[158]

In the epic the oneness of Father and Son, as well as the redeemed is by unanimity of purpose and communion.

Epic,

> "To better life shall yeeld him, where with me
> All my redeemd may dwell in joy and bliss,
> Made one with me as I with thee am one."[159]

The epic too sets forth the glory of the Son as conferred upon him by the Father.

Epic,

> "So spake the Father, and unfoulding bright
> Toward the right hand his Glorie, on the Son
> Blaz'd forth unclouded Deitie; he full
> Resplendent all his Father manifest
> Express'd, and thus divinely answer'd milde."[160]

After the decrees the Son was begotten of the Father, within the limits of time. The decree then was prior to the Fatherhood of God.

Treatise,

> "Thus the Son was begotten of the Father in consequence of his decree, and therefore within the limits of time, for

the decree itself must have been anterior to the execution of the decree, as is sufficiently clear from the insertion of the word today."[161]

In the epic the same serial relationship prevails: God, Decree, Son and Fatherhood.

Epic,
"Hear my Decree, which unrevok't shall stand.
This day I have begot whom I declare
My onely Son, and on this holy Hill
Him have anointed, whom ye now behold
At my right hand."[162]

In a most vital way Milton notes there is a distinction of wills in those who have not the same essence.

Treatise,
"Now it is manifest that those who have not the same will, cannot have the same essence. It appears however from many passages, that the Father and Son have not, in a numerical sense, the same intelligence or will."[163]

Relative to this statement Milton explores various passages of Scr'pture, all of the passages cited leading to three important questions. The passages are as follows: "no man knoweth . . . but my Father only" (Matthew 24:36); "neither the Son, but the Father" (Mark 13:32); "I came down from heaven, not to do mine own will, but the will of him that sent me" (John 6:38); "thinkest thou that I cannot now pray to my Father, and he shall presently give me more than twelve legions of angels?" (Matthew 26:53); "Abba, Father, all things are possible unto thee; take away this cup from me" (Mark 14:36); "I appoint unto you a kingdom, as my Father hath appointed unto me" (Luke 22:29); "Father into thy hands I commend my spirit" (Luke 23:46); "Father save me from this hour." (John 12:27).

Treatise,
"(1) If these prayers be uttered only in his human capacity, which is the common explanation, why does he petition these things from the Father alone instead of from himself, if he were God?

(2) Or rather, supposing him to be at once man and the supreme God, why does he ask at all for what was in his own power?

(3) What need was there for the union of the divine and human nature in one person, if he himself, being equal to the Father, gave back again into his hands everything that he had received from him?"[164]

Epic,
"O Father, O Supream of heav'nly Thrones,
First, Highest, Holiest, Best, thou alwayes seekst
To glorifie thy Son, I always thee,
As is most just; this I my Glorie account,
My exaltation, and my whole delight,
That thou in me well pleas'd, declarst thy will
Fulfill'd, which to fulfil is all my bliss.
Scepter and power, thy giving, I assume,
And gladlier shall resign, when in the end
Thou shalt be All in All, and I in thee
For ever, and in mee all whom thou lov'st."[165]

Milton is definitive as to the relationship of divinity the Son holds to the Father. Even the attributes of divinity do not include him, but belong to the Father alone.

Treatise,

"The Son likewise teaches that the attributes of divinity belong to the Father alone, to the exclusion even of himself."[166]

We list some selections from *Paradise Lost* to show the transference of this view of the Father and the Son.

Epic,

"Scepter and Power, thy giving, I assume
And gladlier shall resign, when in the end
Thou shalt be All in All and I in thee
Forever. . . ."[167]

Epic,

"Son, thou in whom my glory I behold
In full resplendence, Heir of all my might,
Neerly it now concerns us to be sure
Of our omnipotence. . . ."[168]

Epic,

"He said, and on his Son with Rayes direct
Shon full, he all his Father full expresst
Ineffably into his face receiv'd,
And thus the filial Godhead answering spake."[169]

Epic,

". . . Mean while the Son
On his great Expedition now appear'd,
Girt with Omnipotence, with Radiance crown'd
Of Majestic Divine, Sapience and Love
Immense, and all his Father in him shon."[170]

We have reserved for the last citation, that which is the most evident in Milton's total conception of the relationship between the Father and the Son.

Epic,

"Because thou hast, though Thron'd in highest bliss
Equal to God, and equally enjoying
God-like fruition, quitted all to save
A World from utter loss, and hast been found
By Merit more than Birthright Son of God,
Found worthiest to be so by being Good,
Farr more then Great or High."[171]

This view of the relationship of the Son to the Father is common to both the treatise and the epic. The Son's relationship to the Father is one of complete dependence in the fact that the Father delegates to the Son any substance they share. There was an impartation from God to the Son. We note a fine distinction here, namely, that the substance of the Father that was manifest in the Son was the property of the Son not as to nature, but purely as an imparted gift.

What we see of divine substance in the Son, therefore, is not of the intrinsic nature of the Son: rather, it is but the reflection of the Father.

Treatise,

"It must be understood from this, that God imparted to the Son as much as he pleased of the divine nature, nay of the divine substance itself, care being taken not to confound the substance with the whole essence, which would imply, that the Father had given to the Son what he retained numerically the same himself. . . ."[172]

Epic,

"So Spake the Father, and unfoulding bright
Toward the right hand his Glorie, on the Son
Blaz'd forth unclouded Deitie; he full
Resplendent all his Father manifest
Express'd, and thus divinely answer'd milde."[173]

This is in keeping with Milton's view that the Son was both in point of time and in creation the consequence of God's decree. This withholds from the nature of Christ any attribute of eternity, and makes his relationship with the Father, "serial," rather than organic. The treatise expounds this position concerning Christ. To repeat the statement already quoted:

Treatise,
"Thus the Son was begotten of the Father in consequence of his decree, and therefore within the limits of time, for the decree itself must have been anterior to the excution of the decree, as is sufficiently clear from the insertion of the word today."[174]

Milton expresses this same view in the epic.

Epic,
"Hear my Decree, which unrevok't shall stand:
This day I have begot whom I declare
My onely Son, and on this holy Hill
Him have anointed, whom ye now behold
At my right hand."[175]

We reserve further comment respecting the position of Milton as to Christ, until we explore what he has to say about the Holy Spirit. Sufficient is it now to see as respects the Father and Son the lack of any organic and substantial relationship.

We turn now to consider Milton's view concerning Father, Son, and Holy Spirit. This will make it possible to state in formal and complete fashion the implications of Milton's total position respecting the Godhead.

The radical views of Milton's theology, by the standards of his own day, mount in importance as one relates what is further found in the treatise, *De Doctrina Christiana* and directly reflected in the epic, *Paradise Lost.* The way in which this radical development expresses itself in freedom of mind and spirit is basic to the material that constitutes, *Paradise Found*.

Section 5. *The Holy Spirit*, being a synopsis
of the treatise(*)

Scripture is silent respecting the nature of the Holy Spirit, the manner of His origin and existence. We, therefore, are unable to say whether the Holy Spirit was created, generated, or had some other mode of existence.

The name Spirit is used variously throughout the entire Bible, and does not refer alone to the Third Person of the Godhead. It is applied to God, the Father, denoting his power, virtue, or more particularly the divine breath or influence by which everything was created or nourished. Sometimes the Spirit is used with reference to the Son, through whom the Father is so often said to have created all things. Occasionally the Spirit means an angel. More particularly, the Spirit implies that light which was shed on Christ. Finally, the Spirit signifies the person itself of the Holy Spirit, or its symbol, and the gifts the Spirit bestows.

Although the Holy Spirit did not take upon Himself any of the mediatorial functions, as did Christ, and was not engaged by the obligations of a filial relation to pay obedience to the Father, yet *the Holy Spirit must be considered as inferior to both Father and Son.* He is represented and declared to be subservient and obedient in all things; to have been promised, and sent, and given; to speak nothing of himself; and even to have been given as an earnest.

He who sent both the Spirit of his Son and the Son Himself, He on whom we are taught to call, and on whom the Spirit himself calls, is the one God and the only Father.

From this it follows that any ascriptions of divine attributes to the Spirit have no support in Scripture; and this includes the works as well as the divine honors.

(*) *Ibid.*, Vol. XIV, pp. 357-403.

The Holy Spirit is one of three persons in the Godhead, with all power alone and exclusively inherent in the Father. The Son does everything in the name of the Father, and the Spirit everything in the name of the Father and the Son. The Father alone is our God, of whom are both the Son and the Spirit. The Holy Spirit is a minister of God, created of the substance of God, not by necessity but by the free will of God, probably before the foundation of the world but later than the Son, far inferior to him.

The relation of the Spirit to the Christ, and the manner by means of which the glory of the Father shines upon the Son, is set forth in the treatise and in the epic.

Treatise,

"The descent therefore and appearance of the Holy Spirit in the likeness of a dove, seems to have been nothing more than a representation of the ineffable affection of the Father for the Son, communicated by the Holy Spirit under the appropriate image of a dove, and accompanied by a voice from heaven declaratory of that affection."[176]

Epic,

"Thee next they sang of all Creation first,
Begotten Son, Divine Similitude,
In whose conspicuous count'nance, without cloud
Made visible, th' Almighty Father shines,
Whom else no Creature can behold; on thee
Impresst the effulgence of his Glorie abides,
Transfus'd on thee his ample Spirit rests."[177]

Treatise and Epics

This certainly represents, Christ, the Son, as receiving from the Father, *a delegated glory* and Divine Similitude. This glory and this Divine Similitude were not organic to the nature of the Son. This is what Milton meant when he affirmed, "In whose conspicuous count'nance . . . the Almighty Father shines."

Treatise,

"Lest however we should be altogether ignorant who or what the Holy Spirit is, although Scripture nowhere teaches us in express terms, it may be collected from passages quoted above, that the Holy Spirit, inasmuch as he is a minister of God, and therefore a creature, was created or produced of the substance of God, not by a natural necessity, but by the free will of the agent, probably before the foundations of the world were laid, but later than the Son and far inferior to him."[178]

The statement reveals the fact that Milton recognized all three aspects of the Trinity, and offers some indication of their nature. It also suggests somewhat of a view of their relation and degrees of importance. Milton affirms more clearly their serial relationship in these words:

"The power of the Father is inherent in himself, that of the Son and the Spirit is received from the Father; for it has been already proved on the authority of the Son, that the Son does everything in the name of the Father, and the Spirit every thing in the name of the Father and the Son."[179]

What this statement suggests concerning the inferior nature of the Holy Spirit is plainly affirmed by Milton in the following passage.

Treatise,

"The nature of these particulars is such, that although the Holy Spirit be nowhere said to have taken upon himself any mediatorial functions, as is said of Christ, not to be engaged by the obligations of a filial relation to pay obedience to the Father, yet he must evidently be considered

102

as inferior to both Father and Son, inasmuch as he is represented and declared to be subservient and obedient in all things; to have been promised, and sent, and given; to speak nothing of himself; and even to have been given as an earnest."[180]

This is a clear assertion of a lack of co-equality within the Three Persons of the Trinity. There is not only numerical difference, but a difference in essence. Milton does not leave us in doubt about this matter.

Treatise,
". . . it will be universally acknowledged that the Son now at least differs numerically from the Father; but those who differ numerically must differ also in their proper essences, as the logicians express it, is too clear to be denied by any one possessed of common reason. Hence it follows that the Father and the Son differ in essence. That this is the true doctrine, reason shows on every view of the subject. . . ."[181]

In Book eight of the epic one comes face to face with this subtle tri-theism of Milton. The Almighty thus addresses Adam.

Epic,
"What thinkest thou then of mee, and this my State,
Seem I to thee sufficiently possest
Of happiness, or not? who am alone
From all Eternitie, for none I know
Second to mee or like, equal much less."[182]

Adam thus makes reply to God.

Epic,
"Thou in thy self art perfect, and in thee
Is no deficience found; not so is Man,
But in degree, the cause of his desire
By conversation with his like to help,

103

Or solace his defects. No need that thou
Shouldst propagat, already infinite;
And through all numbers absolute, though One."[183]

Milton stands forth in bold position, a position that indicates the wide ramification of freedom of his mind and spirit.
He is a man, not of his century theologically. He is a man
whose unorthodoxy does not belong to the fourth century
Council of Nicea, or the fifth century Council of Chalcedon,
or any of the seventeenth century Church Councils. John Milton
is his own council. The Enlightenment that belongs to the century after John Milton, has found its source in the expansive
mind and spirit of a man whose position is bereft of any orthodoxy but his own.

The Triune God vanishes, for Milton, and even if what is
left be called a Tritheism, it is only because the *created* Son
and the *created* Spirit are *constituted* divine by the will and
decree of the Father. Really, it is not the Father who is re-
sponsible for this creation and constitution, but a poet of un-
surpassed splendor with the Biblical account. Actually, John
Milton was a theist whose God is One. The point of the matter
is that Milton does not stop with the numerical oneness of
God, but proceeds in the creation of the Son whose relation
to the Father is definite, and the Holy Spirit whose relation to
the Father is also definite. Father, Son and Holy Spirit are
manifestations of the oneness of God. In the creation, God
made Himself evident as Father. He made Himself evident as
redeemer, as Son. He made Himself evident in the Third Person, as The Holy Spirit. Historically there is some of the position respecting Christ, of Sabellius who taught in Rome about
215. He departed from Sabellius who held that Father, Son,
and Holy Spirit "are all one and the same."[184] This would be
a Tri-theism; but John Milton held God as One. Milton viewed
the Son and the Spirit, "characteristic of Logos Christology,"[185]

104

in which there is the subordination of Son to the Father, and Spirit to both Father and Son.

"The great advocate of the Logos Christology at this juncture in Rome was Hippolytus (160-170-c. 235), the most learned Christian writer then in the city and the last considerable theologian there to use Greek rather than Latin. . . . Kallistos, (Bishop of Rome) excommunicated Sabellius (c. 217), and charged Hippolytus with being a worshipper of two gods. Hippolytus . . . . became the head of a rival communion in Rome — the first 'counter-pope' — a position he maintained till his banishment in the persecution of 235."[186]

One can readily see the daring views in Milton's theological position. One can readily understand why John Milton expressly planned for the publication of *De Doctrina Christiana,* after his death. One, by degrees, comes to see the liberal mind of John Milton. One stands amazed at the incredible genius of John Milton so artfully to conceal this theological liberalism in the epic. One admires his poetic genius. Agree or not, the poetic mastery of John Milton carries one thoughtfully and gratefully not to what is lost in Paradise, but to *Paradise Found.* Without this kind of liberal theological propensity that grew in dominance with John Milton, we would not have, really have, *Paradise Found.*

In *Paradise Regain'd* John Milton states his position, respecting Christ.

"That all the Angels and Ethereal Powers,
They now, and men hereafter, may discern
From what consummate virtue I have chose
This perfect Man, by merit call'd my Son,
To earn Salvation for the Sons of men."[187]

In *Paradise Lost,* John Milton states more boldly his position respecting Christ.

"Because thou hast, though Thron'd in highest bliss
Equal to God, and equally enjoying
God-like fruition, quitted all to save
A World from utter loss, and hast been found
By Merit more than Birthright Son of God,
Found worthiest to be son by being Good,
Farr more then Great or High."[188]

Even though Christ is perfect Man, He enters upon the relationship He held with the Father not by virtue of a common essence, but "By Merit more than Birthright." This merit in Christ has a parallelism with the merit of Eve and Adam, as they leave traditional Paradise, too small for their great minds and spirits, and merit — and share with us, *Paradise Found.*

Section. 6. The Creation, being a synopsis
of the treatise(*)

Creation is the second species of external efficiency. It is the act in which God the Father, by His Word and Spirit produced everything for the manifestation of His power and goodness.

In Isaiah there is set forth the truth not only making impossible any other God, but also making impossible any co-equal person, with God.[189] God the Father is the primary and efficient cause of all things, with the expression "Word" referring to the Son, and the expression "Spirit" designating not the Third Person but the divine power of God. The Third Person as such therefore had no part in creation; and the Son participated in creation only as the agent of the Father.

When God came to the act of creation, *there was matter already in* existence. This matter was substantially inherent in God and proceeded from Him; therefore matter was good, incorruptible, and eternal.

(*) *Ibid.,* Vol. XV, pp. 2-53.

Creation falls into two classes, namely, those things which are visible, and those invisible. The invisible things consist of the highest heaven, which is the throne and habitation of God, and the heavenly powers, or angels. In his highest heaven is Paradise. The visible creation includes the material universe, and all that is contained in the material universe, especially the human race. With the creation of man, not only the body of man was then made but also the soul. This precludes any preexistence to the soul. When God created man, and infused into him the breath of life, what man received from God was not any portion of God's essence, or even any participation of the divine nature. Rather, he received a measure of the divine virtue or influence, commensurate to the capabilities of the particular individual receiving these blessings. The human soul is not created daily by the immediate act of God, but propagated from the Father to Son, and the power continues in this manner from one generation to another in natural order. Being formed after the image of God, however, man was endued with natural wisdom, holiness, and righteousness.

Treatise,
> "Creation is that act whereby God the Father produced everything that exists by his Word and Spirit, that is, by his will, for the manifestation of the glory of his power and goodness."[190]

Epic,
> "Thy self though great and glorious dost count,
> Or all Angelic Nature joined in one,
> Equal to him begotten Son, by whom
> As by his Word the mighty Father made
> All things, ev'n thee, and all the Spirits of Heav'n."[191]

Milton sets forth matter, pre-existent, good, and used of God as the substance he brought into order and adorned.

Treatise,

"Since, therefore, both Scripture and reason concur in pronouncing that all these things were made, not out of nothing, but out of matter, it necessarily follows that matter must either have always existed independently of God, or have originated from God at some particular point of time."[192]

"For the original matter of which we speak, is not to be looked upon as an evil or trivial thing, but as intrinsically good, and the chief productive stock of every subsequent good. It was a substance, and derivable from no other source than from the fountain of every substance, though at first confused and formless, being afterwards adorned and digested into order by the hand of God."[193]

Epic,

"To whom the winged Hierarch repli'd.
O Adam, one Almightie is, from whom
All things proceed, and up to him return,
If not deprav'd from good, created all
Such to perfection, one first matter all,
Indu'd with various forms, various degrees
Of substance, and in things that live, of life. . . ."[194]

Treatise,

"Previously, however, to the creation of man, as if to intimate the superior importance of the work, the Deity speaks like to a man deliberating . . . 'God said, Let us make man in our own image, after our own likeness.' So that it was not the body alone that was then made, but the soul of man also (in which our likeness to God principally consists); which precludes us from attributing preexistence to the soul which was then formed, a groundless notion sometimes entertained, but refuted . . . 'God formed

man of the dust of the ground, and breathed into his nostrils
the breath of life; thus man became a living soul.' "[195]

Epic,

"Let us make now Man in our image, Man
In our similitude, and let them rule
Over the Fish and Fowle of Sea and Aire,
Beast of the Field, and over all the Earth,
And every creeping thing that creeps the ground.
This said, he formd thee, Adam, thee O Man
Dust of the ground, and in thy nostrils breath'd
The breath of Life; in his own Image hee
Created thee, in the Image of God
Express, and thou becam'st a living Soul."[196]

There is a mental reciprocity of Adam with the Father. Both
Adam and the Father shared, and shared with an unclouded
apprehension from men toward God.

Treatise,

"Man being formed after the image of God, it followed
as a necessary consequence that he should be endued with
natural wisdom, holiness, and righteousness. . . . Certainly
without extraordinary wisdom he could not have given
names to the whole animal creations with such sudden intelligence. . . ."[197]

Epic,

". . . One came, methought, of shape Divine,
And said, thy Mansion wants thee, Adam, rise,
First Man, of Men innumerable ordain'd
First Father, call'd by thee I come thy Guide
To the Garden of bliss, thy seat prepar'd."[198]

The mental ability, as well as the power of apprehension appear in Adam full-grown. Milton describes the sensation of sudden amazement which came with Adam's first recognition of his mental powers.

Epic,
 "But who I was, or where, or from what cause,
 Knew not; to speak I tri'd, and forthwith spake,
 My Tongue obey'd and readily could name
 What e're I saw."[199]

The eloquent tongue of Adam as much as the divine Image itself, is a blessing of the "Sire of Men," a gift to him from God.

Epic,
 "Nor are thy lips ungraceful, Sire of Men,
 Nor tongue ineloquent; for God on thee
 Abundantly his gifts hath also pour'd
 Inward and outward both, his image faire. . . ."[200]

Milton had his own position respecting matter. The material universe resulted from God's action upon the matter He found.

Treatise,
 "It is clear then that the world was framed out of matter of some kind or other. For since action and passion are relative terms, and since, consequently, no agent can act externally, unless there be some patient, such as matter, it appears impossible that God could have created this world out of nothing; not from any defect of power on his part but because it was necessary that something should have previously existed capable of receiving passively the exertion of the divine efficacy."[201]

CHAPTER EIGHT

PROVIDENCE AND THE MORAL ORDER:

Comprising the following six sections

Section 1. General Providence
Section 2. Angels
Section 3. God's Government of Man
Section 4. The Fall
Section 5. The Punishment of Sin
Section 6. The Death of the Body

In order to have the total theological position of John Milton, we are following, section by section, the treatise, *De Doctrina Christiana.* This engages our primary attention. We continue with our purpose to denote and define the parallel affirmations in the epic, as they apply. So what is poetically lodged in *Paradise Lost* and affirmed in parallel fashion in *De Doctrina Christiana,* continues as our adventure. The claim is that this agreement leads into the real theme of *Paradise Lost,* and the true outcome of the epic, in *Paradise Found.*

Section 1. *General Providence,*
being a synopsis of the treatise(*)

The third and remaining species of God's external efficiency, namely his government of the whole creation, is either gen-

(*) *Ibid.,* Vol. XV. pp. 55-97.

111

eral or special. General government extends over the whole creation, and is the means whereby God regards, preserves, and governs with infinite wisdom and holiness, according to the conditions of his decree. Since the spontaneous fall, God preserves mankind and all other things with them in terms of their existence, and not with reference to their primitive perfection. He directs his government even into voluntary actions, but in such a way that there is no infringement on the liberty of the human will. This governing providence of God extends even into sin, not only in his permitting its existence, or in his withdrawal of grace, but also in his impelling sinners to the commission of sin, in his hardening their hearts, and in his blinding their understandings. In all of this we must not consider God as in the smallest instance the author of sin.

It is not the human heart in a state of innocence and purity and of repugnance to evil that is drawn to act wickedly and deceitfully. After the heart has conceived sin, with the action of bringing it forth, the sovereign of all things inclines and disposes it in this or that direction, or towards this or that object.

After the fall of man, God limited human life to a certain period of time, which in the progress of ages, from Adam to David, gradually became more and more contracted. One can shorten the length of his life; but it is in the power of no one to prolong or exceed its perscribed limits. The providence of God is either ordinary or extraordinary. His ordinary providence refers to the immutable order of causes appointed by him in the beginning. His extraordinary providence is that by means of which he or someone empowered by him, produces an effect out of the usual order of nature. Such an event is called a miracle. Miracles are used by God to attest the divine power, to confirm human faith, and by taking away all excuses for unbelief to increase the condemnation of the obdurate.

"His General government is that whereby God the Father regards, preserves, and governs the whole of creation with

112

infinite wisdom and holiness according to the conditions of his decree."[202]

All of this is included under Providence, by means of which God directs the affairs of the universe.

The providence of God is a uniting conception which serves as the organic center of the epic. It appears at the very opening of the epic, for it is against Providence that the Arch-fiend directs his efforts. It was with a realization of his opposition to Providence that Adam in the close of the epic affirms:

"Greatly instructed I shall hence depart,
Greatly in peace of thought, and have my fill
Of knowledge, what this Vessel can containe;
Beyond which was my folly to aspire.
Henceforth I learne, that to obey is best,
And love with fear the onely God, to walk
As in his presence, ever to observe
His providence. . . ."[203]

The opening ascription to Providence and the closing scene of the epic bespeak the experience of universal man in his misuse of his freedom against the Providence of God. The epic opens with the avowed purpose

"That to the highth of this great Argument
I may assert Eternal Providence. . . ."[204]

The closing scene presents both Adam and Eve, "our lingring Parents" looking back to Paradise, but still going forth with Providence as their guide.

"They looking back, all th' Eastern side beheld

113

Of Paradise, so late thir happie seat,
Wav'd over by that flaming Brand, the Gate
With dreadful Faces throng'd and fierie Armes:
Some natural tears they drop'd, but wip'd them soon;
The World was all before them, where to choose
Thir place of rest, and Providence thir guide;
They hand in hand with wandring steps and slow,
Through Eden took thir solitarie way."[205]

Treatise and Epic

It is true to Milton's theological position, both in the treatise and in the epic, that the Providence of God was maintained and continued after the Fall, as well as before. This is evident in the free operation of the human will.

Treatise,
"In this, however, there is no infringement on the liberty of the human will; otherwise man would be deprived of the power of free agency, not only with regard to what is right, but with regard to what is indifferent, or even positively wrong."[206]

Epic,
"So without least impulse or shadow of Fate,
Or aught by me immutablie foreseen,
They trespass, Authors to themselves in all
Both what they judge and what they choose; for so
I formd them free, and free they must remain,
Till they enthral themselves. . . ."[207]

This Providence God maintains over the existence of mankind, after the Fall, but there is the loss of primitive perfection.

Treatise,
"For he preserves mankind, since their spontaneous fall,

and all other things with them, only so far as regards their existence, and not as regards their primitive perfection."[208]

In the epic the same thought of Providence appears.

". . . yet know withal,
Since thy original lapse, true Libertie
Is lost, which alwayes with right Reason dwells
Twinn'd, and from her hath no dividual being:
Reason in man obscur'd, or not obeyd,
Immediately inordinate desires
And upstart Passions catch the Government
From Reason, and to servitude reduce
Man till then free."[209]

God allows the evil will to become perverted, but though wickedness is rampant, he is in control, even directing good from evil.

Treatise,
"Now does God make that will evil which was before good, but the will being already in a state of perversion, he influences it in such a manner, that out of its own wickedness it either operates good for others, or punishment for itself, though unknowingly, and with the intent of producing a very different result."[210]

Out of sin and wickedness, Milton does not see a need for repentance. There is occasion to rejoice that because of sin more good shall spring.

Epic,
"O goodness infinite, goodness immense!
That all this good of evil shall produce,
And evil turn to good; more wonderful
Then that which by creation first brought forth

115

Light out of darkness! Full of doubt I stand,
Whether I should repent me now of sin
By mee done and occasioned, or rejoyce
Much more, that much more good thereof shall spring. . .."[211]

Miracles have a double function: first to withdraw all excuse
for unbelief, because of the unusual witness they bear, and
second, to give evidence of the power of God and thus to
confirm and strengthen our faith.

Epic,
"Thee, Serpent, suttlest beast of all the field
I knew, but not with human voice endu'd;
Redouble then this miracle, ana say,
How cam'st thou speakable of mute, and how
To me so friendly grown above the rest
Of brutal kind, that daily are in sight?
Say, for such wonder claims attention due."[212]

Miracles are to give evidence of God's power, as well as to
confirm our faith.

Epic,
". . . for the Spirit
Power'd first on his Apostles, whom he sends
To evangelize the Nations, then on all
Baptiz'd, shall them with wondrous gifts endue
To speak all Tongues, and do all Miracles,
As did thir Lord before them. Thus they win
Great numbers of each Nation to receave
With joy the tidings brought from Heav'n. . . ."[213]

The relationship between God's government of the universe,
his Providence, and the expulsion of our first Parents from Paradise, constitutes a singular setting for Milton's concept of
sin. This will be explored in a following section under that

specific title. At this point, we simply deal with the Providence of God in respect of the fact of sin. Milton leaves little or no room for any sense of degradation on the part of our first Parents as they leave Paradise.

They appear not to realize the tragedy which sin imposes in a separation from God. Milton admits they have lost true liberty, because reason has become obscured by the Fall, and when reason weakens, all else follows. The sting of sin as an absolute fact separating man from God is markedly absent in Milton. The Providence of God, though modified since the original lapse, escorts the guilty pair from Paradise. There still is fellowship between Providence and the exiles, although the relation is admittedly modified. This very modification, however, suggests a certain *exaltation*. That exaltation is intimated by the Archangel Michael in the words already quoted.

Epic,
". . . onely add
Deeds to thy knowledge answerable, add Faith,
Add Vertue, Patience, Temperance, add Love,
By name to come call'd Charitie, the soul
Of all the rest: then wilt thou not be loath
To leave this Paradise, but shalt possess
A Paradise within thee, happier farr."[214]

Michael has taken away the sting of sin by a pre-figuration of the Providence of God reaching its climax in the "Son of God most High". Adam's exaltation mounts into a celestial humanism as he declares,

Epic,
"O Prophet of glad tidings, finisher
Of utmost hope! now clear I understand
What oft my steddiest thoughts have searcht in vain,
Why our great expectation should be call'd

117

The seed of Woman: Virgin Mother, Haile,
High in the love of Heav'n, yet from my Loynes
Thou shalt proceed, and from thy Womb the Son
Of God most High: So God with man unites."[215]

There is an anomaly, if not a paradox, in the exultation of
the First Pair departing from Paradise, leaving with the participation of Providence. The departure is one thing. Exultation in the departure is another. Leaving with the participation
of Providence is a further irregularity.

This is one aspect of the uniqueness of John Milton. He
cannot be put or remain at home in the company of the reg-
ular. This is the case poetically. This is the case politically.
This is the case religiously. All combine in a genius of interpretation and affirmation, especially evident in the exultation
when expelled from traditional Eden. All combine in the claim
that Providence is on their side.

Epic,
"The World was all before them, where to choose
Thir place of rest, and Providence thir guide:
They hand in hand with wandring steps and slow,
Through Eden took thir solitarie way."[216]

Providence is eternal, and therefore with them, both before
and after the Fall. Even goodness is a larger experience, after
the lapse, than before.[217]

"O goodness, infinite, goodness immense!
That all this good of evil shall produce,
And evil turn to good; more wonderful
Then that which by creation first brought forth
Light out of darkness! Full of doubt I stand,
Whether I should repent me now of sin

118

By mee done and occasioned, or rejoyce
Much more, that much more good thereof shall spring."[218]

Part of the larger experience is the affirmation of the essential part of man in the production of the "Son of God most high."[219] This is what Milton expounds at the very moment of their expulsion from the traditional Eden. We expect tragedy, the tragedy of sin, and we get exultation. We expect separation, and we get participation. The contrast is too great, especially when the participation is in the production of the "Son of God most high." Milton turns what is Biblical into his own emphasis. The contrast between the Biblical and the Renaissantial interpretation of man, places Milton beyond the Renaissance and makes him a man of the Enlightenment. It is Milton of the seventeenth century using the principles of the Enlightenment of the most liberal form, of the eighteenth century, that writes into Paradise, not what is lost, but what is *Paradise Found.*

Section 2. *Angels,* being a synopsis of the treatise(*)

The special government of God is that in reference to angels and men. Both are far superior to the rest of creation. Angels are either good or evil. Of their own accord many of the angels revolted from God, before the fall of man. The good angels are upheld like man before his fall, not by the grace of God, but by their own strength. They are the ministering agents, standing about the throne of God, to praise Him, carrying out the commands of God toward believers, as well as to execute the divine vengeance against the sins of men.

The chief of the good angels is Michael, who presides over the rest of them. The good angels are gifted with excellent intelligence; however, there is much of which they are ignorant.

The evil angels are reserved for punishment. Their knowl-

(*) *Ibid.,* Vol. XV, pp. 97-111.

edge too is great; but their knowledge aggravates rather than diminishes their misery. They have their prince or leader who is the author of all wickedness and the opponent of all good. The devils have their respective ranks. The prince of the devils is known by various names such as Beelzebub, Satan, the Tempter, Abaddon, Apollyon.

Of the ministering angels, seven cover the earth in the performance of their divine duty and attendance upon creation.[220]

Epic,

"Uriel, for thou of those seav'n Spirits that stand
In sight of God's high Throne, gloriously bright,
The first art wont his great authentic will
Interpreter through highest Heav'n to bring,
Where all his Sons thy Embassie attend;
And here art likeliest by supream decree
Like honour to obtain, and as his Eye
To visit oft this new Creation round."[221]

Of the angels, Michael is chief. This is included in *the epic.*

"Go Michael of Celestial Armies Prince. . . ."[222]

The angels have superior intelligence, yet they are ignorant of some things. In keeping with this, Uriel is once beguiled.

Epic,

". . . Which now for once beguil'd
Uriel, though Regent of the Sun, and held
The sharpest sighted Spirit of all in Heav'n. . . ."[223]

Beelzebub is the leader of the devils, and the source of all evil.

Epic,

". . . Thus Beelzebub
Pleaded his devilish Counsel, first devis'd

120

By Satan, and in part propos'd: for whence,
But from the Author of all ill could Spring
So deep a malice. . . ."[224]

There are various positions and degrees among the devils.

Epic,

". . . till at last
Satan, whom now transcendent glory rais'd
Above his fellows, with Monarchal pride
Conscious of highest worth. . . ."[225]

Satan has many names, both in the treatise and the epic.

Epic,

"Satan, now first inflam'd with rage, came down
The Tempter ere th' Accuser of man-kind
To wreck on innocent frail man his loss."[226]

Epic,

". . . .but not so wak'd
Satan, so call him now, his former name
Is heard no more in Heav'n; he of the first
If not the first Arch-Angel, great in Power,
In favour and praeeminence. . . ."[227]

The material in the synopsis and in the relevant extracts
from the epic presents the essence of Milton's views of the
special government of angels. There is little that needs to be
said by way of comment concerning the theological importance
of this material. Both the treatise and the epic join in the traditional belief concerning angels, by Milton.

Section 3. *God's Government of Man,*
being a synopsis of the treatise(*)

The Providence of God covers man before as well as after the Fall. Before the Fall, God placed him in the garden of Eden. He had furnished all to make him happy, but was commanded not to eat of the one tree of knowledge of good and evil, under penalty of death. Adam was not required to work. Only a particular act was forbidden in order to test the fidelity of man, respecting his obedience.

The tree of knowledge of good and evil takes its name from the event; for since Adam tasted it, we know not only evil, but good also, and we know good only by means of evil.

With regard to the Sabbath, God hallowed it to himself, dedicated it to rest, in remembrance of his finished work of creation. From Scripture we do not know whether its institution was made known to Adam, or whether any commandment was given previous to the delivery of the law on Mount Sinai.

With regard to marriage, it is clear that it was instituted, if not commanded, at creation. Marriage consisted in the mutual love of the husband and wife, with the husband having superior rights. After the Fall, this power of the husband was increased.

Marriage has for its purpose either the procreation of children, or comfort and solace of life. Marriage is honorable in itself, and is restricted to no order of men. It is not a command binding on all, but only those who are unable to live with chastity out of this state. Polygamy is allowed by the law of God. Marriage may lawfully be dissolved in divorce, if the prime end and form of the institution are violated. The reason and purpose of marriage is not the nuptial bed, but conjugal love, and mutual help through life.

The test of the obedience of Adam and Eve was in the fruit

(*) *Ibid.*, Vol. XV, pp. 113-179.

of the tree in the center of the Garden. Of this fruit they were
forbidden to eat.

Epic,

"God hath pronounc't it death to taste that Tree,
The only sign of our obedience left
Among so many signes of power and rule
Conferrd upon us. . . ."[228]

This was likewise the tree of knowledge, and was the occasion
of knowing good, by knowing ill.

Epic,

"Out of the fertil ground he caus'd to grow
All Trees of noblest kind for sight, smell, taste;
And all amid them stood the Tree of Life,
High eminent, blooming Ambrosial Fruit
Of vegetable Gold; and next to Life
Our Death the Tree of knowledge grew fast by,
Knowledge of Good bought dear by knowing ill."[229]

The Sabbath was dedicated as a day of rest in remembrance
of God's completed work of creation.

Epic,

". . . Thrice happie men,
And sons of men, whom God hath thus advanc't,
Created in his Image, there to dwell
And worship him, and in reward to rule
Over his Works, on Earth, in Sea, or Air,
And multiply a Race of Worshippers
Holy and just: thrice happie if they know
Thir happiness, and persevere upright.
So sung they, and the Empyrean rung,
With Halleluiahs: Thus was Sabbath kept."[230]

Marriage, as mutual love and help, constituted the relationship of Adam and Eve, although Adam held superior rights, as the husband.

Epic,
> ". . . though both
> Not equal, as thir sex not equal seemd;
> For contemplation hee and valour formd,
> For softness shee and sweet attractive Grace,
> Hee for God only, shee for God in him:
> His fair large Front and Eye sublime declar'd
> Absolute rule. . . ."[231]

Epic,
> "To whom thus Eve with perfet beauty adornd.
> My Author and Disposer, what thou bidst
> Unargu'd I obey; so God ordains,
> God is thy Law, thou mine: to know no more
> Is woman's happiest knowledge and her praise."[232]

After the Fall, the husband had greater power.

Epic,
> "Thy going is not lonely, with thee goes
> Thy Husband, him to follow thou art bound;
> Where he abides, think there thy native soils."[233]

There is a parallelism of thought in both treatise and epic concerning marriage.

Treatise,
> "The end of marriage is nearly the same with the form.
> Its proper fruit is the procreation of children; but
> since Adam's fall, the provision of a remedy against
> incontinency has become in some degree a secondary end.

. . . Hence marriage is not a command binding on all, but only on those who are unable to live with chastity out of this state. . . . Marriage is honorable in itself, and prohibited to no order of men. . . ."[234]

Epic,
". . . nor turned I weene
Adam from his fair Spouse, nor Even the Rites
Mysterious of connubial love refus'd:
Whatever Hypocrites austerely talk
Of puritie and place and innocence,
Defaming as impure what God declares
Pure, and commands to som, leaves free to all.
Our Maker bids increase, who bids abstain
But our Destroyer, foe to God and Man?
Haïle wedded Love, mysterious Law, true source
Of human ofspring, sole proprietie,
In Paradise of all things common else."[235]

Milton draws a distinction between marriage before the Fall, and marriage after the Fall. Before the Fall marriage was inseparable in the nature of the bond between our first Parents. It could not be dissolved even by death.

Epic,
". . . hee
Whose image thou art, him thou shall enjoy
Inseparablie thine, to him shalt beare
Multitudes like thy self, and thence be call'd
Mother of human Race. . . ."[236]

Epic,
". . . to give thee being I lent
Out of my side to thee, neerest my heart
Substantial Life, to have thee by my side

125

Henceforth an individual solace dear;
Part of my Soul I seek thee, and thee claim
My other half. . . ."[237]

Treatise Only

Milton does not carry over into the epic his argument on divorce. The reason is apparent, due to the harmony that prevailed between our first Parents, and due as well to their solitary way. As human beings they were alone in the world.

We notice the condition of obedience for Adam and Eve was in the fruit of the tree in the center of the Garden. This centrality is of more than geographical importance. This centrality takes on philosophical, psychological, and religious proportions. For Milton, this centrality is an inversion of true obedience. Rather than obedience in tension against disobedience; this was "the Tree of knowledge (which) grew fast by." It was,

"Knowledge of Good bought dear by knowing ill."[238]

There was a "knowledge of Good," for Milton, not the possession of Eve and then Adam, before eating of the central fruit. This knowledge is an enlightenment for the First Pair, as they walked their solitary way out of Eden, *hand in hand.* As Milton so dramatically presents the scene, walking out of the restrictions of traditional Eden; there was no sense of loss but an awareness of *Paradise Found.*

Section 4. *The Fall,* being a sypnosis of the treatise(*)

The Providence of God regarding the Fall is evident in the sin of man and in the misery consequent upon it, as well as in his restoration. Sin is the transgression of the law, meaning

(*) *Ibid.,* XV, pp. 179-201.

the innate rule of conscience as well as the special command of God.

Sin has two classifications, namely, that which is common to all men, and that which is personal to each individual. The sin our first Parents committed included all their posterity under sin, when they in disobedience to God ate of the forbidden fruit. This sin had its origin in both the instigation of the devil and in the possibility of our first Parents to fall. This sin was an offence; for it included in one act all the sins against the whole law. Personal sin is that which each has committed independently of the sin which is common to all.

Both kinds of sin, that which is common to all and that which is personal to each, consist of the two following parts: namely, evil concupiscence, or the desire of sinning, and the act of sin itself.

The Providence of God respecting the Fall.

Epic,

". . . But fall'n he is, and now
What rests but that the mortal Sentence pass
On his transgression, Death denounc't that day,
Which he presumes already vain and void,
Because not yet inflicted, as he fear'd,
By some immediate stroak; but soon shall find
Forebearance no acquittance ere day end.
Justice shall not return as bountie scorn'd.
But whom send I to judge them? whom but thee
Vicegerent Son, to thee I have transferr'd
All Judgement whether in Heav'n, or Earth, or Hell.
Easie it might be seen that I intend
Mercie collegue with Justice, sending thee
Mans Friend, his Mediator, his design'd
Both Ransom and Redeemer voluntarie,
And destin'd Man himself to judge Man fall'n."[239]

Sin is the transgression of the law.

127

Epic,

> "Rather how hast thou yeelded to transgress
> The strict forbiddance, how to violate
> The sacred Fruit forbidd'n! some cursed fraud
> Of enemie hath beguil'd thee."[240]

The rule of conscience is innate. Combined with the rule of conscience is the special command of God, both of which comprise the law.

Epic,

> "And I will place within them as a guide
> My Umpire Conscience, whom if they will hear,
> Light after light well us'd they shall attain,
> And to the end persisting, safe arrive."[241]

Both the devil's plan and the possibility of the Fall comprise the origin of sin.[242] The epic combines the action of the devil with the possibility of the Fall.

Epic,

> ". . . and do they onely stand
> By Ignorance, is that thir happie state,
> The proof of thir obedience and thir faith?
> O fair foundation laid whereon to build
> Thir ruine! Hence I will excite thir minds
> With more desire to know, and to reject
> Envious commands, invented with designe
> To keep them low whom knowledge might exalt
> Equal with Gods; aspiring to be such,
> They taste and die. . . ."[243]

Milton dwells upon the manifold nature of this sin of our

first Parents and the heinous nature of it. All sins were included in the first transgression.[244]

Epic,

"For still they knew and ought to have still remember'd
The high Injunction not to taste that Fruit,
Whoever tempted; which they not obeying,
Incurr'd, what could they less, the penaltie,
And manifold in sin, deserv'd to fall."[245]

Treatise and Epic

Milton guards well the difference between Adam and Eve, at the point both of prestige and of intelligence. The burden conclusively is placed upon Eve in her separateness from Adam, at the time of her fall. Milton denotes here the separateness from Adam. What about the separateness from God? This is another matter, later to be explored and developed.

The occasion of the Fall has its origin in the repugnance of the Devil and his aroused envy as he witnesses the unexcelled delight of Adam and Eve, "Imparadis't in one anothers arms."[246]

Epic,

". . . all is not theirs it seems:
One fatal Tree there stands of Knowledge call'd,
Forbidden them to taste: Knowledge forbidd'n?
Suspicious, reasonless, Why should thir Lord
Envie them that? can it be sin to know,
Can it be death? and do they onely stand
By Ignorance, is that thir happie state,
The proof of thir obedience and thir faith?
O fair foundation laid whereon to build
Thir ruine! Hence I will excite thir minds
With more desire to know. . . ."[247]

The Devil's plan strikes at the point of their fidelity to God in abstinence from the forbidden fruit. He directs the strength of the temptation to what they do not have, and by a very subtle entreaty arouses their suspicions. Why should the Lord envy them knowledge? *It is in ignorance they give proof of their obedience and faith.*

If there is one thing that John Milton rejects, it is lack of knowledge and rightful exercise of reason. The penetration, at this point of both the treatise and the epic, is for the full knowledge and the full exercise of reason that makes obedience not only real but just. This thrust forward, by Milton, is one that for him leads, not into the loss of Paradise but *Paradise Found.*

The procedure of the temptation involves both of them, but first and foremost Eve. It is Eve who suggests they divide their labours. The recurrent discourse about something new discovered in the garden, and the exchanged smiles and many looks, interfere with their ceaseless toil as they labour together amid the luxurious growth.

To work in separate places would bring greater accomplishment at the close of day. Regretfully Adam consents to a brief absence, but only with the most definite warning that both had been informed of the Malicious Foe that lurked in the Garden to work them woe.

Epic,
> "If such affront I labour to avert
> From thee alone, which on us both at once
> The Enemie, though bold, will hardly dare,
> Or daring, first on mee th' assault shall light."[248]

It is a subtle procedure by means of which Satan, in the guise of a serpent, draws Eve toward the Tree. He does not identify the tree as the forbidden one, but describes it sumptuously. He arouses in her an appetite for the fruit, by reason of its savory odor, and by reason of the new and capacious wisdom.

When Adam received from Eve the account of her experience with the Serpent and the eating of the fruit, he

Epic,
"Astonied stood and Blank, while horror chill
Ran through his veins, and all his joynt relax'd. . . ."[249]

Milton is careful to have Adam join Eve, *not so much as the result of temptation, as the result of deliberation.* Adam joins Eve as his own rational decision, in order that no different degree may separate them. This is the height of the Enlightenment, to be the development in the century following Milton. the eighteenth century, but expertly used by Milton. In mind, spirit, and interpretation, John Milton was a man in advance of his time. For this reason, great rationalist that he was, Milton read and wrote nothing as lost in Paradise, but everything as *Paradise Found.*

Note, in the epic, the resolve of Milton, in the interpretative role of Adam, to join Eve. With rational deliberation Eve and Adam become conjoined. The reason is that "Death is to mee as Life," as stated in the words below,

Epic,
"And mee with thee hath ruind, for with thee
Certain my resolution is to Die. . . ."[250]

Epic,
"However I with thee have fixt my Lot,
Certain to undergoe like doom, if Death
Consort with thee, Death is to mee as Life. . . ."[251]

Passion has its significant role in this rational deliberation of Adam, but the passion involved has no element of deception. It has all the persuasiveness of perception. As Adam joins Eve in eating the forbidden fruit, Milton makes plain this act is not, as was the case with Eve, the result of his being deceived.

131

Epic,
". . . from the bough
She᾿ gave him of that fair enticing Fruit
With liberal hand: he scrupl'd not to eat
Against his better knowledge, not deceav'd,
But fondly overcome with Femal charm."[252]

For Milton, the occasion of sin is due to a lack of knowledge on the part of Eve. Adam's dominant desire was to give Passion free sway over his reason, in order not to part with Eve. In this surrender Adam failed to heed the warning of Raphael.

Epic,
". . . take heed lest Passion sway
Thy Judgment to do aught, which else free Will
Would not admit; thine and of all thy Sons
The weal or woe in thee is plac't; beware."[253]

In this we have not only the Renaissance, but also that of Classic Greece, with the marked emphasis upon sin as ignorance. In this we find Milton opening the way for the liberalism of the eighteenth century Enlightenment, particularly as seen in Jean-Jacques Rousseau (1712-1778).

"The moralist who did most to prepare for the revolution was Jean-Jacques Rousseau (1712-78). True, he did believe that the perfect man was the natural savage of the woods; but neither he nor the revolutionaries could seriously preach the dissolution of the state into primitive anarchy. They hoped rather for its reform, through simplification and purification; and the model which they proposed was the free republic of Rome and the city-states of free Greece."[254]

Milton holds common ground with Jean-Jacques Rousseau, only

in the liberalism of interpretation. The varied position of actual interpretation places them poles apart. Milton would have no place with the concept of "the perfect man . . . the natural savage of the woods." Milton joins rather with Eve whose sin is occasioned by ignorance.

Ignorance has no part in Milton's deliberate and rational decision to fix his lot with Eve. Then Death would be for him as Life.

Section 5. *The Punishment of Sin,*
being a synopsis of the treatise(*)

After sin, and as the punishment for sin, came death. The consequence of sin involved not merely bodily death, but all the evils that tend to death. Mere bodily death did not follow the sin of Adam on the day of transgression.

There are four degrees of death. The first includes all those evils which lead to death, which came into the world immediately upon the Fall of man, and which are prior to bodily death. The first degree of death includes more particularly, guiltiness, terrors of conscience, and shame.

The second degree of death is spiritual death. In this there is a loss of divine grace, and of innate righteousness, by means of which man in the beginning lived unto God.

Spiritual death does not completely extinguish the divine image in us. Some vestiges of original excellence are visible in the understanding. Some portion of free will remains, both to indifferent actions as well as good works.

Death includes all evils, with everything whose consequence tends to death.

Epic,
"Of Mans First Disobedience, and the Fruit

(*) Milton, *Op. Cit.,* Vol. XV. pp. 203-215.

Of that Forbidden Tree, whose mortal tast
Brought Death into the World, and all our woe. . . ."[255]

Of evil, note first guiltiness.

Epic,
"Love was not in thir looks either to God
Or to each other, but apparent guilt,
And shame, and perturbation, and despaire,
Anger, and obstinacie, and hate, and guile."[256]

Terrors of conscience.

Epic,
"I heard thee in the Garden, and of thy voice
Affraid, being naked, Hid my self."[257]

"O Conscience, into what Abyss of fears
And horrors hast thou driv'n, me; out of which
I find no way, from deep to deeper plung'd!
Thus Adam to himself lamented loud
Through the still Night. . . ."[258]

In death there became obscured first right reason in which
was the life of the understanding.

Treatise,
"This death consists, first, in the loss, or at least in the
obscuration to a great extent of that right reason which
enabled man to discern the chief good, and in which consisted as it were the life of the understanding."[259]

Epic,
"As from unrest, and each the other viewing,

134

Soon found thir Eyes how op'nd, and thir minds
How dark'nd. . . ."[260]

"Thus fenc't, and as they thought, thir shame in part
Coverd, but not at rest or ease of Mind,
They sate them down to weep, nor onely Teares
Raind at thir Eyes, but high Winds worse within
Began to rise, high Passions, Anger, Hate,
Mistrust, Suspicion, Discord, and shook sore
Thir inward State of Mind, calm Region once
And full of Peace, now tost and turbulent:
For Understanding rul'd not, and the Will
Heard not her lore, both in subjection now
To sensual Appetite, who from beneathe
Usurping over sovran Reason claimd
Superior sway. . . ."[261]

Treatise and Epic

The descriptive powers of John Milton are always majestic, but here they reach a nobility of expression unexcelled. It is to be noted, however, that this state of discomfiture arose from *within them, each of them.* It was "Thir inward State of Mind" that was "tost and turbulent." The reason was that,

"Understanding rul'd not, and the Will
Heard not her lore," (cf. 261 above)

Furthermore, and most important, was the fact that Understanding was in subjection, along with the Will, "To sensual Appetite." The sensual had taken over "sovran Reason"; and over Reason was in "Superior sway." (cf. 261 above) Milton remains forever and forever an advocate of Reason, and the direction of the Will by Understanding. This is further reason for the growing anticipation in the epic, not of *Paradise Lost,* but of *Paradise Found.*

135

Section 6. *The Death of the Body,*
being a synopsis of the Treatise(*)

All the labors, sorrow, and diseases which afflict the body are nothing but the prelude to the third degree of death which is called the death of the body. On account of man and the Fall, all nature is subject to mortality. The common definition of the death of the body, which supposes this death to consist in the separation of soul and body, is inadmissible. The body never had life of itself, and therefore cannot be said to die. It is the whole man consisting of body, spirit, and soul, and not just the body, that dies.

The mind is the part principally offending. That the body alone, to which immortality was equally allotted, before death came into the world by sin, should pay the penalty of sin by undergoing death, and that the mind escape, is incredible.

The mind is that which is principally implicated in the transgression. Because of this the whole man — body, spirit, and soul — dies. The saints, the believers of old, the patriarchs, the prophets, and the apostles, without exception held this doctrine.

The fourth and last degree of death, is death eternal, the punishment of the damned.

The labors, sorrows and diseases are the prelude to the third degree of death, the death of the body.[262]

Epic,
". . . why delayes
His hand to execute what his Decree
Fixd on this day? why do I overlive,
Why am I mockt with death, and length'nd out
To deathless pain? how gladly would I meet
Mortalitie my sentence, and be Earth
Insensible, how glad would lay me down
As in my Mothers lap? there I should rest

(*) *Ibid.*, Vol. XV pp. 215-251.

And sleep secure; his dreadful voice no more
Would Thunder in my ears, no fear of worse
To mee and to my offspring would torment me
With cruel expectation."[263]

Through the Fall of man all nature likewise comes under
the curse. Nature "groans" and "weeps." Yet through it all note
the composure of both Adam and Eve. Why this composure?
Was John Milton making this graphic and dramatic description for a significant and further response, by the First Pair?

Epic,
"Earth trembl'd from her entrails, as again
In pangs, and Nature gave a second groan,
Skie lowr'd and muttering Thunder, som sad drops
Wept at compleating of the mortal Sin
Original; while Adam took no thought,
Eating his fill, nor Eve to iterate
Her former trespass fear'd, the more to soothe
Him with her loved societie. . . ."[264]

Treatise and Epic

The whole man, body and spirit, comes in subjection to death.
In the following statement Milton's position is materialistic. Milton's claim is that the spirit of man is "purely human," and
"subject to death." This is not found in his orthodox handling
of creation; but in position cannot avoid heresy regarding matter, and especially spirit.

Treatise,
"First, then as to the body, no one doubts that it suffers
privation of life. Nor will the same be less evident as regards the spirit, if it be allowed that the spirit, according

137

to the doctrine laid down in the seventh chapter, has no participation in the divine nature, but is purely human; and that no reason can be assigned, why, if God has sentenced to death the whole of man that sinned, the spirit, which is the part principally offending, should be alone exempt from the appointed punishment; especially since, previous to the entrance of sin into the world, all parts of man were alike immortal; and that since that time, in pursuance of God's denunciation, all have become equally subject to death."[265]

Epic,
". . . it was but breath
Of Life that sinn'd; what dies and what had life
And sin? the Bodie properly hath neither.
All of me then shall die. . . ."[266]

The mind, too, comes under death, and is depraved.

Treatise,
"Or on the other hand, what could be more absurd than that the mind, which is the part principally offending, should escape the thratened death; and that the body alone, to which immortality was equally allotted, before death came into the world by sin, should pay the penalty of sin by undergoing death, though not implicated in the transgression?"[267]

Epic,
". . . Ah, why should all mankind
For one mans fault thus guiltless be condemn'd,
If guiltless? But from me what can proceed,
But all corrupt, both Mind and Will deprav'd,

Not to do onely, but to will the same
With me?"[268]

The fourth and last degree of death is the punishment of the damned in death eternal.[269]

Epic,
"So judg'd he Man, both Judge and Saviour sent,
And th' instant stroke of Death denounc't that day
Remov'd farr off. . . ."[270]

For Milton, then death is not only final but inclusive of the spirit, the soul, and the body. This makes no room for immortality. Perhaps, in his liberalism, John Milton draws no essential distinction between life with God in mortality, and life with God in immortality. We shall see.

CHAPTER NINE

THE APPROPRIATION OF SALVATION:

comprising the following thirteen sections

Section 1. Restoration and Redemption
Section 2. Christ, the Mediator
Section 3. The Ministry of Redemption
Section 4. Man's Renovation and Calling
Section 5. Regeneration
Section 6. Repentance
Section 7. Saving Faith
Section 8. Ingrafted in Christ
Section 9. Justification and Adoption
Section 10. Christian Fellowship and the Final
          Consummation
Section 11. Grace and Law
Section 12. The Church and the Scriptures
Section 13. Things to Come

The theological material within the epic deals mainly with the nature of the Godhead and the eternal purposes of the Father. Milton includes the plan of salvation, and sets forth the nature of this plan before the actual Fall of man, as well as after the Fall.

This plan of salvation constitutes an essential part of the epic, but because of the nature of the epic it does not comprise so large a body of material as is dealt with in preceding sections.

Section 1. *Restoration and Redemption,* being a synopsis of the treatise(*)

The restoration of man by God delivers him from sin and death, *and elevates him above that state of grace and glory from which he fell.*

This restoration includes both redemption and renovation. Redemption is the voluntary act of Christ whereby his own blood sets free all believers in keeping with the eternal counsel and grace of the Father. Previous to man's confesion of his guilt, and previous to God's sentence of punishment, God promised that he would raise up from the seed of the woman one who should bruise the serpent's head! In this we see the abundant and providential grace of God.

Christ alone is the Redeemer and Mediator. From the time of the Fall the Redeemer was promised; and at the appointed time he was sent. In relation to Christ's character as Redeemer, two points are to be considered, namely, his nature and office.

The nature is twofold: divine and human. The incarnation of Christ, meaning the manner in which he, being God, took upon himself human nature, without ceasing to be numerically the same as before is the greatest mystery of our religion. It is a mystery because it baffles explanation.

We must be content to know merely that the Son of God, our Mediator, was made flesh, and that he is called both God and Man, and that he is such in reality. Scripture remains silent beyond this. Where Scripture is silent, we should not be presumptuous in philosophical reasoning.

The incarnation of Christ consists of two parts: his concep-

(*) *Ibid.*, Vol. XV, pp. 251-283.

tion and his nativity. The efficient cause of his conception was the Holy Spirit, not a Third Person, but the power and spirit of the Father himself.

The restoration of man by God delivers him from sin and death, lifts him above that state of grace and glory from which he fell.[271] The elevation beyond the original grace and glory is, in the epic, that "better life."

Epic,
> ". . . all his works on mee
> Good or not good ingraft, my Merit those
> Shall perfet, and for these my Death shall pay.
> Accept me, and in mee from these receave
> The smell of peace toward Mankinde, let him live
> Before thee reconcil'd, at least his days
> Numberd, though sad, till Death, his doom (which I
> To mitigate thus plead, not to reverse)
> To better life shall yeeld him, where with mee
> All my redeemd may dwell in joy and bliss,
> Made one with me as I with thee am one."[272]

Christ is the sole Redeemer.[273]

Epic,
> "And by thy self Man among men on Earth,
> Made flesh, when time shall be, of Virgin seed,
> By wondrous birth: Be thou in Adams room
> The Head of all mankind, though Adams Son.
> As in him perish all men, so in thee
> As from a second root shall be restor'd,
> As many as are restor'd, without thee none."[274]

The nature of Christ is not only as the seed of woman but the Son of God.[275]

142

Epic,

". . . yet from my Loynes
Thou shalt proceed, and from thy Womb the Son
Of God most High; So God with man unites."[276]

In the conception of Christ, the Power of the Father joined with the Virgin Mother.

Treatise,

"The incarnation of Christ consists of two parts; his conception and his nativity. Of his conception the efficient cause was the Holy Spirit. . . .'that which is conceived in her, is of the Holy Ghost.' . . . 'the Holy Ghost shall come upon thee, and the power of the Highest shall overshadow thee'; by which words I am inclined to understand the power and spirit of the Father himself, as has been shown before; according to Psal. xl. 6. 7. compared with Heb. x. 5, 6. 'A body hast thou prepared me'."[277]

Epic,

"A Virgin is his Mother, but his Sire
The Power of the most High. . . ."[278]

Section 2. Christ, The Mediator,
being a synopsis of the treatise(*)

The office of mediator is the special appointment of God. In this office Christ voluntarily performed and continues to perform on behalf of man that which was necessary for reconciliation with God, and eternal salvation.

Christ has three functions in the mediatorial office, those of prophet, priest, and king. As prophet he instructs his church in heavenly truth, and declares the whole will of his Father.

(*) *Ibid.,* Vol. XV. pp. 285-303.

As priest he once offered himself to God the Father as a sacrifice for sinners, and has always made, and still continues to make intercession for us. As king he governs and preserves, chiefly *by an inward law and spiritual power*, the church which he has purchased for himself. He conquers and subdues its enemies.

The kingdom of Christ is, like his priesthood, eternal. It will endure as long as the world shall last, and as long as there shall be occasion for his mediatorial office.

Under the special appointment of God, Christ voluntarily performed and continues to perform that which is necessary for reconciliation with God and eternal life.[279]

Epic,
"But whom send I to judge them? whom but thee
Vicegerent Son, to thee I have transferr'd
All Judgement whether in Heav'n, or Earth, or Hell.
Easie it might be seen that I intend
Mercie collegue with Justice, sending thee
Man's Friend, his Mediator, his design'd
Both Ransom and Redeemer voluntarie,
And destin'd Man himself to judge Man fall'n."[280]

Christ is Prophet.

Epic,
"To whom the great Creatour thus reply'd.
O Son, in whom my Soul hath chief delight,
Son of my bosom, Son who art alone
My word, my wisdom, and effectual might,
All hast thou spok'n as my thoughts are, all
As my Eternal purpose hath decreed. . . ."[281]

Christ is Priest.

144

Epic,
". . . then clad
With incense, where the Golden Altar fum'd,
By thir great Intercessor, came in sight
Before the Fathers Throne: Them the glad Son
Presenting, thus to intercede began."[282]

"See Father, what first fruits on Earth are sprung
From thy implanted Grace in Man, these Sighs
And Prayers, which in this Golden Censer, mixt
With Incense, I thy Priest before thee bring."[283]

Christ gave himself as Man in satisfaction for man.[284]

Epic,
". . . Be thou in Adams room
The Head of all mankind, though Adams Son.
As in him perish all men, so in thee
As from a second root shall be restor'd,
As many as are restor'd, without thee none.
His crime makes guiltie all his Sons, thy merit
Imputed shall absolve them who renounce
Their own both righteous and unrighteous deeds
And live in thee transplanted, and from thee
Receive new life. So Man, as is most just,
Shall satisfie for Man, be judg'd and die,
And dying rise, and rising with him raise
His Brethren, ransomed with his own dear life."[285]

Christ is King.

We should note here the relationship between the kingship of
Christ, and the emphasis upon the human nature of his sacrifice. The function of Christ as King is *to govern by an inward
and spiritual power,* the Church.[286]

Epic,
"Nor shalt thou by descending to assume

145

Mans Nature, less'n or degrade thine owne.
Because thou hast, though Thron'd in highest bliss
Equal to God, and equally enjoying
God-like fruition, quitted all to save
A World from utter loss, and hast been found
By Merit more then Birthright Son of God,
Found worthiest to be so by being Good,
Farr more then Great or High; because in thee
Love hath abounded more then Glory abounds,
Therefore thy Humiliation shall exalt
With thee thy Manhood also to this Throne;
Here shalt thou sit incarnate, here shalt Reign
Both God and Man, Son both of God and Man,
Anointed universal King, all Power
I give thee, reign for ever, and assume
Thy Merits. . . ."[287]

The kingdom of Christ is eternal.[288]

Epic,

". . . out of one man a Race
Of men innumerable, there to dwell,
Not here, till by degrees of merit rais'd
They open to themselves at length the way
Up higher, under long obedience tri'd,
And Earth be chang'd to Heav'n, and Heaven to Earth,
One Kingdom, Joy and Union without end."[289]

Section 3. *The Ministry of Redemption,*
being a synopsis of the treatise(*)

The effectual discharge of the mediatorial office by Christ,
includes the state of humiliation to which our Redeemer submitted, as well as his state of exaltation.

(*) *Ibid.,* Vol. XV, pp. 303-341.

In his humiliation Christ, the God-Man, voluntarily took upon himself the divine justice in order to fulfill all that was necessary for our redemption. Following the humiliation of Christ was his exaltation.

With his triumph over death, he laid aside the form of a servant, and was exalted by God the Father to a state of immortality and of the highest glory. This exaltation was partly by his own merits, and partly by the gift of the Father, for the benefit of mankind. He arose again from the dead, ascended into heaven, and sitteth on the right hand of God. In both his natures Christ emptied himself, so both the divine and human natures participate in his exaltation: His Godhead by its restoration and manifestation, his manhood by an accession of glory.

The whole ministry of mediation is directed to the satisfaction of divine justice on behalf of all men, as well as to bring the faithful to the image of Christ. This satisfaction made by Christ was not merely sufficient in itself, but effectual so far as the divine will was concerned, for the salvation for all mankind. The humiliation as well as the satisfaction are both evident *in the epic.*

". . . nor can this be
But by fulfilling that which thou didst want,
Obedience to the Law of God, impos'd
On penaltie of death, and suffering death,
The penaltie to thy transgression due,
And due to theirs which out of thine will grow:
So onely can high Justice rest appaid.
The Law of God exact he shall fulfill
Both by obedience and by love, though love
Alone fulfill the Law, thy punishment
He shall endure by coming in the Flesh
To a reproachful life and cursed death,
Proclaiming Life to all who shall believe
In his redemption, and that his obedience

Imputed becomes theirs by Faith, his merits
To save them, not thir own, though legal works.
For this he shall live hated, be blasphem'd,
Seis'd on by force, judg'd, and to death condemnd
A shameful and accurst, naild to the Cross
By his own Nation, slaine for bringing Life;
But to the Cross he nailes thy Enemies,
The Law that is against thee, and the sins
Of all mankinde, with him there crucifi'd,
Never to hurt them more who rightly trust
In this his satisfaction. . . ."[290]

The exaltation of Christ appears in the epic.

Death and resurrection.

Epic,
". . . so he dies,
But soon revives. Death over him no power
Shall long usurp; ere the third dawning light
Returne, the Starres of Morn shall see him rise
Out of his grave, fresh as the dawning light,
Thy ransom paid. . . ."[291]

Benefit to mankind

Epic,
"So in his seed all Nations shall be blest.
Then to the Heav'n of Heav'ns he shall ascend
With victory, triumphing through the aire
Over his foes and thine. . . ."[292]

The exaltation

Epic,

"Therefore thy Humiliation shall exalt
With thee thy Manhood also to this Throne;
Here shalt thou sit incarnate, here shalt Reign,
Both God and Man, Son both of God and Man,
Annointed universal King, all Power
I give thee, reign, for ever, and assume
Thy Merits. . . ."[293]

"Equal to God, and equally enjoying
God-like fruition, quitted all to save
A World from utter loss, and hast been found
By Merit more then Birthright Son of God,
Found worthiest to be so by being Good,
Farr more then Great or High. . . ."[294]

Section 4. *Man's Renovation and Calling,* being a synopsis of the treatise(*)

After the redemption of man, his renovation is next to be considered. His renovation is the change from being under the divine wrath, proceeding into the state of grace. Under the renovation two things come for our consideration: the mode by which man is renewed, and the manifestation of that mode.

The mode by which man is renewed is either natural or supernatural. The natural mode pertains to the natural affections alone, and includes the calling of the natural man, as well as the change that follows in his character. In the call God invites fallen man to accept his propitiation in Christ. Those who believe are called to salvation, and those who refuse to believe are left without excuse.

There is both general and special calling. General calling is

(*) *Ibid.,* Vol. XV, pp. 343-365.

the invitation to the knowledge of the true Deity, issued by God to all mankind. Special calling is God's invitation to particular individuals, the elect as well as the reprobate. By reason of his calling man undergoes a vital and important change. The divine impulse partially renews the natural mind and will of man. This leads him to seek the knowledge of God, and for a time produces a better life. This call of God, and the change which follows, do not of themselves guarantee salvation. The renovation of man necessitates a transformation into a state of grace.[295] In the epic this renovation involves obedience to the law of God which the Saviour provides.

Epic,
". . . who comes thy Saviour, shall recure,
Not by destroying Satan, but his works
In thee and in thy Seed: nor can this be,
But by fulfilling that which thou didst want,
Obedience to the Law of God. . . ."[296]

The invitation is extended to all mankind generally.[297] In the epic the invitation is joined with the original promise to Abraham, that in him "all the families of the earth will be blessed."

Epic,
"And his Salvation, them who shall beleeve
Baptizing in the profluent stream, the signe
Of washing them from guilt of sin to Life
Pure, and in mind prepar'd, if so befall,
For death, like that which the redeemer dy'd.
All Nations they shall teach; for them that day
Not onely to the Sons of Abrahams Loines
Salvation shall be Preacht, but to the Sons
Of Abrahams Faith wherever through the world;
So in his seed all Nations shall be blest."[298]

150

God's calling is issued to individuals and to nations.[299]

A nation called.

Epic,

"A Nation from one faithful man to spring:
Him on this side Euphrates yet residing,
Bred up in Idol-worship; O that men
(Canst thou believe?) should be so stupid grown,
While yet the Patriark liv'd, who scap'd the Flood,
As to forsake the living God, and fall
To worship thir own work in Wood and Stone
For Gods! yet him God the most High voutsafes
To call by Vision from his Fathers house,
His kindred and false Gods, into a Land
Which he will shew him, and from him will raise
A mightie Nation, and upon him showre
His benediction so, that in his Seed
All Nations shall be blest. . . ."[300]

Individuals chosen.

Epic,

"Some I have chosen of peculiar grace
Elect above the rest; so is my will:
The rest shall hear me call, and oft be warnd
Their sinful state, and to appease betimes
Th' incensed Deitie, while offered grace
Invites; for I will cleer thir senses dark,
That may suffice, and soft'n, stonie hearts
To pray, repent, and bring obedience due
To prayer, repentance, and obedience due,
Though but endeavord with sincere intent,
Mine ear shall not be slow, mine eye not shut."[301]

151

Through the calling of God the mind becomes renewed with a desire for divine knowledge.

Treatise,

"The change which takes place in man by reason of his calling, is that whereby the natural mind and will of man being partially renewed by a divine impulse, are led to seek the knowledge of God, and for the time, at least, undergo an alteration for the better."[302]

The change in the natural man does not guarantee his salvation.[303] No one is infallible in terms of faith and conscience.

Epic,

". . . for on Earth
Who against Faith and Conscience can be heard
Infallible? yet many will presume:
Whence heavie persecution shall arise
On all who in worship persevere
Of Spirit and Truth; the rest, farr greater part,
Will deem in outward Rites and specious formes
Religion satisfi'd. . . ."[304]

Something beyond the natural mode of renovation is necessary. That is spiritual renovation.

Section 5. *Regeneration,*
being a synopsis of the treatise(*)

In supernatural renovation man has restored the use of his natural faculties especially his power to make correct judgments, and to exercise free will.

(*) *Ibid.,* Vol. XV, pp. 367-377.

In addition, *the inward man* is created anew, and the mind receives supernatural faculties. This change is wrought by the Word and the Spirit. The old man is destroyed. The inward man is regenerated by God after his own image. All the faculties of his mind, as well as both his body and soul, become as it were a new creature. The death and resurrection of Christ is the means for this regeneration.

Treatise,

"The intent of supernatural renovation is not only to restore man more completely than before to the use of his natural faculties, as regards his power to form right judgment, and to exercise free will; but to create afresh, as it were, *the inward man,* and infuse from above new and supernatural faculties into the minds of the renovated. This is called regeneration, and the regenerate are said to be planted in Christ."[305]

Repentance.

Epic,

"Thus they in lowliest plight repentant stood
Praying, for from the Mercie-seat above
Prevenient Grace descending had remov'd
The stonie from thir hearts, and made new flesh
Regenerate grow instead. . . ."[306]

The better convenant.

Epic,

"Up to a better Cov'nant, disciplin'd
From shadowie Types to Truth, from Flesh to Spirit,
From imposition of strict Laws, to free
Acceptance of large Grace . . ."[307]

All this regeneration is the result of Christ's death and resurrection.[308] From his grave Jesus usurped Satan and his dominion over men.

Epic,
 "When Jesus son of Mary second Eve,
 Saw Satan fall like Lightning down from Heav'n.
 Prince of the Aire; then rising from his Grave
 Spoild Principalities and Powers, triumpht
 In open show, and with ascension bright
 Captivity led captive through the Aire,
 The Realm it self of Satan long usurpt,
 Whom he shall tread at last under our feet;
 Eeven hee who now foretold his fatal bruise,
 And to the Woman thus his Sentence turn'd."[309]

Treatise and Epic

In Restoration and Redemption, John Milton claims that in
salvation God elevates man above that state of grace and glory
from which he fell.[310] In the epic Milton calls this the "better"
life."
 In this "better life" all the redeemed by Christ shall come
where,

Epic,
 "To better life shall yeeld him, where with mee
 All my redeemd may dwell in joy and bliss,
 Made one with me as I with thee am one."[311]

The Death and Resurrection of Christ is the means of the
Regeneration of the inward man, and

Treatise,
 "infuse from above new and supernatural faculties into

154

the minds of the renovated."[312]

The recapitulation of these affirmations of John Milton, in both treatise and epic, point the way toward a rational affirmation of Eden larger than the Biblical Eden, and to nothing at all lost in Paradise, with everything pointing to *Paradise Found.* In the Biblical Eden obedience was a condition that for Milton constituted something short of Paradise. The renovation of the Saviour, Jesus Christ, for John Milton in this "better life" provides what they wanted, "obedience to the Law of God."[313] This is structured into both the treatise and epic which now has as its true title, *Paradise Found.*

Section 6. *Repentance,*
being a synopsis of the treatise(*)

Repentance and faith follow as the effects of regeneration. Being a gift from God, repentance involves a perception of the sorrow to God by our sin. This sorrow brings with it a detestation and avoidance of sin. All of this involves a turning to God for his mercy, with the earnest desire to follow righteousness.

Repentance, known as conversion, is general when a man is converted from a state of sin to a state of grace. Repentance is particular, when one who is already converted repents of some individual sin.

In contrition both Adam and Eve plan to confess their guilt, so great is their desire to depart from evil.

Epic,
"What better can we do, then to the place
Repairing where he judg'd us, prostrate fall
Before him reverent, and there confess
Humbly our faults, and pardon beg, with tears
Watering the ground, and with our sighs the Air

(*) *Ibid.,* Vol. XV, pp. 379-393.

155

Frequenting, sent from hearts contrite, in sign
Of sorrow unfeign'd, and humiliation mee.
Undoubtedly he will relent and turn
From his displeasure; in whose look serene,
When angry most he seem'd and most severe,
What else but favor, grace, and mercie shon?
    So spake our Father penitent, nor Eve
Felt less remorse: they forthwith to the place
Repairing where he judg'd them prostrate fell
Before him reverent, and both confess'd
Humbly thir faults, and pardon beg'd, with tears
Watering the ground, and with thir sighs the Air
Frequenting, sent from hearts contrite, in sign
Of sorrow unfeign'd, and humiliation meek."[314]

Their conversion to good comes with their repentance and faith.

Epic,
"Thus they in lowliest plight repentant stood
Praying for from the Mercie-seat above
Prevenient Grace descending had remov'd
The stonie from thir hearts, and made new flesh
Regenerate grow instead."[315]

Section 7. *Saving Faith,* Being a synopsis
of the treatise(*)

Saving faith is the persuasion to believe, relying solely on
the promise of God. This faith is a gift the Father has bestowed
upon us in Christ, including eternal life. Knowledge of God,
even though at first imperfect, is the source from which faith
proceeds in its progress to good. Yet the seat of faith is not
the understanding but the will. Hope comes from faith and
is an assurance of things to come.

(*) *Ibid.,* Vol. XV. pp. 393-409.

Treatise,
"Saving faith is a full persuasion operated in us through
the gift of God, whereby we believe, on the sole authority
of the promise itself, that whatsoever things he has promised in Christ are ours, and especially the grace of eternal
life."[316]

Adam was persuaded to believe because of the promise.

Epic,
". . . For since I saught
By Prayer th' offended Deitie to appease,
Kneel'd and before him humbl'd all my heart,
Methought I saw him placable and mild,
Bending his eare; perswasion in me grew
That I was heard with favour; peace returnd
Home to my Breast, and to my memorie
His promise, that thy Seed shall bruise our Foe;
Which then not minded in dismay, yet now
Assures me that the bitterness of death
Is past, and we shall live. Whence Haile to thee,
Eve rightly call'd, Mother of all Mankind,
Mother of all things living, since by thee
Man is to live, and all things live for Man."[317]

In the epic the law of faith will be upon their hearts to guide
them.

Epic,
". . . but from Heav'n
Hee to his own a Comforter will send,
The promise of the Father, who shall dwell
His Spirit within them, and the Law of Faith
Working through love, upon thir hearts shall write,
To guide them in all truth. . . ."[318]

157

Hope is born of faith.

Treatise,
> "From faith arises hope, that is, a most assured expectation through faith of those future things which are already ours in Christ."[319]

Both the imperfect knowledge which Adam had in terms of his understanding apart from faith, as well as the hope which springs from faith, are readily discerned in this passage.

Epic,
> "O Prophet of glad tidings, finisher
> Of utmost hope! now clear I understand
> What oft my steddiest thoughts have searcht in vain. . . ."[320]

Section 8. *Ingrafted in Christ,* being a synopsis of the treatise (*)

Ingrafting in Christ follows upon regeneration, repentance and faith. One is ingrafted in Christ when by faith he is made a partaker of Christ, and is ready to become one with him.

This ingrafting, combined with regeneration, results in newness of life and increase. Newness of life is also called self-denial, and is that by which we are said to live unto God. In this newness of life we comprehend spiritual things and love holiness.

In the comprehension of spiritual things God produces a condition of the mind in which the ignorance of believers is removed. They are enabled to perceive heavenly things. Therefore, by divine teaching they know what is necessary for salvation and true happiness. In this life there is possible only an imperfect comprehension of spiritual things.

Love springs forth from the hearts of those in whom the

(*) *Ibid.,* Vol. XVI, pp. 3-23.

Spirit has placed a sense of the divine love. Those whose hearts are thus filled become dead to sin and alive unto God. *They bring forth good works with freedom.* This is holiness.

The increase within the regenerate is either absolute or relative. Absolute refers to internal, and relative to external. Absolute increase refers to those gifts we have received by being ingrafted in Christ. Perfection is not to be expected in the present life; yet we are to strive after it as the one goal of our existence.

There is a victory to be gained. Those who strive after perfection in Christ, even though imperfect, are frequently called in Scripture "perfect," and "blameless," and "without sin." This is because sin, though still dwelling in them, does not reign over them.

Transplanted into Christ

Epic,
"As in him perish all men, so in thee
As from a second root shall be restor'd,
As many as are restor'd, without thee none.
His crime makes guiltie all his Sons, thy merit
Imputed shall absolve them who renounce
Thir own both righteous and unrighteous deeds,
And live in thee transplanted, and from thee
Receive new life. So Man, as is most just,
Shall satisfie for Man, be judg'd and die,
And dying rise, and rising with him raise
His Brethren, ransomd with his own deer life."[321]

Guidance into all truth

Epic,
". . . but from Heav'n
Hee to his own a Comforter will send,

159

The promise of the Father, who shall dwell
His Spirit within them, and the Law of Faith
Working through love, upon thir hearts shall write,
To guide them in all truth, and also arme
With spiritual Armour. . . ."322

Love is the soul of all the rest

Epic,

". . . add Love
By name to come call'd Charitie, the soul
Of all the rest. . . ."323

Perfection is the one aim of all existence. *One Man perfect* is the salvation of the world.

Epic,

"O thou who future things canst represent
As present, Heav'nly instructer, I revive
At this last sight, assur'd that Man shall live
With all the Creatures, and thir seed preserve,
Farr less I now lament for one whole World
Of wicked Sons destroyd, then I rejoyce
For one Man found so perfect and so just,
That God voutsafes to raise another World
From him."324

Treatise and Epic

The fidelity of parallelism between the treatise, *De Doctrina Christiana,* and the epic, *Paradise Lost,* gives an accumulation of assurance that John Milton was writing of one position, over the course of the same time, and with the commonly avowed purpose. That purpose was to write about the life, "Happier farr." This constitutes the material of *Paradise Found.*

Section 9. *Justification and Adoption,*
being a synopsis of the treatise(*)

Thus far we have considered the absolute or internal increase of the regenerate. Now we deal with that which is relative or external. This increase has reference either to the Father exclusively, or to the Father and Son together.

That which has reference to the Father exclusively is called justification and adoption. Justification is God's goodness to those of faith who are regenerate and grafted in Christ. They are set free from sin and are considered just in God's sight. Works are the effects of faith, not the cause of justification; therefore we are justified by faith without the works of the law, but not without the works of faith. Peace of mind follows upon a consciousness of justification.

Adoption signifies those whom God takes as his children. They are those who are justified through faith. In our adoption we receive a new nature, and have a conformity to his glory.

Justification is God's goodness to those of faith.

Epic,
"The bloud of Bulls and Goats, they may conclude
Some bloud more precious must be paid for Man,
Just for unjust, that in such righteousness
To them by Faith imputed, they may finde
Justification towards God, and peace
Of Conscience, which the Law by Ceremonies
Cannot appease, nor Man the moral part
Perform, and not performing cannot live."[325]

(*) *Ibid.,* Vol. XVI pp. 25-55.

161

Epic,
> "As in him perish all men, so in thee
> As from a second root shall be restor'd,
> As many as are restor'd, without thee none.
> His crime makes guiltie all his Sons, thy merit
> Imputed shall absolve them who renounce
> Thir own both righteous and unrighteous deeds,
> And live in thee transplanted, and from thee
> Receive new life."[326]

Peace of conscience

Epic,
> ". . . that in such righteousness
> To them by Faith imputed, they may finde
> Justification towards God, and peace
> Of Conscience. . . ."[327]

God adopts those justified by faith. All nations are open for this adoption.

Epic.
> ". . . for from that day
> Not onely to the Sons of Abrahams Loines
> Salvation shall be Preacht, but to the Sons
> Of Abrahams Faith wherever through the world;
> So in his seed all Nations shall be blest."[328]

Section 10. *Christian Fellowship and the Final Consummation,* being a synopsis of the treatise (*)

The increase of the regenerate with reference to the Father

(*) *Ibid.,* Vol. XVI, pp. 57-97.

and Son consists in our union and fellowship with the Father through Christ the Son, as well as our glorification after the image of Christ.

From this union there is a fellowship and participation of the various gifts and merits of Christ. "He that eateth my flesh, and drinketh my blood, dwelleth in me, and I in him."[329] Out of this fellowship there are constituted the members of Christ's body, known as "The Communion of Saints." The total fellowship of the regenerate with the Father and Christ, and of the members of Christ's body among themselves, is the mystical body known as "The Invisible Church."

Of this, Christ is the head. Since the body of Christ is mystically one, the fellowship is likewise mystical. It is not restricted to place or time. It is composed of indivduals of widely separated countries, and of all ages, from the foundation of the world.

Imperfect glorification signifies our adoption by the Father. In this glorification we are conscious of grace already, and have an expectation of future glory to such an extent that we are already in a state of blessedness.

Along with regeneration and increase there is a preservation in the faith, also the work of God. Regeneration, increase, and preservation in the faith, considered on the part of God, and their effects, as faith, love, considered on the part of man, or as acting in man, give an assurance of salvation.

On the part of God, however, the primary cause is his election of believers. Having been justified by faith and received into union with Christ, one has an assurance of salvation, if he continue in faith and love. Only God's preserving power can make possible the final perseverence of the saints. With this perseverence, and as long as nothing is wanting in the utmost maintenance of their faith and love, they will attain to everlasting life. The perfection of glorification is not attainable in the present life.

Fellowship in one kingdom through Jesus Christ

163

Epic,

". . . and in a moment will create
Another World, out of one man a Race
Of men innumerable, there to dwell,
But here, till by degrees of merit rais'd
They open to themselves at length the way
Up hither, under long obedience tri'd,
And Earth be chang'd to Heav'n, and Heav'n to Earth,
One Kingdom, Joy and Union without end.
Mean while inhabit laxe, ye Powers of Heav'n,
And thou my Word, begotten Son, by thee
This I perform, speak thou, and be it don. . . ."[330]

Participation in Christ's merits. His merits will save them

Epic,

"Proclaiming Life to all who shall believe
In his redemption, and that his obedience
Imputed becomes theirs by Faith, his merits
To save them, not thir own. . . ."[331]

A pre-figurament of the reward that awaits the good.

Epic,

". . . Him the most High
Rapt in a balmie Cloud with winged Steeds
Did, as thou sawst, receave, to walk with God
High in Salvation and the Climes of bliss,
Exempt from Death; to shew thee what reward
Awaits the good. . ."[332]

Section 11. *Grace and Law,* being a synopsis
of the treatise(*)

(*) *Ibid.,* Vol. XVI, pp. 99-219.

In the development thus far we have considered renovation as it is in this life. Now we trace its manifestation and exhibition in the covenant of grace. This covenant was first declared by God. "I will put enmity between thee and the woman, and between thy seed and her seed. It shall bruise thy head, and thou shalt bruise his heel."[333] "For this purpose the Son of God was manifested, that he might destroy the works of the devil."[334] Moses exhibited a shadowing forth of the covenant in the liberation from Egyptian bondage, and in the brazen serpent.

The Mosaic Law was intended for the Israelites alone, with a promise of life to such as should keep them, and a curse on such as should be disobedient. The purpose was that they might have recourse to the righteousness of the promised Savior. Through them the hope was for all other nations to be led under the Gospel.

The Gospel is the new covenant, superior to the law, and announced by Christ, as well as written in the hearts of believers by the Holy Spirit. The promise of eternal life in the Gospel is extended to all in every nation who shall believe.

The love of our neighbor remains unchanged. Only the tablet of the law is changed, with the injunctions now written by the Spirit in the hearts of believers.

Christian liberty is the freedom from enfranchisement we have obtained through Christ. This is both a freedom from the bondage of sin and the rule of man. In this freedom we are sons rather than servants, serving God by the guidance of the Spirit of Truth.

The covenant of grace was appropriately sealed. Under the law the sealing of the covenant consisted in circumcision and the passover. Under the Gospel it consists in Baptism and the Supper of the Lord. Believers are immersed, signifying union with Christ in his death, burial, and resurrection. Since infants are unable to receive instruction; baptism, and the Lord's Supper must wait for them until they are able to understand and receive the meaning.

The sacraments have no salvation in themselves as such, but

are symbolical of the actual blessings. Confirmation, penance, extreme unction, orders, and marriage have no divine establishment in the sealing of the covenant.

The new covenant is manifested in the hearts of believers

Epic,

"Thus they in lowliest plight repentant stood
Praying, from the Mercie-seat above
Prevenient Grace descending had remov'd
The stonie from thir hearts, and made new flesh
Regenerate grow instead. . . ."[335]

The imperfect nature of the law directs to a better covenant.

Epic,

"So law appears imperfect, and but giv'n
With purpose to resign them in full time
Up to a better Cov'nant, disciplin'd
From shadowie Types to Truth, from Flesh to Spirit,
From imposition of strict Laws, to free
Acceptance of large Grace, from servil fear
To filial, works of Law to works of Faith."[336]

Salvation is open to all peoples and nations by faith

Epic,

"For death, like that which the redeemer dy'd.
All Nations they shall teach; for from that day
Not onely to the Sons of Abrahams Loines
Salvation shall be Preacht, but to the Sons
Of Abrahams Faith wherever through the world;
So in his seed all Nations shall be blest."[337]

Baptism is the sign of a pure life as well as preparation for death

Epic,

"And his Salvation, them who shall beleeve
Baptizing in the profluent stream, the signe

166

Of washing them from guilt of sin to Life
Pure, and in mind prepar'd, if so befall,
For death, like that which the redeemer dy'd."[338]

Treatise and Epic

There is a continued parallelism between the treatise, *De Doctrina Christiana*, and the epic, *Paradise Lost*, with a manifold body of material that builds into the idyllic, and the life "Happier farr" which forms the material of *Paradise Found*.

Section 12. *The Church and the Scriptures*, being a synopsis of the treatise(*)

The visible church comprises those who are called. Those who have received the call, whether actually regenerate or otherwise, are the visible church.

The tokens of the visible church are, pure doctrine; the proper external worship of God; genuine evangelical love; and the right administration of the seals of the covenant.

Christ alone is the head of both the visible church as well as the mystical church. There is no earthly head over the church, such as the Roman pontiffs. No Scriptural basis can be found for such an office. The visible church is either universal or particular.

The universal church consists of ministers and people. It includes all the called in every part of the world, who worship the Father through Christ, either individually or collectively.

Ministers work under a divine commission in their various offices within the church. Extraordinary ministers extend the church into new areas, or reform its corrupt practices.

The writings of the prophets, apostles, and evangelists composed under divine inspiration, are called the Holy Scriptures. The Scriptures are for the use of all men, of all classes. They are adapted for daily reading or hearing. The Scriptures are a

(*) *Ibid.*, Vol. XVI, pp. 219-337.

sufficient guide to salvation, due to their own simplicity as well as divine illumination. Scripture is open to individual interpretation, under the guidance of the Spirit and with the mind of Christ.

There is in the Gospel as two-fold Scriptures, the external and the internal. The external Scripture is the written word. The internal Scripture is that written in the hearts of believers by the Holy Spirit. Of the two the Spirit is the more certain guide. The written word can be faulty, but never the Spirit.

A society of believers, joined by the bond of brotherhood, and united in the common effort to edify believers, is called a particular church. Ministers of a particular church are called presbyters and deacons. The people have the privilege to choose the minister. It is Scriptural for a minister to receive a remuneration; however it is more desirable to serve gratuitously. When a remuneration is given it must be spontaneous, and a voluntary act, without interference by the civil power.

Discipline is the bond by which a particular church is held together. Church discipline is the polity of the members of the church by means of which they fashion their lives according to Christian doctrine, and govern their public meetings.

When a new member is received into a particular church, he must agree to fashion his life for the improvement of his brethren as well as his own life. The administration of discipline is the responsibility of the entire body of the church, including all the members. The church has unusual power against her enemies. It is a lack of faith to conclude that the civil magistrate is necessary for proper administration of the power and the authority of the church.

The visible church includes those who are called in every part of the world; for all nations receive the tidings of heaven.

Epic,
    ". . . for the Spirit
    Powrd first on his Apostles, whom he sends

168

To evangelize the Nations, then on all
Baptiz'd, shall them with wondrous gifts endue
To speak all Tongues, and do all Miracles,
As did thir Lord before them. Thus they win
Great numbers of each Nation to receave
With joy the tidings brought from Heav'n. . . .[339]

No human institution or hierarchy within the church is possible. Christ alone is the universal king.[340] This affirmation,
located in the treatise, is matched by the equivalent affirmation in the,

Epic,
"Therefore thy Humiliation shall exalt
With thee thy Manhood also to this Throne;
Here shalt thou sit incarnate, here shalt Reign
Both God and Man, Son both of the God and Man,
Anointed universal King. . . ."[341]

Those who have fashioned places of power in the church are
wolves.

Epic,
". . . but in thir room, as they forewarne,
Wolves shall succeed for teachers, grievous Wolves
Who all the sacred mysteries of Heav'n
To thir own vile advantages shall turne
Of lucre and ambition, and the truth
With superstitions and traditions taint,
Left onely in those written Records pure,
Though not but by the Spirit understood.
Then shall they seek to avail themselves of names,
Places and titles, and with these to joine
Secular power, though feigning still to act
By spiritual. . . ."[342]

The truth is in the Word, interpreted by the Spirit.

Epic,
"Who all the sacred mysteries of Heav'n
To thir own vile advantages shall turne
Of lucre and ambition, and the truth
With superstitions and traditions taint,
Left onely in those written Records pure,
Though not but by the Spirit understood."[343]

Secular power in the church is a misuse of the Spirit of God.

Epic,
"Then shall they seek to avail themselves of names,
Places and titles, and with these to joine
Secular power, though feigning still to act
By spiritual, to themselves appropriating
The Spirit of God, promis'd alike and giv'n
To all Beleevers; and from that pretense,
Spiritual Lawes by carnal power shall force
On every conscience; Laws which none shall finde
Left them inrould, or what the Spirit within
Shall on the heart engrave. What will they then
But force the Spirit of Grace it self, and binde
His consort Libertie. . . ."[344]

Women must maintain silence in church.[345] Eve is counselled
to seek from Adam what concerns her faith.

Epic,
". . . go, waken Eve;
Her also I with gentle Dreams have calm'd
Portending good, and all her spirits compos'd
To meek submission: thou at season fit
Let her with thee partake what thou hast heard,
Chiefly what may concern her Faith to know."[346]

170

The consolidation of thought alike in the treatise, *De Doctrina Christiana,* and in the epic, *Paradise Lost,* writes into Paradise nothing essentially lost. Even the companionship of our first Parents, hand in hand, but with Adam in the lead, is the companionship of *Paradise Found.*

Section 13. *Things To Come,* being a synopsis of the treatise(*)

Reference has already been made to the imperfect glorification to which believers attain in this life. Perfect glorification is effected in eternity. Perfect glorification begins from the period of Christ's second coming to judgment, and the resurrection of the dead. Only the Father knows the day and hour of Christ's coming; hence it will be sudden.

Certain signs will mark its approach. These are either general or peculiar. The general signs relate to the destruction of Jerusalem, the type of Christ's advent, false prophets, false Christs, wars, earthquakes, persecution, pestilence, famine, and the gradual decay of faith and charity down to the very day itself.

The peculiar signs are, an extreme recklessness, impiety, an almost universal apostasy, the revealing of antichrist, and his destruction by the spirit of the mouth of Christ. The dead will rise. A sudden change will take place upon the living.

In the last judgment Christ will judge the evil angels, and the whole race of mankind. Then will be pronounced that sentence, "Come ye blessed of my Father, inherit the kingdom prepared for you from the foundation of the world."[347] "Depart from me, ye cursed, into everlasting fire, prepared for the devil and his angels."[348] This sentence will be executed in the pun-

(*) *Ibid.,* Vol. XVI, pp. 337-381.

ishment of the wicked, and the perfect glorification of the righteous. Christ then takes up his reign on earth. There shall be no end of his kingdom.

Our glorification will be accompanied by the renovation of heaven and earth. The final judgment shall consume the bad as well as the unclean world in a great conflagration. The world shall burn, and with it bad men and angels. From her ashes shall spring a new heaven and a new earth. Then there shall be no need for a regal scepter. God shall be all in all.

Epic,
". . . under thee as Head Supreme
Thrones, princedoms, Powers, Dominions I reduce:
All knees to thee shall bow, of them that bide
In Heaven, or Earth, or under Earth in Hell;
When thou attended gloriously from Heav'n
Shalt in the Sky apeer, and from thee send
The summoning Arch-Angels to proclaime
Thy dread Tribunal: forthwith from all Windes
The living, and forwith the cited dead
Of all past Ages to the general Doom
Shall hast'n, such a peal shall rouse thir sleep.
Then all thy Saints assembl'd, thou shalt judge
Bad men and Angels, they arraignd shall sink
Beneath thy Sentence; Hell, her numbers full,
Thenceforth shall be for ever shut. Mean while
The World shall burn, and from her ashes spring
New Heav'n and Earth, wherein the just shall dwell,
And after all thir tribulations long
See golden days, fruitful of golden deeds,
With Joy and Love triumphing, and fair Truth.
Then thou thy regal Scepter shalt lay by,
For regal Scepter then no more shall need,
God shall be All in All."[349]

The second advent of Christ will dissolve the present world in a great conflagration, out of which new heavens and earth will be raised. Then all will be eternal joy and bliss.

Epic,

". . . Truth shall retire
Bestuck with slandrous darts, and works of Faith
Rarely be found: so shall the World goe on.
To good malignant, to bad men benigne,
Under her own waight groaning till the day
Appeer of respiration to the just,
And vengeance to the wicked, at return
Of him so lately promis'd to thy aid
The Womans seed, obscurely then foretold,
Now amplier known thy Saviour and thy Lord,
Last in the clouds from Heav'n to be reveald
In glory of the Father, to dissolve
Satan with his perverted World, then raise
From the conflagrant mass, purg'd and refin'd,
New Heav'ns, new Earth, Ages of endless date
Founded in righteousness and peace and love
To bring forth fruits Joy and eternal Bliss."[350]

Treatise and Epic

We have come through thirteen sections under the theme of salvation. Each of these sections, and all of them together, have designated a consolidation of mind in the treatise, *De Doctrina Christiana,* and the epic, *Paradise Lost.*

From this manifold and unitary treatment of Salvation, John Milton affirms the New Heaven and New Earth to come with golden days, fruitful of golden deeds. This is the adverse of anything lost, and the affirmation of *Paradise Found.*

CHAPTER TEN

THE CHRISTIAN ETHIC:

comprising the following two sections

Section 1. The Service of God
Section 2. The Service of Men

The second book of *De Doctrina Christiana* deals especially with questions of Christian conduct. The evident and organic relationship we have noted thus far between the treatise and the epic still continues in this second book; however, there is a disproportion at this point between the amount of relevant material in the treatise and that in the epic.

This is due to the fact that the epic comes to a close with the departure of our First Parents from the Garden. The second book of the treatise deals with man's relationship both to God and to his neighbor, after the Fall.

The theology man has constructed since the expulsion from the Garden has become both voluminous and complex. The treatise bears witness to the truth of this, since in the epic Milton gives little room to these relationships of the fallen couple, either toward God or toward man.

Book two of *De Doctrina* . . . is conveniently divided into two sections. The first comprises the relationship of man toward God, with all that is involved in the way of worship. The second section deals with all that is involved in the way of man's relationship to his neighbor.

Section 1. *The Service of God,* being a
synopsis of the treatise(*)

The subject of the first book was Faith, or the knowledge of God. The second treats of the worship or love of God. Milton here deals with such questions as Good Works and their Proximate Causes; the benefits and forms of Worship; Oaths and the lot; Zeal; and the Lord's day and Festivals.

The true worship of God is in good works. We perform good works by the Spirit of God and through faith. Those works redound to the glory of God and our salvation as well as the edification of our neighbor. Faith alone brings justification not agreement with the decalogue. That which justifies alone is able to perform any good work; therefore faith is essential to good works.

The essence of the matter is that there is in good works a conformity, not with the written law, but with the unwritten law of the Spirit, given by the Father; hence the works of believers are the works of the Spirit itself.

God is the primary cause of good works. The proximate causes of good works are good habits, also called virtues, in which is included the whole of our duty toward God and men.

The general virtues belong partly to the understanding, and partly to the will. Those belonging to the understanding are wisdom and prudence. When we diligently search after the will of God and direct our actions accordingly, we are wise. Prudence is the correct discernment of what is proper in given situations and circumstances. The virtues which belong to the will are sincerity, promptitude, and constancy. Sincerity means proper conduct on all occasions in which we act with earnest determination. Promptitude means actions that are occasioned with a ready and willing spirit. Constancy is a determination to do right, from which nothing can divert us.

Special virtues refer to a particular branch of our duty; namely, to our duty towards God, or towards man. Our duty towards

(*) *Ibid.,* Vol. XVII, pp. 2-193.

God relates to his immediate worship or service, being either internal or external. Internal worship consists in the belief in one true God, and the worship of Him. Devout affections towards God are love, trust, hope, gratitude, fear, humility, patience, obedience.

External worship, commonly called religion, is our worship of God after the form and manner which He has Himself set down. The parts into which religion is divided are the invocation or adoration of God, and the sanctification of His name in all the circumstances of life. Under invocation are included, first, supplication and thanksgiving; secondly, oaths and the casting of lots.

Supplication is the request for God to give what is lawful, for us and for others. The posture of the body is not important to effective prayer. It is not necessary that our prayers be audible. Set forms of worship are superfluous. All places are equally suitable for prayer; however, for private prayer, a retired place is most proper. A religious fast assists prayers, as do vows; however a religious fast is abstinence not so much from eating and drinking, as from sin. Addresses to God, and particularly thanksgiving are frequently accompanied by singing and hymns in honor of the divine name.

Another species of invocation consists in oaths, and in the casting of the lot. In an oath we call God to bear witness to the truth of our statement, with a curse upon us if we are false.

The casting of lots is an appeal for God to decide in a perplexing situation. Invocations to angels or saints and any form of idolatry are in opposition to God.

So far we have treated of the invocation or adoration of God. Now we come to the sanctification of the divine name under all circumstances, particularly in respect to place and time. Zeal is the ardent desire to hallow the name of God. It includes indignation against anything that violates religion.

The circumstances of worship are the same as of all things nature, place and time. Public worship, before Mosaic times, was not confined to any definite place. Under the law it took place partly in the synagogues and partly in the temple. Under the Gospel, any convenient place is proper. Before Mosaic times we do not know the time of public worship. With Moses it was the Sabbath. Under the Gospel no one day is appointed for divine worship in preference to another. The church may set apart a day for the assembly of its members. This may conveniently take place every seven days, and particularly on the first day of the week.

Now let us look for the relationship of these various ideas, in the epic.

Good works lead to our elevation, the benefit of our neighbor, and especially the glory of God. From works of law we proceed upward to works of faith, under the new Covenant in Christ.

Epic,
"So Law appears imperfet, and but giv'n
With purpose to resign them in full time
Up to a better Cov'nant, disciplin'd
From shadowie Types to Truth, from Flesh to Spirit,
From imposition of strict Laws, to free
Acceptance of large Grace, from servile fear
To filial, works of Law to works of Faith.[351]

Good works are evidence of God working in us. The perfection of our works is by way of Christ.

Epic,
". . . let mee
Interpret for him, mee his Advocate
And propitiation, all his works on mee
Good or not good ingraft, my Merit those
Shall perfet, and for these my Death shall pay."[352]

God hears even the least utterance, when we pray. Even sighs are heard and received, sighs and prayers.

Epic,
". . . sighs now breath'd

177

Unutterable, which the Spirit of prayer
Inspir'd, and wing'd for Heav'n with speedier flight
Then loudest Oratorie."[353]

Epic,

"See Father, what first fruits on Earth are sprung
From thy implanted Grace in Man, these Sighs
And Prayers, which in this Golden Censer, mixt
With Incense, I thy Priest before thee bring."[354]

The place of prayer is of no consequence.

Epic,

". . . God attributes to place
No sanctitie, if none be thither brought
By men who there frequent, or therein dwell."[355]

An oath binds us to God, in fidelity to the truth of what we say. Even God pronounced His will with a mighty oath.

Epic,

". . . so was his will
Pronounc'd among the Gods, and by an Oath
That shook Heav'ns whol circumference, confirm'd."[356]

Zeal is reverence toward God and indignation against anything that violates religion.

Epic,

"Abdiel, then whom none with more zeale ador'd
The Deitie, and divine commands obeid,
Stood up, and in a flame of zeale severe
The current of his fury thus oppos'd."[357]

Section 2. *The Service of Men,* being a
synopsis of the treatise(*)

In this section Milton deals with such questions as the duty of man towards himself, and the duty of man towards his

(*) *Ibid.,* Vol. XVII, pp. 193-421.

neighbor. In our duty towards men we may be considered as serving God, so long as this total duty is done in obedience to the divine command. The virtues connected with our duty towards man, are partly those which each individual owes to himself, and partly those which we owe to our neighbors. These virtues are neither general or special. The general virtues are love and righteousness.

Milton treats of the duties we owe our neighbors in the characters of Noah, Abraham, and Isaiah.

Noah

Epic,

> "At length a Reverend Sire among them came,
> And of thir doings great dislike declar'd,
> And testifi'd against thir wayes; hee oft
> Frequented thir Assemblies, whereso met,
> Triumphs or Festivals, and to them preachd
> Conversion and Repentance, as to Souls
> In Prison under Judgements imminent:
> But all in vain: which when he saw, he ceas'd
> Contending, and remov'd his Tents farr off;
> Then from the Mountain hewing Timber tall,
> Began to build a vessel of huge bulk,
> Measur'd by Cubit, length and breadth, and highth."[358]

Abraham

Epic,

> "A Nation from one faithful man to spring:
> Him on this side Euphrates yet residing,
> Bred up in Idol-worship: O that men
> (Canst thou believe?) should be so stupid grown,
> While yet the Patriark liv'd, who scap'd the Flood,
> As to forsake the living God, and fall
> To worship thir own work in Wood and Stone
> For Gods! yet him God the most High voutsafes
> To call by Vision from His Fathers house,

179

His kindred and false Gods, into a Land
Which he will shew him, and from him will raise
A mightie Nation, and upon him showre
His benediction so, that in his Seed
All Nations shall be blest."[359]

Isaiah

Epic,

". . . the like shall sing
All Prophecie, That of the Royal Stock
Of David (so I name this King) shall rise
A Son, the Womans Seed to thee foretold,
Foretold to Abraham, as in whom shall trust
All Nations, and to Kings foretold, of Kings
The last, for of his Reign shall be no end."[360]

Virtues have a special function.

Treatise,

"The special virtues which regulate our desire of external
advantages, have reference either to bodily gratifications,
or to the possessions which enrich and adorn life."[361]

Special virtues have various classifications: temperance, sobriety,
chastity, modesty, decency.

Temperance

Treatise,

"The virtue which prescribes bounds to the desire of bodily
gratification, is called temperance."[362]

Epic,

"I yield it just, said Adam, and submit,
But is there yet no other way, besides
These painful passages, how we may come
To death, and mix with our connatural dust?
There is, said Michael, if thou well observe
The rule of not too much, by temperance taught

In what thou eatst and drinkst, seeking from thence
Due nourishment, not gluttonous delight,
Till many years over thy head return:
So maist thou live, till like ripe Fruit thou drop
Into thy Mothers lap, or be with ease
Gatherd, not harshly pluckt, for death mature."[363]

Sobriety

Treatise,
"Sobriety consists in abstinence from immoderate eating and drinking."[364]

Epic,
"Thus when with meats and drinks they had suffic'd,
Not burd'nd Nature."[365]

Chastity and Modesty

Treatise,
"Chastity consists in temperance as regards the unlawful lusts of the flesh."[366]
"Modesty consists in refraining from all obscenity of language or action, in short, from whatever is inconsistent with the strictest decency of behavior in reference to sex or person."[367]

Epic,
"Giver of all things faire, but fairest this
Of all thy gifts, now enviest, I now see
Bone of my Bone, Flesh of my Flesh, my Self
Before me; Woman is her Name, of Man
Extracted; for this cause he shall forgoe
Father and Mother, and to his Wife adhere;
And they shall be one Flesh, one Heart, one Soule.
    She heard me thus, and though divinely brought,
Yet Innocence and Virgin Modestie,
Her vertue and the conscience of her worth."[368]

181

Decency

Treatise,

"Decency consists in refraining from indecorum or lasciviousness in dress or personal appearance."[369]

Epic,

"So much delights me as those graceful acts,
Those thousand decencies that daily flow
From all her words and actions mixt with Love."[370]

Moderation in the possession of temporal things becomes evident in the virtues of contentment, frugality, patience, industry, and a liberal spirit.

Contentment

Treatise,

"Contentment is that virtue whereby a man is inwardly satisfied with the lot assigned him by divine providence."[371]

Epic,

"Thy Love, the sole contentment of my heart."[372]

Frugality

Treatise

"Frugality consists in avoiding expense, so far as is seemly, and in wasting nothing which is capable of being applied to an useful purpose."[373]

Epic,

". . . small store will serve, where store
All seasons, ripe for use hange on the stalk;
Save what by frugal storing firmness gains
To nourish, and superfluous moist consumes:
But I will haste and from each bough and break,
Each Plant and juicest Gourd will pluck such choice
To entertain our Angel guest."[374]

Industry

Treatise,

"Industry is that by which we honestly provide for ourselves the means of comfortable living."[375]

Epic,

". . . thou shalt eate th' Herb of th' Field,
In the sweat of thy Face shalt thou eat Bread."[376]

A Liberal Spirit

Treatise,

"Liberality is a temperate use of our honest acquisitions in the provision of food and raiment, and of the elegancies of life."[377]

Epic,

". . . Author of this Universe . . .
So amply, and with hands so liberal
. . . hast provided all things."[378]

Fortitude and patience are special virtues enabling us to resist evil. Christ is the great pattern of fortitude, as seen in both His life and death.

Fortitude

Treatise,

"Fortitude is chiefly conspicuous in repelling evil, or in regarding its approach with equanimity."[379]

Epic,

"Henceforth I learne, that to obey is best,
And love with fear the onely God, to walk
As in his presence, ever to observe
His providence, and on him sole depend,
Mercifull over all his works, with good
Still overcoming evil, and by small
Accomplishing great things, by things deemd weak

Subverting worldly strong; and worldly wise
By simply mee; that suffering for Truths sake
Is fortitude to highest victorie,
And to the faithful Death the Gate of Life;
Taught this by his example whom I now
Acknowledge my Redeemer ever blest."[380]

Patience

Treatise

"Patience consists in the endurance of misfortunes and injuries."[381]

Epic,

"Ere thou from thence depart, know I am sent
To show thee what shall come in future dayes
To thee and to thy Offspring; good with bad
Expect to hear, supernal Grace contending
With sinfulness of Men; thereby to learn
True patience, and to temper joy with fear
And pious sorrow, equally enur'd
By moderation either state to beare,
Prosperous or adverse: so shalt thou lead
Safest thy life, and best prepar'd endure
Thy mortal passage when it comes."[382]

We have considered the duties of man towards himself. Now we turn to the same virtues in their relationship to our neighbor. Love towards our neighbor means that we love him as ourselves. Milton differentiates between the two by classifying humanity, goodwill and compassion under absolute love, and brotherly love and friendship under reciprocal love.

Treatise,

"Charity towards our neighbor consists in loving him as ourselves."[383]

184

Compassion sums up these virtues of absolute love as enumerated by Milton. Adam felt this when Michael showed him many sights of Death.

Epic,
   "Adam could not but wept,
   . . . compassion quell'd
   His best of Man, and gave him up to tears
   A space, till firmer thoughts restrained excess."[384]

In our relations with our neighbor we must regulate both our actions and our affections concerning him. Special duties towards our neighbor regard his internal and external good.

His internal good is consulted by a regard to his safety and honor; his external, by a concern for his good name and worldly interests. This regard should extend not merely to the present life, but to the eternal state. If we conduct ourselves toward our neighbor with due respect and refrain from all action that would injure him in his relationships with others, we support and sustain his good name.

The virtues by which we promote the worldly interests of our neighbor are integrity and beneficence. Integrity consists in refraining from the property of others. It also means honesty and uprightness in dealing with our neighbor. Beneficence means helping our neighbor out of our abundance.

Thus far we have treated of these virtues or special duties which man owes to his neighbor simply as such. The virtues or duties originating are either private or public.

Private duties are partly domestic and partly those outside our own house. Under domestic duties are comprehended the reciprocal obligations of husband and wife, parent and child, brethren and kinsmen, master and servant.

The duties towards those not of our own house are almsgiving and hospitality.

Treatise,

"Almsgiving consists in affording relief to the poor, especially to such as are brethren, in proportion to our means, or even beyond them, without ostentation, and from the motive of true charity.[385]

Hospitality consists in receiving under our own roof or providing for the kind reception of the poor and strangers; especially such as are recommended to us by the churches, or by our brethern in the faith."[386]

Epic,

"So saying, with dispatchful looks in haste
She turns, on hospitable thoughts intent
What choice to chuse for delicacie best."[387]

Public duties are of two kinds, political and ecclesiastical. Political duties include the obligations of the magistrate and the people to each other and to foreign nations. The magistrate is to encourage religion and the service of God, public worship in particular, and to reverence the Church. Religion therefore is to be protected by the magistrate, not forced upon the people.

Public ecclesiastical duties consist in the reciprocal obligations of ministers and of the church considered collectively and individually.

In these sections Milton has detailed the virtues and duties comprising the sum total of the relationship of man toward God, and man towards his neighbor.

After such a detailed presentation of this relationship, it is interesting to note Masson's judgment on the value of the Church in Milton's later life. "Milton, in his last years, belonged to no religious communion, and attended no place of worship. . . ."[388]

PART III

THE AFFIRMATION OF ORTHODOXY

CHAPTER ELEVEN

ORTHODOXY RESTATED

The purpose of this part of our work, known as the Affirmation of Orthodoxy, is to set forth the doctrine of the Christian Faith concerning Sin, Soul and Body, God, the Divinity of Christ, and the Trinity.

On these aspects of Christian doctrine we have indicated in previous sections of this study, Milton held opinions considered as unorthodox. It is to these unorthodox views of Milton we now turn our attention.

No attempt at all is made to present a history of doctrine. Every effort has been made to give the true orthodox position, as that position has been accepted by the Protestant church, as well as endorsed by contemporary leaders in the Christian Faith.

There are essentially two principles that are the distinguishing characteristics of Protestant theology. One is the sole reliance upon the Holy Scriptures as the authority both for faith and practice. The other is that man can receive justification before God on the basis of faith alone. Both of these distinguishing characteristics of Protestant theology stem from the concept of sin as having such reality that a thorough-going separation results between man and God.

"It was in their profound sense of the reality of sin, and of its dominion in the human will, that the Protestants laid the foundations of their theology."[389]

Such a concept of sin that it resulted, from the human side in an absolute separation from God, dominated the thinking of

189

both Protestant and Catholic alike. Only indirectly did Pelagian interrogations respecting the reality and dominion of sin over the human will enter into the Protestant controversy.

The issue was drawn between Catholic and Protestant at the point of man's reconcilement with God. Both sides of the dispute accepted the orthodox view of the Trinity as set forth in the Council of Nicea, that Christ was "of the same substance with the Father." Both accepted the divine and human natures existing in Christ, as declared by the Creed of Chalcedon. With the exception of the followers of Zwingli and the earlier influence of Scotus, both parties in the dispute accepted the Augustinian view of sin and the Anselmic view of the atonement. The crux of the problem lay in the manner by which the human soul, burdened with the awful consequences of sin, could obtain forgiveness and reconciliation with God. For both sides, sin constituted a basic and thorough-going separation between man and God.

Sin

Because of sin, man was in a constant and sustained otherness to God. From the human side sin left man in a state of complete depravity. Of himself man was utterly helpless to relieve his spiritual destitution. This was Scriptural in the view of Saint Paul,

"For the good that I would I do not, but the evil which I would not, that I do. Now if I do that I would not, it is no more I that do it, but sin that dwelleth in me. I find then a law, that when I would do good, evil is present with me. For I delight in the law of God after the inward man. But I see another law in my members, warring against the law of my mind, and bringing me into captivity to the law

of sin which is in my members. O wretched man that I am!
Who shall deliver me from the body of this death?"[390]

This view constituted a most complete otherness to God, a
thorough-going depravity occasioned by sin. So complete was
the otherness to God, that the result was death itself.

Augustine (354-430) followed Paul in this Scriptural view
of sin and death.

> "For, though a man be delighted with the law of God
> after the inner man, what shall he do with that other law
> in his members which warreth against the law of his mind,
> and bringeth him into captivity to the law of sin which is in
> his members? For thou art righteous, O Lord, but we have
> sinned and committed iniquity, and have done wickedly,
> and thy hand is grown heavy upon us, and we are justly
> delivered over unto that ancient sinner, the king of death;
> because he persuaded our will to be like his will, whereby
> he abode not in Thy truth. What shall wretched man do?
> Who shall deliver him from the body of this death. . . .?"[391]

Along with Paul and Augustine, Martin Luther (1483-1546)
held that sin had the same tragic separation of man from God.
In fact it was the trenchant sense of sinfulness that started Luther
in the religious revival resulting in the Protestant Reformation.[392]

John Calvin (1509-1564) likewise emphasized the spiritual
destitution of man in his separation from God because of sin.

> "These two things therefore should be distinctly observed:
> first, that our nature being so totally vitiated and depraved,
> we are, on account of this very corruption, considered as
> convicted and justly condemned in the sight of God, to
> whom nothing is acceptable but righteousness, innocence,
> and purity. And this liableness to punishment arises not from
> the delinquency of another; for when it is said that the sin
> of Adam renders us obnoxious to the Divine judgment, it

191

is not to be understood as if we, though innocent, were undeservedly loaded with the guilt of his sin; but, because we are all subject to a curse, in consequence of his transgression, he is therefore said to have involved us in guilt. Nevertheless we derive from him, not only the punishment but also the pollution to which the punishment is justly due. Wherefore Augustine, though he frequently calls it the sin of another, the more clearly to indicate its transmission to us by propagation, yet, at the same time, also asserts it properly to belong to every individual. And the Apostle himself expressly declares, that "death has therefore passed upon all men, for that all have sinned," that is, have been involved in original sin, and defiled with its blemishes."[393]

The Westminster Confession is an exposition of Calvin's theology. In this confession sin is given a full explanation as a tragic separation of man from God, in which state all humanity is spiritually destitute.

"Our first parents being seduced by the subtility
and temptation of Satan, sinned in eating the forbidden
fruit. This their sin God was pleased according to his
wise and holy counsel to permit, having purposed to
order it to his own glory.
. . . .
By this sin they fell from their original righteousness and
communion with God, and so became dead in sin, and wholly
defiled in all the faculties and parts of soul and body.
. . . .
They being the root of all mankind, the guilt of this sin
was imputed, and the same death in sin and corrupted nature
conveyed to all their posterity, descending from them by
ordinary generation.
. . . .
From this original corruption, whereby we are utterly

192

indisposed, disabled and made opposite to all good, and
wholly inclined to all evil, do proceed all actual
transgressions.

. . . .

This corruption of nature, during this life doth remain
in those that are regenerated, and although it be
through Christ pardoned and mortified, yet both itself,
and all motions thereof, are truly and properly sin.

. . . .

Every sin, both original and natural, being a transgression
of the righteous law of God, and contrary there-unto, doth
in its own nature, bring guilt upon the sinner, whereby he
is bound over to the wrath of God, and curse of the law,
and so made subject to death, with all miseries spiritual,
temporal, and eternal."[394]

This Wesminster Confession was adopted by the English Parliament in 1648.

There is in Milton a rational alleviation of the doctrine of
sin, so important in the orthodox view. He presents no thorough-
going separation of Adam and Eve from God as they leave
Paradise. In this respect there is no final tragedy to sin. There
is no Fall, and therefore no real redemption. Paradise is not
actually lost, and the title of the epic is a misnomer. In what
sense has there been a real "loss" of paradise when Milton can
end the epic with such an optimistic note as

Epic,
". . . then wilt thou not be loath
To leave this Paradise, but shalt possess
A paradise within thee, happier farr."[395]

There is no room left for the orthodox degradation because of
the separation sin imposes. Instead Milton presents Adam and

193

Eve departing from Paradise conscious of their partnership with Providence in the Seed that shall bruise the Serpent.

Epic,

". . . Then let us seek
Some safer resolution, which methinks
I have in view, calling to minde, with heed
Part of our Sentence, that thy Seed shall bruise
The Serpents head; piteous amends, unless
He meant, whom I conjecture, our grand Foe
Satan, who in the Serpent hath contriv'd
Against us this deceit: to crush his head
Would be revenge indeed."[396]

This partnership with Providence is organic to their penitence. Milton presents it that way; hence the full value of the atonement is utterly lacking. What place has the fact of grace in a view that presents Adam and Eve as having a basic partnership in the retaliation against Satan? Instead of dwelling upon their lost estate occasioned by sin, Milton has them exult in their partnership with God. It is no wonder that Milton makes this view basic to *Paradise Regain'd*. What Christ has done in his victory over Satan, men are to follow as an example, and this is their redemption! The view of Christ, of our relation to him, and of the Father, which Milton presents near the close of *Paradise Regain'd*, is but the logic of the view of the Fall.

"Heard thee pronounc'd the Son of God belov'd,
Thenceforth I thought thee worth my nearer view
And narrower Scrutiny, that I might learn
In what degree or meaning thou are call'd
The Son of God, which bears no single sence;
The Son of God I also am, or was,
And if I was, I am; relation stands;

194

All men are Sons of God; yet thee I thought
In some respect far higher so declar'd."[397]

The Socratic principle of virtue residing in knowledge constitutes the philosophical basis of *Paradise Regain'd*. In each temptation Christ surveyed all the implications, and brought to light the fallacy. In that was his virtue and victory. Milton says in essence that this is the example to follow. In *Paradise Lost* Milton conceded the Socratic principle that "Knowledge is virtue." It was virtuous for Adam and Eve to have become enlightened with the "Paradise within, happier farr." There is no proper appreciation of the ultimate and tragic consequences of sin. We see Milton here in the clutches of the self-sufficient individualism of the Renaissance. He moves to his conclusion by way of Greek intellectualism. This is Milton living in the seventeenth century, but exercising principles of the eighteenth century Enlightenment. It is Milton, acclaimed the voice of English Protestantism.

Soul and Body

Scripture teaches that the body and the soul have distinct entities. At the creation God made the body out of the dust of the earth, and then infused into it the breath of life, so that man became a living soul.[398] Christ treated the body and the soul as two distinct attributes.

"Fear not them which kill the body, but are not able to kill the soul."[399]

Saint Paul deals separately with the body and the soul. He speaks of being absent from the body and present with the Lord. He affirms that when this earthly tabernacle is dissolved there is a home of the soul, eternal in the heavens.[400] Augustine deals separately with body and soul. In fact the principle of

195

discernment itself is attributed by him to the faculty of the soul.

"For examining when it was that I admired the beauty
of bodies celestial or terrestrial; and what aided me in
judging soundly on things mutable, and pronouncing,
'This ought to be thus, this not'; examining, I say,
when it was that I so judged, seeing I did so judge,
I had found the unchangeable and true Eternity of
Truth, above my changeable mind. And thus by degrees,
I passed from bodies to the soul, which through the
bodily senses perceives."[401]

Calvin asserts the essential distinction between soul and body.

"Now unless the soul were something essentially distinct
from the body, the Scripture would not inform us that
we dwell in houses of clay, and at death quit the
tabernacle of the flesh; that we put off the corruptible,
to receive a reward at the last day, according to the
respective conduct of each individual in the body.
. . . .
For when the whole man is called mortal, the soul is
therefore made subject to death, nor, on the other
hand, when man is called a rational animal, does reason
or intelligence therefore belong to the body."[402]

The essential distinction between soul and body was incorporated into the Westminster Confession.

"The bodies of men after death return to dust, and see
corruption, but their souls (which neither die nor sleep),
having an immortal subsistence, immediately return to God
who gave them."[403]

In the following statement Milton's materialistic position is made evident by his insistence that the spirit of man is "purely human" and "subject to death." This is the focal point of his heresy regarding matter, and is not found in his handling of creation.[404]

Treatise,
"First, then as to the body, no one doubts that it suffers
privation of life. Nor will the same be less evident
as regards the spirit, if it be allowed that the spirit,
according to the doctrine laid down in the seventh
chapter, has no participation in the divine nature, but
is purely human; and that no reason can be assigned, why,
if God has sentenced to death the whole of man that
sinned, the spirit, which is the part principally
offending, should be alone exempt from the appointed
punishment; especially since, previous to the entrance
of sin into the world, all parts of man were alike
immortal; and that since that time, in pursuance of
God's denunciation, all have become equally subject to
death."[405]

This same heresy is carried over into the epic, where Milton likewise declares that all parts of man are subject to death.

Epic,
". . . it was but breath
Of Life that sinn'd; what dies but what had life
And sin? the Bodie properly hath neither.
All of me then shall die."[406]

For Milton then death is not only final but inclusive of the spirit, the soul, and the body. This leaves no room for personal immortality.

Throughout the theological treatise of Milton, we have been conscious of a brilliant mind at work upon Scripture. There has subsumed this large task a conscious adherence to reason as the criterion for evaluating Christian truth. Calvin holds that the Scriptures are the basis of faith. He disparages any procedure in which the speculative faculties of man regulate the extent or the nature of God's message in Scripture. Likewise the essential nature of God's character is not made known to man by way of man's rational faculties.

> "What is taught in the Scriptures concerning the immensity and spirituality of the essence of God, should serve not only to overthrow the foolish notions of the vulgar, but also to refute the subtleties of profane philosophy.
>
> . . . .
>
> Although God, to keep us within the bounds of sobriety, speaks but rarely of his essence, yet, by those two attributes, which I have mentioned, he supersedes all gross imaginations, and represses the presumption of the human mind. For, surely his immensity ought to inspire us with awe, that we may not attempt to measure him with our senses; and the spirituality of his nature prohibits us from entertaining any earthly or carnal speculations concerning him."[407]

The Westminster Confession asserts the knowledge of God to be separate from man's ability to discern or find out by speculation.

> "In his sight all things are open and manifest; his knowledge is infinite, infallible and independent upon the creature, so as nothing is to him contingent or uncertain."[408]

198

In this affirmation the Westminster Confession refers to the declaration of Paul.

"O the depth of the riches both of the wisdom and knowledge of God! How unsearchable are his judgments, and his ways past finding out."[409]

Both in the treatise and in the epic Milton declares that in Scripture God accommodates himself to the comprehension of man, and is not exhibited as he really is.

Treatise,
"For granting that both in the literal and figurative descriptions of God, he is exhibited not as he really is, but in such a manner as may be within the scope of our comprehensions, yet we ought to entertain such a conception of him, as he, in condescending to accommodate himself to our capacities, has shown that he desires we should conceive."[410]

It is a serious matter to say that in Scripture God is exhibited "not as he really is, but in such a manner as may be within the scope of our comprehensions." In essence that is saying that God does not give to man the truth of himself. This places within the heart of the Eternal a conflict and a limitation: a conflict, because God cannot deal with the comprehension of man without being false to His true nature. It is a limitation because God cannot represent Himself to the intellectual level of man's comprehension without taking on some of the abnormalities of that level. The worst of all abnormalities He takes upon himself is falsity itself. In a brilliant work, Henry Mansel deals with this problem.

"The purpose of the foregoing Lectures will have been answered, if they can only succeed in clearing the way for a candid and impartial inquiry; by showing what are the limits within which it must be confined, and what kind of reasoning is inadmissible, as transgressing those limits. The conclusion which an examination of the conditions of human thought unavoidably forces upon us is this: There can be no such thing as a positive science of Speculative Theology; for such a science must necessarily be based on an apprehension of the Infinite; and the Infinite, though we are compelled to believe in its existence, cannot be positively apprehended in any mode of the human Consciousness."[411]

No matter how benevolent the purpose of God is for man, if He denies His essential nature of perfect truth to perform even that benevolent act, He defeats His immediate as well as his ultimate purpose. If man ever came to the beneficent state where he could discern the true nature of God, along with that power of discernment would go the insight that God at first gave a false view of Himself. That false view was not due, he would also discern, to his intellectual limitations, but to the fact that God *chose* an imperfect method of representing Himself. It hardly needs to be mentioned, that this false view of God would evoke in man nothing but distrust, once he was aware of it. Further, If God has by His own initiative given this false view of Himself in Scripture, that but serves as a wedge for other false presentations within the compass of Scripture. This undermines the fidelity with which Milton deals with Scripture. The amazing thing is that this came from the pen of him was acclaimed the voice of English Protestantism.

Orthodox Protestantism staunchly maintains both the omnipotence of God and the immortality of the soul. This orthodoxy bases its contention not upon a rational venture, but upon an affirmation of faith.

"Christianity as a religion with supernatural reference is not a logical demand but a great moral appeal. It is a faith to be accepted, not a philosophy to be constructed."[412]

200

H. R. Mackintosh declares,

"God is omnipotent in the sense that he is able to realize
perfectly whatever he wills. . . . All things are possible with
God; that is the strongest affirmation of the divine omnipotence even in the Bible. It takes the almightiness of
God to save a man, now or at the End."[413]

Paul Tillich affirms,

"God is 'beyond' the split between essence and existence,
as well as being (in a static sense) and becoming."[414]

As Milton joined a disbelief in the omnipotence of God with
a disbelief in the immortality of the soul, so Mackintosh likewise joins the omnipotence of God with salvation, in a great
orthodox affirmation. What makes the latter arthodox is not
just the radical difference in conviction, but the experiential
nature of salvation itself, wrought in the believer's soul.

In Paul Tillich's affirmation, God is ontologically before any
possible distinction between the contemporary dissension over
which is prior: essence or existence. In the same significant and
sound manner, with Tillich, God is also ontologically before the
distinction between being and becoming. Let us put it concisely.
God is, before any apprehension of God by any other than God,
is possible.

The Divinity of Christ

In his treatment of the divinity of Christ, Calvin maintained
that the Son, before time began, remained with God. He found
the scriptural basis for this assertion from both John and Paul.

John,
"In the beginning was the Word, and the Word was with
God, and the Word was God. The same was in the begin-
ning with God."[415]

201

Paul,

". . . Christ Jesus, who being in the form of God, thought it not robbery to be equal with God. . . ."[416]

Calvin declares that this "proves his eternity, his true essence, and his divinity."[417]

This view was set forth in the Westminster Confession, and the orthodox statement of faith for English Protestantism of Milton's day.

"In the unity of the Godhead there be three persons, of one substance, power and eternity; God the Father, God the Son, and God the Holy Ghost. . . ."[418]

The relation of the Son to the Father, for Milton, does not have about it the organic relation of one common substance.[419] There is a dependence of the Son upon the Father. This dependence is denoted in the fact that the Father imparts to the Son any substance they share. That which we see of the divine nature of the Son is then not the intrinsic nature of the Son but the reflection of the Father's nature.

Epic,

"So spake the Father, and unfoulding bright
Toward the right hand his Glorie, on the Son
Blaz'd forth unclouded Deitie; he full
Resplendent all his Father manifest
Express'd and thus divinely answer'd milde."[420]

It was the result of the decree of God, and therefore in point of time successive to the Father, that the Son was created. Coming as the result of God's decrees, the Son does not share an eternal relationship with the Father. His relationship with the Father is serial rather than organic. The highest view of Christ one can grant to Milton, then, is that Christ, Son of God as all men are Sons of God, provided for sinners the perfect pattern and hence the way of life. This is not the true

Christian position. Rather this is a Pelagian and Socinian humanism![421]

Epic,

"Hear my Decree, which unrevok'd shall stand
This day I have begot whom I declare
My onely Son, and on this holy Hill
Him have anointed, whom ye now behold
At my right hand."[422]

The Son becomes created as the Son by the decree and will of the Father. In the same fashion Christ is constituted divine by the will and decree of the Father. Christ is not divine in and of himself. Under this view there was a time when Christ was not the Son of God. In his ministry he demonstrated his merit, and thus came into the Sonship by the beneficence of the Father.

Epic,

". . . and hast been found
By Merit more then Birthright Son of God,
Found worthiest to be so by being Good,
Farr more then Great or High."[423]

The divinity Christ attained as a human achievement merited for him Sonship with the Father. This makes the divinity rest lightly upon him. What has been found by God to be worthy of merit may just as readily be denied the Son.

The Trinity

When we take seriously the divinity of Christ, we open the way for the orthodox view of the Trinity. Calvin held this historic view, and found the basis for it in Scripture.

"When the Scripture speaks of one God, it should be understood of a unity of substance; and that when it speaks of three in one essence, it denotes the Persons in this trinity."[424]

203

This view was the orthodox statement of faith for English Protestantism of Milton's day.[425] The Trinity was comprised of one substance with three distinct Persons, The Father, The Son, and the Holy Spirit. In the substance They share one common essence. In their Persons they have a characteristic individuality, peculiar to each one and incommunicable; yet each has all the attributes of the divine essence. In this position Calvin was true to the historic statement of the Church, in the Athanasian Creed.

". . . we worship one God in Trinity, and Trinity in Unity; neither confounding the Persons: nor dividing the Substance. For there is one Person of the Father: another of the Son: and another of the Holy Ghost. But the Godhead of the Father, of the Son, and of the Holy Ghost, is all one: the Glory equal, the Majesty coeternal. Such the Father is: such is the Son: and such is the Holy Ghost. . . ."[426]

Milton recognizes the three aspects of The Trinity, and states their degrees of importance. Both power and deity are integral to the Father. The Son has a power and deity delegated to him by the Father. The Holy Spirit is subject to both Father and Son. In this way the serial relationship of the Son to the Father is continued in reference to the Holy Spirit. Like the Son, the Holy Spirit was created by no necessity, but by the free will of the Father. This took place before the foundations of the world, and after the creation of the Son.

"Lest however we should be altogether ignorant who or what the Holy Spirit, is, although Scripture nowhere teaches us in express terms, it may be collected from passages quoted above, that the Holy Spirit, inasmuch as he is a minister of God, and therefore a creature, was created or produced of the substance of God, not by a natural necessity, but by the free will of the agent, probably before the foundations of the world were laid, but later than the Son and far inferior to him."[427]

There was then full authority invested in the Father, with a power and a spirit delegated to the Son; and finally, a relationship of both Father and Son to the Holy Spirit. In the serial relationship the Holy Spirit held the inferior position. The Holy Spirit had no filial relationship to the Father. The Holy Spirit labored under no mediatorial functions. In function and service the Holy Spirit performs acts of obedience, and is represented in Scripture as an agency of both Father and Son.

"The nature of these particulars is such, that although the Holy Spirit be nowhere said to have taken upon himself any mediatorial functions, as is said of Christ, not to be engaged by the obligations of a filial relation to pay obedience to the Father, yet he must evidently be considered as inferior to both Father and Son, inasmuch as he is represented and declared to be subservient and obedient in all things; to have been promised, and sent, and given; to speak nothing of himself; and even to have been given as an earnest."[428]

There is therefore clearly manifest a tri-theistic view of the Godhead. Milton endorses the three Persons, but only the Father is absolute. The Son and the Holy Spirit proceed from the Father, but are dependent upon his will both as to their origin and nature. In short, the heresy of Milton is at the point that the Son and the Holy Spirit proceed from the Father's will, and not from the Father's nature. The heresy continues in the fact that there is no bond between the Son and the Holy Spirit, other than the fact that both proceed from the will of the Father. For their divinity they are dependent upon the Father's will. Just as it was the will of the Father to make them divine, it may equally be his will to revoke that divinity.

205

The epic declares the absolute unity of God. It likewise declares in the same passage that God is under no necessity to become Father.

Epic,

"Thou in thy self are perfect, and in thee
Is no deficience found; not so is Man,
But in degree, the cause of his desire
By conversation with his like to help,
Or solace his defects. No need that thou
Shouldst propagat, already infinite;
And through all numbers absolute, though One."[429]

The tri-theism of Milton is subtly woven into the texture of the epic. The Almighty addresses Adam, and declares that in his nature he has been alone and absolute from all eternity.

Epic,

"What thinkest thou then of mee, and this my State,
Seem I to thee sufficiently possest
Of happiness, or not? who am alone
From all Eternitie, for none I know
Second to mee or like equal much less."[430]

Milton is a heretic in his tri-theism. This assertion is not dogmatic. Milton is a heretic not by an assertion, but by the very fact he challenges the Christian Faith at the very point where that challenge is fatal.[431]

The new emphasis in theology affirms that the Revealer and the Word revealed are one. This oneness has a definite relation to the doctrine of the Trinity. It has a focal significance in the fact that the Word is a Person. We therefore are not dealing with an idea whose time has come. We are dealing with a Person who is eternal, as well as divine.[432]

We are dealing with Christ, as himself Revelation in the Word. He is both the Word, and he came to reveal the Word.

There is   time-eternity relationship here. The God who is in Christ still remains the Other, the One who wills to manifest himself, of transcendental majesty, clouded in the sheerest mystery.[433] Thus there is a singularity of Being in eternity which therefore does not become exhausted in Christ the Word.

Orthodox Protestantism, either in its historical or modern form, affirms the divinity of Christ to be a divine disclosure. It is not the climax of a human achievement. It is a revelation. More than that, it is the Revelation. It is an eternal fact, with its basis in the organic nature of the Godhead.

"God Himself reveals himself personally in Jesus Christ.
This is revelation in the complete sense of the word:
the identity of the One who reveals and of that which
is revealed. Here God Himself speaks, but not in a mere
message — for there is more than a prophet, but in the
existence of this Person. It is this which constitutes
the mystery of revelation, and also its authority, the
absolutely new element, in its very essence absolutely
unique. If this were not the meaning of revelation,
then Christ would be a mere symbol, merely the bearer
of an Idea, of a Gospel which could be detached from His
own Person. But this would not then be a revelation;
for he would then be less than a prophet, nor more. It
is only this identity of the divinely authoritative
Word and the Person which constitutes the fact that He
is "more than a prophet." Thus His Person is not the
transparent veil through which gleams the divine, but
He is Himself the Divine; hence He is not that which is
divine, but God."[434]

Revelation does not mean that we know in Christ all there is to be known about God. There is still the worshipper on bended knee with bowed head before the mystery of God's eternal and majestic love. This constitutes the highest devotion to the Trinity. It is not an argument from reason, but a rational defense of faith itself.

CHAPTER TWELVE

THE OFFICE OF MEDIATOR

The office of the Mediator brings us to the theological crux of this work. This is the perplexing matter for anyone dealing with Milton's total theological position. We found that Milton presented the relation of the Son to the Father in terms of an attainment, not as an organic relationship, in terms of substance. Even the glory of the Son was a delegated glory from the Father. It was a Divine Similitude but did not bespeak any essential identity.

Treatise,
"Certain, however, it is whatever some of the moderns may allege to the contrary, that the Son existed in the beginning, under the name of the logos or word, and was the first of the whole creation, by whom afterwards all other things were made both in heaven and earth."[435]

Epic,
"Thee next they sang of all Creation first,
Begotten Son, Divine Similitude,
In whose conspicuous cont'nance, without cloud
Made visible, th' Almighty Father shines."[436]

Treatise,
"The Son likewise teaches that the attributes of divinity belong to the Father alone, to the exclusion even of himself."[437]

Epic,

"Effulgence of my Glorie, Son belov'd,
Son in whose face invisible is beheld
Visibly, what by Deitie I am,
And in whose hand what by Decree I doe. . . ."[438]

Milton recognized the three persons of the Trinity but after the fashion of Socinus (1539-1604).[439] The Father, the Son, and the Holy Spirit held various degrees of importance in a serial relationship. There was a numerical difference in this serial relationship, with the Son inferior to the Father, and the Holy Spirit inferior to the Son. The skepticism of the Renaissance, and the rationalism of the Enlightenment had taken hold upon Milton in this thorough-going interpretation of the Godhead.

A definitive study could be made of the influence of Socinus upon Milton at this point; however, it is sufficient to point out here certain unmistakable parallels. The execution of Servetus turned the attention of Socinus to a study of the Trinity.[440] His speculations on the Trinity were not made public until after his death. In like respect, we find Milton arranged for the posthumous publication of *De Doctrina Christiana*; and therefore of the public avowal of the Trinitarian heresy, so artfully concealed in the epic. Socinus guarded well the freedom of man as essential; and we find with Milton that freedom is both his political and theological position. With Socinus the Fall clouded the rational concourse of man with his Creator; and therefore eternal life was impossible for man as a rational discovery. The result of this rational obliquity was that God in His goodness deposited with man both the Scriptures, and the life of Christ as an example. The merits of Christ in His achievements brought Him a divinity which previously was not His. These merits and this attained divinity enabled Christ to receive the prayers of humanity, and to present them to the Father. It is just this position as to the Office of Mediator that Milton presents. It is clearly stated in the *epic*.

". . . To Heav'n thir prayers
Flew up, nor missd the way, by envious windes
Blown vagabond or frustrate: in they pass'd
Dimentionless through Heav'nly dores; then clad
With incense, where the Golden Altar fum'd,
By thir great Intercessor, came in sight
Before the Fathers Throne: Them the glad Son
Presenting, thus to intercede began.
See Father, what first fruits on Earth are sprung
From thy implanted Grace in Man, these Sighs
And Prayers, which in this Golden Censer, mixt
With Incense, I thy Priest before thee bring,
Fruits of more pleasing savour from thy seed
Sow'n with contrition in his heart, then those
Which his own hand manuring all the Trees
Of Paradise could have produc't, ere fall'n
From innocence. Now therefore bend thine eare
To supplication, heare his sighs though mute;
Unskilful with what words to prayer, let mee
Interpret for him, mee his Advocate
And propitiation, all his works on mee
Good or not good ingraft, my Merit those
Shall perfet, and for these my Death shall pay.
Accept me, and in mee from these receave
The smell of peace toward Mankinde, let him live
Before thee reconcil'd, at least his days
Numberd, though sad, till Death, his doom (which I
To mitigate thus plead, not to reverse)
To better life shall yeeld him, where with mee
All my redeemd may dwell in joy and bliss,
Made one with me as I with thee am one."[441]

There is a deep and wide chasm between divinity approached, as Milton does, from the human to the divine, and the revelation of God upon the human scene, in Christ. Even if we grant to

Milton this achieved divinity of Jesus, there is still a difference. The approach from the human to the divine culminates in a divinity that is conferred. This we found to be Milton's approach. He makes it fundamental to both the treatise and the epic.

What we see of divine substance in the Son is not of the intrinsic nature of the Son, but what the Father has imparted to him. There is a difference in essence between the Father and the Son, and this gives Milton a kinship with the heretic Arius.[442] Milton also affirms on the part of Christ the attainment to merit and thus to a delegated divinity, and this gives him a kinship with the heretic Socinus.[443] We let Milton speak for himself, in both the treatise and the epic, concerning this heresy.

Treatise,

"However this may be, it will be universally acknowledged
that the Son now at least differs numerically from the
Father; but that those who differ numerically must
differ also in their proper essences, as the logicians
express it, is too clear to be denied by any one possessed
of common reason. Hence it follows that the Father and
the Son differ in essence. That this is the true doctrine,
reason shows on every view of the subject."[444]

Epic,

"What thinkst thou then of mee, and this my State,
Seem I to thee sufficiently possest
Of happiness, or not? whom am alone
From all Eternities, for none I know
Second to mee or like, equal much less."[445]

"Thou in thy self art perfet, and in thee
Is no deficience found; not so is Man
But in degree, the cause of his desire
By conversation with his like to help,
Or solace his defects. No need that thou

211

Shouldst propagat, already infinite;
And through all numbers absolute, though One."[446]

A delegated divinity, the result of attainment.

Epic,
> "Because thou hast, though Thron'd to highest bliss
> Equal to God, and equally enjoying
> God-like fruition, quitted all to save
> A World from utter loss, and hast been found
> By Merit more then Birthright Son of God,
> Found worthiest to be so by being Good,
> Farr more then Great or High. . . ."[447]

All of this, when considered in its totality, constitutes the severest kind of limitation upon Christ as Mediator. With Milton's view of Christ, as not being co-substantial with the Father, but by merit holding the relationship of Son to the Father, the Christian Faith loses its unique and distinctive message of salvation. The Christian Faith,

> ". . . is to be construed as itself a datum; a divine gift, not a human instrument; an apocalypse rather than an deduction; a word, an action, a life, and an experience, proceeding directly from that same eternal source whence came creation itself; an Omega which completes the movement beginning in a primal Alpha."[448]

There is no final assurance the delegated divinity will continue endlessly. That divinity, conferred because of merit, bespeaks no necessary metaphysical bond of organic unity. What was conferred so readily, may just as easily be revoked! What was attained so demonstrably as a human achievement, may just as readily be denied as deficient in the eyes of God,

Epic,

". . . who am alone
From all Eternitie, for none I know
Second to mee or like, equal much less."[449]

This cuts into the very character of God as Father. God *becomes* a Father, and is not Father by the constitutive nature of his very Being. This denotes a chosen beneficence on the part of God toward man.

". . . No need that thou
Shouldst propagat, already infinite;
And through all numbers absolute, though One."[450]

Man may be restored by the merited Sonship of Christ. This constitutes the office of Mediator, according to Milton. In contrast to this view of the Mediator as one who has merited Sonship, there is the orthodox view as stated in the Westminster Confession.

"The Son of God, the second person in the Trinity, being very and eternal God, of one substance, and equal with the Father, did, when the fulness of time was come, take upon him man's nature, with all the essential properties and common infirmities thereof, yet without sin; being conceived by the power of the Holy Ghost, in the womb of the Virgin Mary, of her substance. So that two whole, perfect and distinct natures, the Godhead and the manhood, were inseparably joined together in one person, without conversion, composition or confusion. Which person is very God and very man, yet one Christ, the only Mediator between God and man."[451]

Brunner expresses the orthodox view of the office of Mediator.

213

"We do not need to posit Christ as the subject of a transaction in order to speak of His work. If we speak rightly of His Person, in accordance with His Nature, we also bear witness to His work of revelation and atonement. He *is* what He does and He *does* what He is, and both these statements mean that He reunited man, who is separated, indeed practically severed from his divine origin, with God. He does this by the very fact that He is a Person, because in so far as His being a Person is, as such, already God's reconciling act. For He is indeed the Incarnate Word, in Him and in His being God is the One who has come to us. Thus in His very Nature the gulf between God and man has been bridged. He Himself is the bridge which God throws across to us, over which God comes to us."[452]

When the mediation rests upon a merited Sonship, not upon a Sonship integral to the nature of God himself, salvation arises not from the organic oneness of the Triune God, but from a humanly demonstrated achievement.

Epic,
". . . let me
Interpret for him, mee his Advocate
And propitiation, all his works on mee
Good or not good ingraft, my Merit those
Shall perfet."[453]

Sin,
This view of the office of Mediator corresponds with Milton's concept of sin. Sin for Milton was a moral obliquity, with reason in default to passion and inordinate desire. This is plainly stated.

Epic,
". . . yet know withall,
Since thy original lapse, true Libertie

214

Is lost, which alwayes with right Reason dwells
Twinn'd, and from here hath no dividual being:
Reason in man obscur'd, or not obeyed,
Immediately inordinate desires
And upstart Passions catch the Government
From Reason, and to servitude reduce
Man till then free."[454]

Sin, therefore, is a deficiency at the point of reason,[455] and
this is a Greek, not a Biblical conception. What Eve did in
her rational inferiority to Adam, implicated Adam because of
his devotion toward Eve. Milton maintains his conviction of
the supremacy of man to woman in his understanding of the
Fall. He presents Eve falling under temptation, due to her be-
guilement, at the point of her reason. Adam joined in the rational participation of the forbidden fruit, in order to dwell
unfettered with Eve, in her lot.

Epic,
". . . from the bough
She gave him of that fair enticing Fruit
With liberal hand: he scrupl'd not to eat
Against his better knowledge, not deceav'd,
But fondly overcome with Femal charm."[456]

Epic,
"Rather how hast thou yeelded to transgress
The strict forbiddance, how to violate
The sacred Fruit forbidd'n! some cursed fraud
Of Enemie hath beguil'd thee yet unknown,
And mee with thee hath ruind, for with thee
Certain my resolution is to Die. . . ."[457]

So Milton liquidates the Orthodox conception of sin in his
emphasis upon sin as a rational tangent away from truth, rather

than as a moral and spiritual chasm into which man has fallen in his chosen separation from God.

"For the God of the Christian religion is a God who cares so much about *moral reality* that the only way open to him if he would at one and the same time preserve that reality and save the human race from the inevitable issue of both its sinful status and its more specific sinful deeds was by — *atonement*. Made by whom? Made by himself. Creation and atonement must have the same source."[458]

One is simply repelled by Milton's exaltation over sin, as he presents Adam in pleased contemplation of the goodness that will follow the expulsion from the Garden.

Epic,
"So spake th' Archangel Michael, then paus'd,
As at the Worlds great period; and our Sire
Replete with joy and wonder thus repli'd.
    O goodness infinite, goodness immense!
That all this good of evil shall produce,
And evil turn to good; more wonderful
Then that which by creation first brought forth
Light out of darkness! full of doubt I stand,
Whether I should repent me now of sin
By mee done and occasioned, or rejoyce
Much more, that much more good thereof shall spring. . . ."[459]

In what sharp contrast this concept of sin, with its attendant effect upon man, stands to orthodoxy. A contemporary theologian expressed the orthodox view of sin, with the emphasis rightfully placed upon the infinite self-cost to God to make atonement.

"What, then, is Christianity as belief? It is the belief that God, of whom and through whom are all things, at infinite

216

self-cost did in Jesus Christ manifest and satisfy his holy love for the purpose of making an atonement for the sins of the world and opening a way for men from death unto life.

What is Christianity as experience? It is the realization of sin forgiven; the knowledge of God reconciled; the sense of peace within; a sure confidence in the face of the ills of life; an inner glow which to the believer himself is the indubitable evidence to the presence and the favor of his Lord; a satisfaction and an inspiration in the fellowship of those who are of like mind; and the possession of an expansive love which takes the form of an increasing "passion for souls." What is Christianity as a way of life? It is such forms of behavior as are everyway compatible with the purpose to glorify Christ and exhibit him before the world. It is Christlikeness, when that is properly understood. It is love triumphant; it is selfless living; it is sacrificial but joyous endeavor to make every individual life, every human relationship, ever social institution, so expressive of the will of God, "that in all things Jesus Christ, who is the image of the invisible God, might have the preeminence."[460]

Milton never came to the place where he would admit that while he was intellectually examining Christ, he found Christ spiritually examining him. Had this occurred, had Milton allowed the Christ entrance into his life as love and forgiveness and redemption — there would have been a different Milton. This is as much as to say that for all his splendid writings, Milton lacked a deep and abiding awareness of the Master. No wonder Keats brought judgment on Milton in the words, "Life to him would be death to me."[461]

CHAPTER THIRTEEN

THE DENOUEMENT OF MILTON

Milton declares the freedom of the human will, but maintains at the same time that nothing with which the free will of man works is absolute. Is that not what he means in the statement:

Treatise,
"We must conclude, therefore, that God decreed nothing absolutely, which he left in the power of free agents."[462]

Milton proves that statement to his own satisfaction by Scriptural reference. The astounding fact is that God left to man's freedom the choice of the divine plan and purpose, and more important than all, the choice of God Himself. Yet Milton declares, "that God decreed nothing absolutely, which he left in the power of free agents."[463] In *Paradise Lost* there is the parallel reference of this thought.

Epic,
". . . such discourse bring on,
As may advise him of his happie state,
Happiness in his power left free to will,
Left to his own free Will, his Will though free,
Yet mutable; whence warne him to beware
He swerve not too secure."[464]

The freedom of the human will which Milton declares has a definite relation to the spirit characteristic of the Renaissance,

218

and in advance of his time, of the Enlightenment, in its emancipation of the individual. It speaks more of the humanism of Erasmus than of the evangelical fervor of Luther. Milton, as we have already seen, defines Predestination as that decree,

Treatise,
"Whereby God in pity to mankind, though foreseeing that they would fall of their own accord, predestinated to eternal salvation before the foundation of the world those who should believe and continue in the faith; for a manifestation of the glory of his mercy, grace, and wisdom, according to his purpose in Christ."[465]

He therefore maintains the doctrine of predestination, but in a somewhat superficial sense. He does not renounce the traditional aspects of grace, of election, or of predestination, but he certainly depletes them of their vitality. This he does by maintaining always unimpaired the principle of the freedom of the human will. This freedom of the human will remains unimpaired even when both Adam and Eve are ushered by the Archangel Michael from the Garden. In the familiar lines which follow we find not only the key to the understanding of the entire epic of *Paradise Lost,* but also the ever dominant emphasis which human freedom and liberty receive at the hands of Milton. This is the denouement of Milton.

Epic,
". . . onely add
Deeds to thy knowledge answerable, add Faith,
Add Vertue, Patience, Temperance, add Love,
By name to come call'd Charitie, the soul
Of all the rest; then wilt thou not be loath
To leave this Paradise, but shalt possess
A paradise within thee, happier farr."[466]

Adam and Eve pay the forfeit of Paradise, but in exchange they have a paradise within them, "happier farr." Is that paradise within them not the unconquerable freedom of the human will! On the contrary, the orthodox Protestant position would declare with emphasis:

"Christianity is based on the fact of this freedom
This is why Christianity can have a doctrine of sin."[467]

Even the judgment of God against them, and the loss of Paradise, had no profound effect upon the freedom of the exiles' wills. Rather did they find the full and more complete exercise of their freedom after the Fall; for there followed the Fall and the departure from Paradise, the "paradise within them, happier farr," and a paradise achieved of the will.

At this point where we have given such emphasis to the unconquerable freedom of the human will which Milton maintains, we remember the passage in *Samson Agonistes,* of which we said: Unlike Samson, Milton had no fault which he was ready to confess.[468] Samson confesses his fault in the lines,

"Nothing of all these evils hath befall'n me
But justly; I my self have brought them on,
Sole Author I, sole cause."[469]

The pride of Milton has a definite relation to the indomitable freedom of the will which he always maintained, even at such great cost. The cost becomes of infinite significance personally for Milton when we follow the natural course of this position. We therefore lift this question, with its important relation to this whole procedure: What importance has the sacrifice of Christ to a person (in this case, Milton) who makes no room for confession? What importance has the Atonement for a person who leaves no sense of guilt upon Adam and Eve when they leave the Garden, but rather ascribes to them a new-found exaltation in the now complete exercise of their wills? Perhaps we discern here the reason why in *Paradise Regain'd* Milton centers the victory of Christ over Satan, rather in the temptation experiences in the wilderness, than in the struggle upon the Cross! A victory thus centered gives Christ an exemplary function, and not, as would be the case had Milton centered the victory of Christ in the Cross, an atoning function.

We have evidence to justify the assertion: that he who was the voice of English Protestantism did not believe in the traditional doctrine of Predestination which was fundamental in the recognized theology of the Reformation, whether in the form given it by Luther or in the form given it by Calvin. And we have evidence to justify the assertion that he who was the voice of English Protestantism, by reason of his emphasis upon the complete supremacy of the free human will, found small place personally for the Atonement and for the Saviourhood of Christ. The First Pair were authors of their own revolt. Any accusation under which they reside is of their own making.[470]

Epic,
". . . They therefore as to right belonged,
So were created, nor can justly accuse
Thir maker, or thir making, or thir Fate,
As if predestination over-rul'd
Thir will, dispos'd by absolute Decree
Or high foreknowledge; they themselves decreed
Thir own revolt, not I."[471]

This, we must discern, is the subtle message of Milton in the great epic of the English language. It is proper to dwell upon it, especially as one witnesses Milton first a Puritan in his own right, then a Presbyterian, and finally a defender of the cause of liberty. This witness of Milton is progressive in the fact that his own pride and will were of such proportions that the restrictions of the Puritans, and, by contrast, the more generous bounds of Presbyterianism, were alike too inhibitive for so liberal a

221

mind. We therefore see Milton involved in the progressive movement toward liberalism. In this sense, he was both a man of the Renaissance and of the Enlightenment, in literature and theology. He helped to open the way for the liberalism in the century following him, of the eighteenth century Enlightenment.[472]

PART IV

THE LURE OF THE IDYLLIC

CHAPTER FOURTEEN

THE LURE OF THE IDYLLIC

In the mind of Milton we found poetic genius early declared and constantly maintained. We found an increasing passion for freedom, as declared in the poetic, the polemic, and now expressly the religious developments of his day.

We saw Milton, when academically ready to enter the church, remove himself to Horton, his father's estate in Buckinghamshire. There we saw him in concentration upon the Greek classics.[473]

Milton found growing upon him the ambition to write in such a way that what he wrote would have the quality of endurance. This ambition never forsook him. It did not forsake him, when he took Mary Powell for his wife. The tumult and storm that entered his domestic life, when Mary departed him, for the Cavalier home of her parents did turn Milton's literary powers away from their true course, for a time. We would like, if possible, to remove from the literary account of John Milton, his writings on divorce. At the same time, these writings revealed something more than compensation for the lost companionship of a wife. These writings, in the context of domestic tension and tumult, sharpened by stimulation, the developing literary powers of Milton.

This ambition was further developed in the twenty years Milton gave his literary powers to the Commonwealth. From one point of view these powers may have been deferred from their main task. Over these twenty years, however, these same literary powers of John Milton came into a dimension of bravery. There was also developed his powers of expression. All this was in the

225

cause of a Commonwealth whose ideal and structure were worthy of the dedication of his life. In the midst of tortuous events, including Milton's endorsement of regicide, there moved upon Milton the idyllic. Like a Rembrandt portrait whose dark background sharpens and gives light to the foreground, these events did the same for Milton.

The darkness was of a Commonwealth at first beleaguered and then dispelled. What was lost for Milton was one Commonwealth. Within there was a far greater development of the idyllic, in a Paradise to be found and proclaimed. Twenty years of polemical investment brought light out of darkness. This light was literary. This light was idyllic. This light was religious, and even Biblical.

This light was invested not in any loss of Paradise, but in *Paradise Found.* This idyllic would no longer be in submission to any turbulence without. The idyllic would boldly break forth. This dimension of boldness, sharpened by adverse stimulation in the loss of the Commonwealth, made its singular contribution in the idyllic, yet to come into literary expression.

Blindness, bankruptcy, domestic loneliness, national failure in the Commonwealth inverted themselves in a combined contribution. This contribution was to write. This writing would be a motion out of what was lost to what was found.

Eyesight was lost. Milton's money was lost. Real home life was lost. His daughters with sight, at times, would not read to their sightless father. The Commonwealth shattered at his feet prompted Milton to write of a Commonwealth whose cause can never be lost or stayed. This cause was idyllic, in *Paradise Found.*

Civil liberty now destroyed, Milton would write classically of a religious liberty, never to be destroyed. This was the growth of the Biblical theme upon him. This was the growth of a liberty of mind, heart, and soul, larger than any traditional configurement of Eden.

Taken together, all was the *a priori* right of a mind to true freedom. This was the regnancy of Milton's mind. This was the lure of the idyllic that found incomparable largness, liberty, and literary excellence in the Epic. The Epic was not to be an experience of loss, but a *Paradise Found.*

In only one respect did Milton depart from this avowed and growing dedication to the idyllic. That was in the posthumous publication of a prose document, the treatise, by name, *De Doctrina Christiana.* This was the declaration of his faith, systematically, thoughtfully, deliberately, finally. The Epic would contain this faith, but with the artistry of the poetic, the true nature of what Milton thus put into bold lines and straightforward declarations, would be evident, only when treatise and epic came into parallelism.

The lure of the idyllic was for Milton the deep desire to move from incompleteness to completeness. Read the *Sonnet On His Blindness.* Read again, *Samson Agonistes* where Milton expressly desired that eyesight had not, by God in creation, been limited to two small orbs. In his liberalism, here majestically stated, Milton reached for the idyllic, in his desire that sight had been like feeling. Feeling was liberally spread throughout the surface of the body.

Appraise John Milton, as you will, in his lack of orthodoxy, give him the theological severity in judgment he deserves; one yet confronts with empathy his reach for the idyllic. It was the reach to move from incompleteness to completeness. It was the reach for domestic tranquility. It was the reach for what would not be a lost cause, namely: the Commonwealth under Cromwell. With all England against him, at the time the Commonwealth came to its close; Milton reached for a Commonwealth that would have no close.

The idyllic, as we have built up in parallel after parallel of treatise and epic, is finally victorious, not on the side of what is lost but of what is affirmed in, *Paradise Found.*

There is role playing in the closing book of the Epic. It is Eve and Adam, hand in hand, departing the traditional Eden.

More significantly it was Milton who placed Eve and Adam, hand in hand. It was Milton who saw that in their departure from Eden, they were not losing anything. It was Milton who, in the Epic of the English language, affirmed Providence, the Providence of God was on their side, in their departure together from Eden. It was Milton who saw they departed Eden, not with Fate upon them, but with the greatness of faith within them. It was Milton's own faith, and for Milton, the idyllic finally achieved. Under the escort of the Archangel Michael who,

Epic,
". . . . . paus'd
As at the Worlds great period."[474]

The "great period" was the occasion of their departure from Eden. It was then that Milton put in the words

". . . . . and our Sire
Replete with joy and wonder thus repli'd.
O goodness infinite, goodness immense!
That all this good of evil shall produce
And evil turn to good; more wonderful
Then that which by creation first brought forth
Light out of darkness! full of doubt I stand,
Whether I should repent me now of sin
By mee done, and occasioned, or rejoyce
Much more, that much more good thereof shall spring."[475]

When expulsion is expected, as they depart, Milton is certain to move toward the idyllic. Milton is eager for incompleteness to become completeness. Instead of expulsion, Milton puts into Adam and Eve, exaltation. When tragedy is their expected lot, Milton makes sure to affirm the idyllic, in triumph. This triumph is also placed by Milton into the voice of "our Sire."

Epic,

"To God more glory, more good will to Men
From God, and over wrauth grace shall abound."[476]

It was Milton's own faith. It was Milton's own idyllic finally achieved. It was Milton, therefore, who put into this departing episode from Eden, the words spoken by their escort, the Archangel Michael. The words were spoken by Michael to Adam and Eve! — and to all their successors in humanity. These words are idyllic.

Epic,

". . . . then wilt thou not be loath
To leave this Paradise, but shalt possess
A Paradise within thee, happier farr."[477]

This was and is, for John Milton, *Paradise Found.*

CHAPTER FIFTEEN

THE INWARDNESS OF PARADISE FOUND

There is a future and a past in any Paradise, especially in *Paradise Found.*

"The present can be fully alive only in tension between past and future. This is the fruitfulness of utopia — its ability to open up possibilities."[478]

These words of the great theologian, Paul Tillich, stress not only tension of past and future, but the inwardness of possibilities. The past is in the adequate comprehension of the structure of the very beginning. It is inward. Rightly to appraise the posture of circumstances in which one is a participant, is a part of knowing whether Paradise is, or is not.

The condition of obedience, for John Milton, was something less than Paradise. It was more. It was a tension in the center of Paradise. It was a prophetic tension. It was an eschatological tension. Because of the prescience of God, later made known to the nescience of man, it was more than accidental. It was planned that way. This pushed Milton back upon the Godhead, and creation.

If creation by God had the condition of obedience, to save the Godhead there must be in the structure of the Godhead, the desire to start out again. This means, as Milton rightfully places it, the Providence of God must be on both sides of the lapse of man. In fact the Providence of God must be active before the first act of creation, active in creation, and continuously active in the outcome of creation.

In this sense, the Providence of God placed with Adam and Eve as they left traditional Eden, is necessary to save the integrity of God Himself. It is cosmic. It saves man's integrity in *Paradise Found*. In this, it is creative. There is fulfillment in God first, and then fulfillment in man.

"Every utopia is but one manifestation of what man has as inner aim and what he must have for fulfillment as a person. This definition stresses the social as much as the personal, for it is impossible to understand the one apart from the other. A socially defined utopia loses its truth if it does not at the same time fulfill the person, just as the individually defined utopia loses its truth if it does not at the same time bring fulfillment to society."[479]

What Paul Tillich affirms in these words in his writing entitled, *Critique and Justification of Utopia*[480] is concisely expressed. Individual fulfillment and social fulfillment go together. Furthermore, this combined individual and social fulfillment is inward. The inwardness has a truth expressed in both individual and social fulfillment. This is the justification of Utopia.

In a deep sense, man is ever a pilgrim. He is a pilgrim but not a stranger. The Pilgrims with their Puritan background had the nostalgia to start out again. They crossed the Atlantic and came to America. This was the deep desire, not only to preserve what they had, but to recover pure religious origins, and to keep them pristine.

In *The Quest for the Earthly Paradise*, Mircea Eliade draws important implications.

"Christopher Columbus did not doubt that he had come near the Earthly Paradise. He believed that the fresh water currents he encountered in the Gulf of Paria originated in

231

the four rivers of the Garden of Eden. For Columbus, the search for the Earthly Paradise was not a chimera. The great navigator accorded an eschatological significance to this geographic discovery. The New World represented more than a new continent open to the propagation of the Gospel. The very fact of its discovery had an eschatological implication.

"Indeed, Columbus was persuaded that the prophecy concerning the diffusion of the Gospel throughout the whole world had to be realized before the end of the world — which was not far off."[481]

To go to the Pilgrims, as they landed in America, we must recall how little, and yet how very much they brought. They brought seed and not a harvest. The seed was more than what they planted in the ground. The seed was an inwardness which bore fruit, "thirty, sixty, and a hundred-fold."[482]

"More than any other modern nation the United States was the product of the Protestant Reformation seeking an Earthly Paradise in which the reform of the Church was to be perfected."[483]

Salvation is more than a concept within creation. Salvation is a part of the cosmic reality that pushes man beyond any island or garden Paradise. Salvation, for Milton, pushes man beyond any Eden and makes Paradise to be found within. The inwardness is first of God Himself, then of man.

The within is wherever man is, and God is with and for man. This means everywhere. Just as Utopia literally means "no where" — *Paradise Found* means everywhere. So there is not only an expansiveness about the inwardness of *Paradise Found;* there is also the reality.

The future begins for Milton when Adam and Eve left traditional Eden. Up to then Providence was under the condition of obedience or disobedience, with disobedience known by God.

232

With disobedience in the background and the grace of God in the present and in the foreground, there is *Paradise Found.* Paradise is Found because in Christ Jesus God's mercy, grace, and wisdom unfold. They unfold for Adam and Eve, in keeping with God's Providence.

There is the might of the Son, in keeping with the eternal purpose, expressed in the

Epic,

"O Son, in whom my Soul hath delight,
Son of my bosom, Son who art alone
My word, my wisdom, and effectual might,
All hast thou spok'n as my thoughts are, all
As my Eternal purpose hath decreed:
Men shall not quite be lost, but sav'd who will,
Yet not of will in him, but grace in me
Freely voutsaft; once more I will renew
His lapsed powers, though forfeit and enthrall'd
By sin to foul exorbitant desires;
Upheld by me, yet once more he shall stand
On even ground against his mortal foe.
By me upheld, that he may know how frail
His fall'n condition is, and to me ow
All his deliv'rence, and to none but me."[484]

The horizontal experiences of Adam and Eve, when they were only horizontal ended correctly in the loss for them. The vertical experience that came into their experience as they departed Eden was the redemptive. Milton makes the redemptive rational, involving communication and participation. The rational becomes real in the Son of God, so that "God with man unites."

The vertical refers to the Kingdom of God, the Kingdom of Heaven, the Kingdom of Justice, the consummation of God with man in rational love. The horizontal refers to what becomes constituted as history. Paul Tillich affirms

"The vertical order participates in the horizontal order that is, the Kingdom of God actualizes itself in historical events. It both actualizes itself and at the same time is resisted, suppressed, vanquished. Yet it is this fighting Kingdom of God in history that cannot disillusion because it does not confer utopian finality to any place or time in history. Rather it always makes itself known again and again in ever new actualizations, so that the truth of utopia is always borne out. This reciprocal participation of the two orders is the solution to the problem of utopia."[485]

The horizontal cannot survive without the vertical. In an equally deep sense the vertical cannot continue as real unless it participates in the actualization of what in the horizontal is *Paradise Found.*

BIBLIOGRAPHY

This is a complete, rather than a selected bibliography. It includes not only the books incorporated in the body of the work, but all the important volumes consulted.

I. PRIMARY SOURCES

The Holy Bible, authorized or King James Version, Philadelphia: John C. Winston Company, 1933.

Milton, John, *An Index to the Columbia Edition of the Works of John Milton.* Two Volumes. New York: Columbia University Press, 1940.
Volume I. A-K, 1073 pp.
Volume II. L-Z, 2141 pp.
Prepared by Frank Allen Patterson assisted by French Rowe Fogle. A two-volume concordance of marked value, serving as a key to the prolific writings of Milton. The work has been compiled with meticulous care, with references and cross-references thoroughly listed.

————, *The Works of John Milton.* 18 Volumes. New York: Columbia University Press, 1931-38.
This is the only complete edition of the works of John Milton, being both exhaustive as well as definitive. The translation of *De Doctrina Christiana* is based upon the original work of Bishop Charles R. Sumner.
Volume One, Part One contains the shorter English poems edited by Frank Allen Patterson; the Italian poems edited, with a translation, by Arthur Livingston; the Latin and Greek poems edited by W. P. Trent in collaboration with Thomas Ollive Mabbott, with a translation by Charles Knapp.
Volume One, Part Two contains *Samson Agonistes* edited by Frank Allen Patterson; notes to the shorter English poems, to the Italian poems, to the Latin and Greek poems, to *Samson Agonistes.*

Volume Two, Part One contains *Paradise Lost* edited by Frank Allen Patterson, Book I to the end of Book VIII.

Volume Two, Part Two contains *Paradise Lost* edited by Frank Allen Patterson, Book IX to the end of Book XII; *Paradise Regain'd* edited by Frank Allen Patterson; notes to *Paradise Lost* and *Paradise Regain'd*.

Volume Three, Part One contains *Of Reformation Touching Church-Discipline in England*, edited by Harry Morgan Ayres; *Animadversions upon the Remonstrants Defence, against Smectymnuus* edited by Harry Morgan Ayres; *The Reason of Church-government urg'd against Prelaty*, edited by Harry Morgan Ayres; *An Apology against a Pamphlet call'd a Modest Confutation* of the *Animadversions of the Remonstrant against Smectymnuus,* edited by Harry Morgan Ayres.

Volume Three, Part Two contains *The Doctrine and Discipline of Divorce* edited by Frank Allen Patterson and the late Chilton Latham Powell; and notes of the *Anti Prelatical Tracts* contained in Volume Three Parts One and Two.

Volume Four contains *The Judgement of Martin Bucer concerning Divorce* edited by Chilton Latham Powell; *Tetrachordon* edited by Chilton Latham Powell; *Colasterion* edited by Chilton Latham Powell; *Of Education* edited by Allan Abbott; *Areopagitica: for the Liberty of Unlicenc'd Printing* edited by William Haller; Notes.

Volume Five contains *The Tenure of Kings and Magistrates* edited by William Haller; *Eikonklastes* edited by William Haller; Notes.

Volume Six contains *A Treatise of Civil power in Ecclesiastical causes* edited by William Haller; *Considerations touching the likeliest means to remove Hirelings out of the church* edited by William Haller; *A Letter to a Friend, Concerning the Rupture of the Commonwealth* edited by William Haller; *The Present Means, a brief Delineation of a Free Commonwealth. . . . In a Letter to General Monk* edited by William Haller; *The Readie & Easie Way to Establish a Free Commonwealth* edited by William Haller; *Brief Notes upon a late Sermon, Tit'd, the Fear of God and the King &c,* edited by William Haller; *Of True Religion, Heresie, Schism, Toleration* edited by William Haller; *Articles of Peace. . . . Observations* edited by Frank Allen Patterson; *A Declaration or Letters Patents of the Election of this Present King of Poland* edited by Frank Allen Patterson; *Accedence Commenc't Grammar* edited by George Philip Krapp.

236

Volume Seven contains *John Milton, an Englishman his Defence of the People of England against Claudius anonymous, alias Salmasius his Defence of the King* edited by Clinton W. Keyes, with a translation by Samuel Lee Wolff; Notes.

Volume Eight contains *John Milton an Englishman his Second Defence of the People of England against the infamous libel, entitled, the Cry of the Royal Blood to Heaven, against the Engligh Parricides* edited by Eugene J. Strittmatter with the translation of George Burnett, London, 1809, revised by Moses Hadas; Notes.

Volume Nine contains *John Milton an Englishman his Defence of Himself in answer to Alexander More, & c.* edited by Eugene J. Strittmatter with the translation of George Burnett, London 1809, revised by Moses Hadas; Notes.

Volume Ten contains *The History of Britain* edited by George Philip Krapp; *A Brief History of Moscovia* edited by George Philip Krapp; Notes.

Volume Eleven contains *A Fuller Institution of the Art of Logic* edited and translated by Allan H. Gilbert; Notes.

Volume Twelve contains *The Familiar Letters of John Milton* edited by Donald Lemen Clark with the translation of David Masson; *The Prolusions of John Milton* edited by Donald Lemen Clark with a translation by Bromley Smith; *An Early Prolusion by John Milton and Miscellaneous Correspondence in Foreign Tongues* edited and translated by Thomas Ollive Mabbott and Nelson Glenn McCrea; *English Correspondence by John Milton and Mylius, 1651-1652* collected, edited, and translated by Thomas Ollive Mabbott and Nelson Glenn McCrea.

Volume Thirteen contains *The State Papers of John Milton* collected and edited by Thomas Ollive Mabbott and J. Milton French.

Volume Fourteen contains *De Doctrina Christiana* Book I, Chapters 1-6, edited, with the translation of Charles R. Sumner, D.D., by James Holly Hanford and Waldo Hilary Dunn.

Chapter 1 *Of the Definition of Christian Doctrine, and the Several Parts Thereof.*

Chapter 2 *Of God.*

Chapter 3 *Of the Divine Decrees.*

Chapter 4 *Of Predestination.*

Chapter 5 *Prefatory Remarks.*

Chapter 6 *Of the Holy Spirit.*

Volume Fifteen contains *De Doctrina Christiana* Book I, Chapters 7-20 edited, with the translation of Charles R. Sumner, D.D., by James Holly Hanford and Waldo Hilary Dunn.

Chapter 7 *Of the Creation.*

Chapter 8 *Of the Providence of God, or of His General Government of the Universe.*

Chapter 9 *Of the Special Government of Angels.*

Chapter 10 *Of the Special Government of Man Before the Fall, Including the Institutions of the Sabbath and of Marriage.*

Chapter 11 *Of the Fall of Our First Parents, and of Sin.*

Chapter 12 *Of the Punishment of Sin.*

Chapter 13 *Of the Death of the Body.*

Chapter 14 *Of Man's Restoration and of Christ as Redeemer.*

Chapter 15 *Of the Office of the Mediator . . . and of his Threefold Functions.*

Chapter 16 *Of the Ministry of Redemption.*

Chapter 17 *Of Man's Renovation, including His Calling.*

Chapter 18 *Of Regeneration.*

Chapter 19 *Of Repentance.*

Chapter 20 *Of Saving Faith.*

Volume Sixteen contains *De Doctrina Christiana* Book I, Chapters 21-23 edited with the translation of Charles R. Sumner, D.D., by James Holly Hanford and Waldo Hilary Dunn.

Chapter 21 *Of Being Ingrafted in Christ and its Effects.*

Chapter 22 *Of Justification.*

Chapter 23 *Of Adoption.*

Chapter 24 *Of Union and Fellowship with Christ and His Members, Wherein is Considered the Mystical or Invisible Church.*

Chapter 25 *Of Imperfect Glorification, Wherein are Considered the Doctrine of Assurance and Final Perseverance.*

Chapter 26 *Of the Manifestation of the Covenant of Grace, Including the Law of God.*

Chapter 27 *Of the Gospel and Christian Liberty.*

Chapter 28 *Of the External Sealing of the Covenant of Grace.*

Chapter 29 *Of the Visible Church.*

Chapter 30 *Of the Holy Scriptures.*

Chapter 31 *Of the Particular Churches.*

Chapter 32 *Of Church Discipline.*

Chapter 33 *Of Perfect Glorification, Including the Second Advent of Christ, the Resurrection of the Dead, and the General Conflagration.*

Volume Seventeen contains *De Doctrina Christiana* Book II, Chapters 1-17 edited with the translation of Charles R. Sumner, D.D., by James Holly Hanford and Waldo Hilary Dunn.

Volume Eighteen contains *The Uncollected Writings of John Milton* edited by Thomas Ollive Mabbott and J. Milton French with translation by Nelson Glenn McCrea and Others.

II. SECONDARY SOURCES

BIOGRAPHY AND INTERPRETATION

Arnold, Matthew. *Essays in Criticism.* (Second Series) London: Macmillan and Company, 1888, pp. 331.

Essay on "Milton" pp. 56-68 is interesting because it was delivered as an address in St. Margaret's Church, Westminster, on Feb. 13, 1888, at the unveiling of a Memorial Window to Catherine Woodcock Milton, presented by an American. Arnold shows

239

through a brief summary of the life of Milton that "Excellence is not commone and abundant . . . it dwells among rocks hardly accessible, and a man must wear his heart out before he can reach her." Milton, for Arnold, is a standard of poetic excellence.

Bacon, Sir Francis. *The Works* . . . New York: Hurd and Houghton, 1877, pp. 438.

Beeching. H. C., *The Poetical Works of John Milton*. London: Oxford University Press, 1928, pp. 554.

This edition of Milton's poetry is a reprint from the earliest printed copies. It contains the only reprint of the Minor Poems in the old spelling of the small octave of 1645.

Belloc, Hilaire, *Milton*. Philadelphia: J. B. Lippincott Company, 1935, pp. 313.

Written by a Catholic with the conviction that Milton gave the last and decisive blow to the Catholic tradition in England. As to the contention of the book it is very incisive. There are many brilliant insights into Milton as a literary artist.

Belloc contends that Milton is the exponent of English orthodox Protestantism, and then having set forth Milton's theological position with his Arianism, views on divorce, and the like, states, "The *De Doctrina*, I say is neglected; yet not only in our judgment of Milton, but as a landmark in the break-up of European religion, it is of the highest moment. It shows on the surface of English Protestantism like the first thin crack one finds on the ice of a frozen pond, which will soon grow to a broad fissure, until the general ruin of the whole surface in the full thaw." (p. 290) The author regards the heresy of Milton as the occasion of the break-up of the Catholic tradition in England.

————, *Selected Essays*. Philadelphia: J. B. Lippincott Company, 1936, pp. 319.

"The Sonnets of Milton," pp. 133-164. Belloc points out that the sonnet measures a poet's ability; then he criticizes Milton for both a "spendthrift spirit in words," as well as for ignoring that which is essential to the effect of a sonnet, namely the contrast of the octave with the sextet. He admits that Milton has some good sonnets, but is not impressed by the entire lot.

Brydges, Sir Egerton. *Paradise Lost by John Milton*. Philadelphia: G. S. Appleton, 1851.

In addition to a life of Milton, the publisher contends that this is the First, Complete and Perfect edition of *Paradise Lost*.

Bush, Douglas. *The Renaissance and English Humanism*. Toronto: University of Toronto Press, 1939, pp. 134.

The author declares Milton was the "last great exponent of Christian Humanism in its historical continuity" (p. 101). He emphasizes the passionate belief of Milton in the freedom of the will, and the dignity of human reason.

Cambridge History of English Literature. New York: G. P. Putnam's Sons, 1911-27, 15 Volumes.

Volume 7. Chapter 5, pp. 108-161. "Milton," by George Saintsbury. Milton is "admittedly, in the least disputed sense of that much debated term, 'the grand style,' the grandest style of English poets."

Corson, Hiram. *An Introduction to the Prose and Poetical Works of John Milton.* New York: The Macmillan Company, 1899, pp. 303.

Here is given great importance to the work of Milton in the cause of political and religious liberty as a polemic prose writer, ". . . it was in a large measure due to those pamphlets that in a a few years — fourteen after Milton's death — the constitutional basis of the monarchy underwent a quite radical change for the better. . . ." (p. xv)

Dryden, John. *The Poetical Works of* . . . Boston: Houghton, Mifflin and Company, Vol. I, n. d. pp. 394.

Famous quotation comprises the entire poem, entitled *Under Mr. Milton's Picture, Before his Paradise Lost* and appears on page 324 of this edition of the works of John Dryden.

Elliott, G. R. *The Cycle of Modern Poetry.* Princeton: Princeton University Press, 1929, pp. 194.

With singular insight the author discerns the subtle interweaving of the idyllic motive throughout the entirety of the great epic. The interpretation of Paradise unique with Milton in his emphasis upon the "Paradise within" is here laconically set forth.

Elton, Oliver. *The English Muse.* London: G. Bell and Sons, 1936, pp. 464.

Of importance for this study is the view of the author concerning the theme of *Paradise Lost.*

Encyclopaedia of Religion and Ethics. James Hastings. Volume 8, pp. 641-648. "John Milton" by H. J. C. Grierson.

This article by an authority in the field of literature is helpful, not only because of its literary evaluation of Milton but also because of the importance given to *De Doctrina* in an understanding of the purpose of *Paradise Lost.*

Fletcher, Harris Francis. *The Use of the Bible in Milton's Prose.* Urbana: University Press, 1929, pp. 176.

241

Points out the singular importance of the use of the Bible by Milton, especially in *De Doctrina Christiana.* Denotes the Bible Milton used was the Latin Bible translated by Junius and Tremellius.

Grierson, Sir Herbert J. C. *Cross Currents in English Literature of the 17th Century.* London: Chatto and Windus, 1929, pp. 341.
Of special value in discerning the humanistic and secular revival due to a study of the classics; and in contrast, the emphasis later upon the revival of early Christianity maintaining the great doctrines of sin and death, and grace and all that is involved in an escape from John Bunyan's "City of Destruction."

————, *Milton and Wordsworth.* New York: The Macmillan Company, 1937, pp. 185.
A comparison of the reactions of Milton and Wordsworth to the political events of their respective days. The contrast is drawn between Milton's passionate devotion to human freedom in his public pronouncements, and Wordsworth's battle for freedom fought out privately. Wordsworth expressed his intense feeling in his personal interest in nature. His philosophy is not alone of nature, but, deeper than that, of the inner heart of man. Writing in a century when intellectual tradition was in high respect, Milton projected his convictions to the public. Due to the Romantic Revival and the reaction against intellectual tradition, Wordsworth "turned to the senses and the imagination, from political speculation to the individual, to all the subtle but profound reactions of his emotional nature to its natural and human environment." (p. 162)

————, *Seventeenth Century Studies.* Oxford: The Clarendon Press, 1938, pp. 415.
A memorial volume presented to Sir Herbert by authorities writing on *Seventeenth Century Studies.*
E. M. W. Tillyard writes on "Milton and the English Epic Tradition" pp. 211-234. He agrees with Basil Willey that a sacred subject alone would find credence in the growing scientific consciousness of his day. But he goes on to state there are many heroic stories in the Bible, providing copious possibilities for an Arthurian type of epic. Tillyard manifests his definitive interpretative ability in the observation that Milton could not write an epic in praise of his nation for he was firmly convinced that in a time of crisis England had failed.

Hanford, James Holly. *A Milton Handbook.* New York: F. S. Crofts. 1936, pp. 366.

This book provides, in brief compass, the essential material for a basic understanding of Milton as a Poet, both by means of his prose as well as his poetry. Important extracts from the prose writings are given to show the years of diligent study and steadfast purpose which made possible the successful writing of the great epic.

————, *"Milton and the Return to Humanism"* Studies in Philology, XVI (April 1919), pp. 126-147.
Shows the bent of Milton's mind toward a reliance upon the rational as an interpretation of human freedom. "Outward freedom and inward control or freedom with discipline is the authentic humanistic formula which Milton applies in all the domains of education, politics, morality, religion and art." (p. 144) The basic claim of this humanism is the spiritual dignity of man, with the control of the lower nature by the higher as being essential for salvation.

Havens, Raymond Dexter. *The Influence of Milton on English Poetry.* Cambridge: Harvard University Press, 1922.
This work traces the great influence of Milton upon the poetry of the 18th and 19th centuries.

Houston, Percy Hazen. *Main Currents of English Literature.* New York: F. S. Crofts and Company, 1936, pp. 526.
Of special value was the chapter entitled, "The Seventeenth Century," pp. 124-180.

Ivimey, Joseph. *John Milton.* London: Effingham Wilson, 1832, pp. 397.
In this work, the author states his purpose, to show Milton as Patriot, Protestant and Non-Conformist. The prose writings of Milton are used as the basis of most of the biographical material.

Keats, John. *Letters.* London: Macmillan and Company, 1921, pp. 398.
Many references are made in these letters to Milton. Of particular interest was his comparison of Wordsworth and Milton, pp. 105-109.

Kelley, Maurice. *This Great Argument.* Princeton: University Press, Princeton, New Jersey, 1941.
The author necessarily becomes involved in the theology of Milton, due to the nature of his work especially with *De Doctrina Christiana.* The primary emphasis of his work was that of the literary value of a comparative study of *De Doctrina Christiana* and *Paradise Lost.*

Lang, Andrew. *History of English Literature.* New York: Longmans, Green and Company, 1933.
A good history of English literature in one volume.

243

Langdon, Ida. *Milton's Theory of Poetry and Fine Art.* New Haven: Yale University Press: 1924, pp. 342.

Beauty of construction and high inspiration are organic, the one to the other. This, the author exemplifies, is well portrayed in the fine art and poetic ability of Milton. The philosophical principle of this discernment is essentially Platonic. The beauty of the seen has its heavenly counterpart in the inspiration of the unseen.

Legouis, Emile. *A History of English Literature.* New York: The Macmillan Company, 1927. Volume I, *The Middle Ages and the Renaiscence* (650-1660), pp. 387.

Primarily written for students of English in the Universities of France, but was so favorably received in Great Britain that it was translated into English.

Lewis, C. S. *A Preface to Paradise Lost.* Oxford: University Press, 1943, pp. 133.

The author brings his own special style of thought and writing to bear upon *Paradise Lost.* His plea for the orthodox interpretation of the theology within the epic is without defense, when he states that heretical elements exist in it. His attempt to reduce the importance of the heresy in favor of the epic itself contains little merit.

Macaulay, Thomas Babington, *The Works of* . . . 8 Volumes. New York: Longmans, Green and Company, 1897. Essay on "Milton" Volume 5, pp. 1-45. "He lived at one of the most memorable eras in the history of mankind, at the very crisis of the great conflict between Oromasdes and Arimanes, liberty and despotism, reason and prejudice. That great battle was fought for no single generation, for no single land. The destinies of the human race were staked on the same cast with the freedom of the English people. Then were first proclaimed those mighty principles which have since worked their way into the depths of the American forests, which have aroused Greece from the slavery and degradation of two thousand years, from one end of Europe to the other, have kindled an unquenchable fire in the hearts of oppressed, and loosed the knees of the oppressors with an unwonted fear. . . ." (p. 23)

Martz, Louis L., *Milton, A Collection of Critical Essays,* Prentice-Hall, Englewood Cliffs, New Jersey, 1966, 212 pages.

Just as the title indicates this is a collection of critical essays, on John Milton. Only by opening this book does one find that there are authors and titles, such as, T. S. Eliot, *"A Note on the Verse of John Milton";* and particularly, *"The Crisis of Paradise*

Lost," by E. M. W. Tillyard, and *"Milton's Counterplot"* by Geoffrey Hartman. In *"Milton's Counterplot,"* Geoffrey Hartman affirms: "Paradise Lost was written not for the sake of heaven or hell but for the sake of the creation. . . . The center around which and to which all actions turn is whether man can stand though free to fall, whether man and the world can survive their autonomy. The issue may not therefore be determined on the supernatural level by the direct clash of heaven and hell, only by these two arbiters: man's free will, and God's foreknowledge." (p. 108)

Masson, David, *The Life of John Milton narrated in connexion with the Political, Ecclesiastical, and literary History of his Time.* 6 Volumes. London: Macmillan and Company, 1881-1894.

This work is considered an authoritative source for the accurate portrayal of the life of Milton and the important events of his time. It has the merit of readability. The contents of each volume are here given as a helpful index to the life of Milton.

Volume One 1608-1639, pp. 834.

Book One 1608-1625 includes Milton's ancestry and kindred; the Spread Eagle, Bread Street, Old London; Education at home and at St. Paul's School.

Book Two. 1625-1632 includes Cambridge and its Dons in 1625; Milton's seven years at the University, with the incidents of that period; Academic studies and results.

Book Three. 1632-1638 includes history of the reign; biography.

Book Four. April 1638-July 1639 contains an account of the continental journey of Milton.

Volume Two. 1638-1643, pp. 608.

Book I. April 1638-November 1640. History: The Scottish Presbyterian revolt, and its effect on England. Biography: Milton back in England: his *Epitaphium Damonis,* and literary projects.

Book II. November 1640-August 1642. History: First two and twenty months of the Long Parliament. Biography: Milton in Aldersgate Street; his anti-episcopal pamphlets.

Book III. August 1642-July 1643. History: Commencement of the Civil War: the Long Parliament continued: meeting of the Westminster Assembly. Biography: Milton still in Adersgate Street: his marriage.

Book IV. English Presbyterianism and English Independency: their history to 1643.

Volume Three. 1643-1649, pp. 729.

Book I. July 1643-March 1644. History: First eight months of the Westminster Assembly: Civil War and the Long Parliament continued: Biography: Milton still in Aldersgate Street: his marriage misfortune: his first divorce treatise.

Book II. March 1644-March 1645. History: The year of Marston Moor: Civil War, the Long Parliament, and Westminster Assembly continued. Struggle of Independency with Presbyterianism: toleration controversy; English sects and sectaries — Presbyterian settlement voted new model of the army. Biography: Milton among the sectaries: his second divorce pamphlet, *On Education, Areopagitica, Tetrachordon,* and *Colasterion.*

Book III. April 1645-August 1646. History: Sixteen months of the new model army, of the Long Parliament and Westminster Assembly continued. Battle of Naseby and its consequences — episode of Montrose in Scotland; Flight of the king to the Scots and conclusion of the Civil War. Progress of the toleration controversy and of the struggle between the Presbyterians and the Independents. London and Lancashire Presbyterianized. Biography: Return of Milton's wife: his removal from Aldersgate Street to Barbican: first edition of his poems: three more sonnets: continued Presbyterian attacks on Milton: his retaliation: troubles of the Powell family.

Book IV. August 1646-January 1649. History: The last two years and a half of the reign of Charles I. Biography: Milton in Barbican and in High Holborn. Private and public anxieties: Ode to Rous, two more sonnets, and translation of nine Psalms: other works in progress: Letters to and from Carlo Dati.

Volume Four. 1649-1654, pp. 642.

Book I, January 1649-July 1649. History: Foundation and beginnings of an English Republic. Biography: Milton's adhesion to the Republic: His *Tenure of King's and Magistrates*: commencement of his Latin secretaryship.

Book II. July 1649-April 1653. History: Annals of the Commonwealth from the first through a fragment of the fifth year.

Biography: Milton's life through the period of the Commonwealth, with his Secretaryship under five successive Councils of State.

Book III. April 1653-September 1654. History: Cromwell's interim dictatorship and elevation to the protectorate. Biography: Milton's life and secretaryship through this period.

Volume Five. 1654-1660, pp. 703.

Book I. September 1654-June 1657. History: Oliver's first protectorate continued. Biography: Milton's life and secretaryship through the first protectorate continued.

Book II. June 1657-September 1658. History: Oliver's second protectorate. Biography: Milton's life and secretaryship through the second protectorate.

Book III. September 1658-May 1660. History: The protectorate of Richard Cromwell, the anarchy, Monk's march and dictatorship, and the restoration. Biography: Milton's life and secretaryship through Richard's protectorate, the anarchy, and Monk's dictatorship.

Volume Six. 1660-1674, pp. 840.

Book I. May 1660-1661. History: The year of the restoration. Biography: Milton through the year of the restoration.

Book II. May 1661-August 1667. History: The Clarendon administration continued: Davenant's revived laureateship, and the first seven years of the literature of the restoration. Biography: Milton's life from 1661-1667: with *Paradise Lost*.

Book III. August 1667-November 1674. History: English politics and literature from 1667 to 1674. Biography: The last seven years of Milton's life.

Book IV. Posthumous Miltoniana.

More, Paul Elmer. *Shelburne Essays*. Boston: Houghton Mifflin Company, 1906, pp. 283. "The Theme of Paradise Lost," p. 239. Fourth Series. More rightly believes the theme of *Paradise Lost* has been misunderstood. With clarity and his usual excellence of interpretation, he strikes forth the real motive and theme of the great epic.

Murry, John Middleton. *Heroes of Thought,* Julian Messner, Incorporated, New York, 1938, pp. 368. Three chapters (pp. 142-177), on John Milton give an appreciative and yet scathing criticism of Milton's position in religious thought and literature, as well as the politico-religious position of the individual in a growing democracy. In this latter respect Milton and Cromwell are well contrasted. Cromwell's passion for the toleration of the individual lay in his protection of others, while Milton's passion in the same direction was a matter of his own self-assertion.

Parker, William Riley. *Milton's Debt to Greek Tragedy in Samson Agonistes*. Baltimore: The Johns Hopkins Press, 1937, pp. 260. In this work the author shows the wide extent of indebtedness Milton has to Aeschylus, Sophocles, and Euripedes, in *Samson Agonistes*.

Pattison, Mark. *Milton*. New York: Harper and Brothers. 1899, pp. 215.
A small but complete account of the life of Milton with his literary works used as commentaries on his life.

Pinto, V. De Sola. *The English Renaissance*. New York: Robert M. McBride and Company. 1938, pp. 381.
Of particular value was his chapter on "Elizabethan Literature," pp. 64-87.

Saintsbury, George. *A History of English Criticism*. New York: Dodd, Mead and Company, 1911, pp. 551.
A great volume in extensive and scholarly treatment of the subject.

Sampson, Alden. *Studies in Milton*. New York: Moffat, Yard and Company, 1913, pp. 310.
The author makes a comparison of Milton with George Fox, maintaining a similarity in spiritual life.

Saurat, Denis. *Milton, Man and Thinker*. New York: The Dial Press, 1925, pp. 363.
Saurat conceives Milton's writings to be a projection of his own qualities of character in which pride reigns supreme. The author overdraws this principle, especially in reference to the pride of Milton. We are indebted to Saurat in his emphasis upon the unorthodox thinker Milton was. At the same time his interpretation of Milton lacks a broad acquaintance with the total life and literature of Milton's day.

Sewell, Arthur. *A Study in Milton's Christian Doctrine*. London: Oxford University Press, 1939, pp. 214.
Sewell argues that *Christian Doctrine* was for Milton a statement of the theological problems he confronted, rather than a reasoned conclusion of his religious convictions. At times Sewell argues with credence, but there are many reasons for the belief that *Christian Doctrine* comprised Milton's theological position, that are left untouched by Sewell.

Smart, John S. *The Sonnets of Milton*. Glasgow: Maclehose, Jackson and Company, 1921, pp. 195.
This work is an authority on the sonnets, and is indispensable for a clear and concise view of this phase of Milton's poetic ability.

Stoll, Elmer Edgar. *Poets and Playwrights*. Minneapolis: The University of Minnesota Press, 1930, pp. 295.
The author maintains there was a romantic vein in the poetry of Milton. The lack of despair in the departure of Adam and

Eve from Paradise was a part of this. Milton closed the epic in everything but strict Puritan fashion.

Taylor, George Coffin. *Milton's Use of Du Bartas.* Cambridge: Harvard University Press, 1934, pp. 129.
This work sets forth the influence of Sylvester's translation of Du Bartas *Divine Weekes and Workers* upon the composition of *Paradise Lost.* At length Taylor presses quite rigidly the dependence of Milton upon this work.

Tennyson, Alfred. *The Poetical Works of* . . . New York: Harper and Brothers, 1871, pp. 250. Poem on "Milton," p. 224.

Thaler, Alwin. *Shakspere's Silences.* Cambridge: Harvard University Press, 1929, p. 279.
Of particular interest for this work was the chapter on "Milton in the Theatre," pp. 209-256.

Tieghem, Paul Van. *Outline of the Literary History of Europe Since the Renaissance.* New York: The Century Company, 1930, pp. 361.
An introductory work in comprehensive form of the general movement of modern literature.

Tillyard, E. M. W. *Milton.* London: Chatto and Windus, 1930, pp. 396.
This volume represents the work of an authority on the seventeenth century, particularly focussed on Milton. The work considers Milton's mental development with special relation to *Paradise Lost.*

——, *The Miltonic Setting.* London: Cambridge University Press, 1938, pp. 208. This is a study of Milton against the background of the seventeenth century, with a commentary on his present poetic status. The author points that Milton was a Protestant only in the extended meaning of the term when it implies the aloneness of the individual before God. Such an interpretation gives an individual full freedom to adopt his own position, and this is what Milton plainly did.

Wordsworth, William. *The Poetical Works of* . . . London: Oxford University Press, 1928, pp. 986.
"Scorn not the Sonnet," p. 260.
"Excursion," p. 865.
"Milton," p. 307.

HISTORY

Bowden, Witt, Michael Karpovich, and Abbott Payson Usher. *An Economic History of Europe Since 1750.* New York: American Book Company, 1937, pp. 948.

This work traces the growth of the modern business enterprise from its fundamental development in the sixteenth and seventeenth centuries to the present time. Particular reference is given to the social and economic development of the sixteenth and seventeenth centuries in the growth of commerce and trade between countries, including as well commerce with the New World. "It is hardly too much to say that all the fundamental elements of modern business enterprise were developed during the sixteenth and seventeenth centuries. The basic features of the new social structure were worked out, but they were applied on a relatively small scale, and the economic changes found no adequate expression in the political life of the time." (p. 23)

Campbell, Douglas. *The Puritan In Holland, England, and America.* New York: Harper and Brothers, 1892. Volume I, 509, pp. Volume II, 588 pp.

These two volumes present a comprehensive picture of the Puritan and his rise to leadership in both the Old World and the New. "I have chosen as a title 'The Puritan in Holland, England, and America' because the Puritan, who has done so much for the modern world, was not the product of any one race or country. He was born out of the uprising against the abuses of the Church of Rome. He came to maturity in upholding liberty against the assaults of kingly power. In him was represented the principle of religious and civil freedom." (Volume I, pp. xxvi, xxvii)

Clark, G. N. *The Seventeenth Century.* Oxford: Clarendon Press. 1929. pp. 372.

The writer treats the seventeenth century for its immense activity and transition as related in various fields from economics to painting and architecture. The book guards against the interpretation of historical phenomena in terms of one single principle, but shows the connection between the various fields of interpretation. This is good background material for interpretation, especially in religion and literature.

Davies, Godfrey, *The Early Stuarts 1603-1660.* Oxford: The Clarendon Press, 1937, pp. 439.

A thorough and scholarly treatment of the years indicated in the title. This is one of the volumes in the series included in the Oxford History of England. The author gives a comprehensive picture of the various phases of life, particularly a political and constitutional history, England's foreign relations including trade with the colonies, religious history, education and science, the arts and literature.

Fisher, George P. *The Reformation.* New York: Charles Scribner's Sons, 1902, pp. 620.

Very helpful because it is not only an accurate Church History of the period but gives the important relationship of political and social elements influencing the course of events. Written by a Protestant, this is a remarkably impartial account of the Reformation.

———, *History of Christian Doctrine.* New York: Charles Scribner's Sons, 1923, pp. 583.
A reference work of the highest excellence for the doctrinal history of the Christian Faith.

Gardiner, Samuel R. *History of the Commonwealth and Protectorate.* 4 Volumes London: Longman's, Green, and Company, 1903.
A splendidly detailed account of the history of the period making for accuracy in documenting historical events.

———, *A Student's History of England.* Volume II. London. Longman's Green, and Company, 1909, pp. 606.
This work in outline form gives a perspective of the movement of events from the beginning of the Reign of Henry VIII to the constitutional victory of Parliament in 1689. This has a larger and more detailed account in the four volumes mentioned above.

Green, John Richard. *History of the English People.* Volume III, New York: Harper and Brothers, n. d. pp. 451.
This volume is a history of Puritan England from 1603 to 1660 and of the Restoration from 1660-67. In a detailed and expansive way this work deals with the history of England and the part played by the Puritans, especially associated with the significant leadership and writings of Milton. The second phase of the work deals with the Revolution of 1688 and the permanence of the constitutional victory achieved in the supremacy of Parliament over that of the King.

———, *A Short History of the English People.* New York: A. L. Burt Company, 1886, pp. 538.
This recognized historian has summarized his splendid history of the people of England into this compact and thorough volume. Of special value in this work is the perspective Green gives of the time of Milton in relation to the entire history of England. "The whole history of English progress since the Restoration, on its moral and spiritual sides, has been the history of Puritanism." p. 186.

Highet, Gilbert. *A Classical tradition.* Oxford: Oxford University Press, 1949. Greek and Roman influences on Western Literature.

Hulme, Edward Maslin. *A History of the British People.* New York: The Century Company, 1924, pp. 717.
This work traces the political, economic, social, and religious

conditions in the life of the British people, to the commanding position they hold today.

Larson, Laurence M. *History of England and the British Commonwealth.* New York: Henry Holt and Company, 1924, pp. 911.

Especially helpful because of the political development of the period pertaining to the life and times of Milton.

Manuel, Frank E. *Utopias and Utopian Thought,* Houghton Mifflin Company, New York, 1965, pp. 321.

A collection of essays on Utopias with an interpretation by each of the authors. The thought on Utopias has five divisions, each one in its own perspective and character. The divisions are: I. Historical Dimension; II. Utopia Is Dead; III. Limitations on Utopia: IV. Utopia As Practice; V. Utopia The Eternal Human. The proliferation of various types of Utopias is engaging; also the omission of any contribution of John Milton is singular.

McConnell, Francis J., *John Wesley,* The Abingdon Press, New York, N. Y., 1939, pp. 355.

One of the most disturbing and thought provoking accounts of John Wesley, the founder of Methodism. The scholarship is excellent. At points there is an accent on the liberal in interpretation; however this serves academic tension and growth of insight, when compared with other biographies.

Plato, The Dialogues of, (Two Volumes). Translated into English by Benjamin Jowett, Random House, New York, N. Y., 1937. Volume I, pp. 879. Vol. II, pp. 939.

Probably the most consummate interlacing of thought upon thought, upon the important subjects of humankind.

Though Socrates did not leave a written word, his pupil, Plato, conveyed these interlocutary discussions of his master to succeeding generations. In the procedure there is the graduation from Socrates to Plato, with the various stages in the developing thought of Plato.

The Critias is one of these dialogues dealing with Utopia, as is *The Republic,* and in its own way, *The Laws.*

Stowell, W. H., *A History of the Puritans and Pilgrim Fathers.* New York: Worthington Company, 1888, pp. 508.

Traces the rise of the Puritans from the English reformers to the reign of Charles the Second.

Tatham, G. B. *The Puritans in Power.* Cambridge: University Press, 1913, pp. 282.

Deals with the influence of the Puritan Revolution upon the Church of England from the viewpoint of its immediate and material results.

Walker, Williston. *A History of the Christian Church.* New York: Charles Scribner's Sons, 1944, pp. 624.
An authoritative Church history in one volume.

Willey, Basil. *The Seventeenth Century Background.* London, Chatto and Windus, 1934, pp. 315.
A study of poetry and religion against the background of the thought of the century, particularly the growth in the demand for scientific truth. Against this consciousness, Willey maintains that a Scriptural theme could alone find credence.

Wolfe, Don M. *Milton in the Puritan Revolution.* New York: Thomas Nelson and Sons, 1941, pp. 496.
A closely reasoned and finely developed account of the rise of the revolutionary spirit in the 17th century life of England, from the religious and theological concept of individualism in Puritanism, and beyond Puritanism, as exemplified by Milton. Wolfe traces the lodgement of this spirit in *Paradise Lost.*

Workman, Herbert B. *The Dawn of the Reformation.* London: The Epworth Press, 1933, pp. 310.
Volume I, "The Age of Wyclif." An especially fine and reliable treatment of the life of Wyclif, in his own time, as well as the influence of his life that registered through the Lollards who maintained "a continuity of dissent" until the reform movement of the sixteenth century.

THEOLOGY

Allen, Alexander, V. G., *The Continuity of Christian Thought,* New York: Houghton Mifflin Company, 1894.
A study of modern theology in the light of its history. Of particular value was the chapter on "The Greek Theology."

Augustine, *The Confessions of* . . . New York: E. P. Dutton and Company, 1913, pp. 348.
A compendium of person theology with great importance for later orthodoxy.

Ayer, Joseph Cullen, Jr. *A Source Book for Ancient Church History.* New York: Charles Scribner's Sons, 1913, pp. 707.
An excellent one volume source covering that period of Church history from the Apostolic Age to the close of the Conciliar period.

Brunner, Emil. *The Mediator.* New York: The Macmillan Company, 1934, pp. 622.

253

An authoritative work on that which is central to the Christian Faith, namely the doctrine of Christ. Brunner's directness becomes incisive for decision. God confronts man in Jesus Christ. He is the Revelation. He is the Word. He is the Message. And He is the Messenger. He is God, inasmuch as He is Son. To accept Him is to accept Truth in its personal manifestation.

Of particular value in our task is the distinction between Christ the Word, as Truth becomes personal, and the so-called abstract Idealism of speculative philosophy. Christ is not only the Platonic Messenger of eternal Truth manifest in time. He is that Truth Himself.

Calvin, John, *The Institutes of the Christian Religion*. Philadelphia: Presbyterian Board of Education, 1936. Volume I 838 pp. Volume II, 812 pp. This work was occasioned by the desire to set forth the elementary principles of the Christian Faith for the Protestants among the French. It was of such a character that it became the definitive statement of the Protestant theology of the Reformation.

Evans, J. M., *Paradise Lost, and The Genesis Tradition,* Clarendon Press, Oxford University, 1968. 314 pages.

This book is mainly a study of a Tradition in three parts. Part One, The Exegetical Tradition; Part Two, The Literary Tradition; Part Three, Paradise Lost and the Tradition.

The book accomplishes what the title indicates. It is a study of Genesis, from the viewpoint of tradition, and then an application of this tradition to *Paradise Lost.* At points the statements are most penetrating, as for example, "God's behaviour, for example, appears to be malicious, and Adam's inexplicable." (p. 2) "Thus, according to J, the Fall does not seem to have been a fall at all. On the contrary, it was an over-abrupt rise, a momentary transition from a state of naive innocence to one of precocious maturity; it was a cautionary tale of a child who grew up too quickly, not a demi-god who fell." (p. 19) "As in the Jahwist document, therefore, the Fall consisted in eating the fruit too soon and so growing up too quickly." (p. 80)

"In fact Adam and Eve's moral awareness was complete before the Fall, and the reason they were prohibited from partaking of this one tree was (so they might know that they enjoyed the fruition only by God's grace and charity, and that He is the Lord and Creator of all things)." p. 89. The facets of insight and interpretation flash upon one suddenly and almost unexpectedly from the pen of this author.

His work, however, is a development within The Genesis Tradi-

254

tion, interpreted by the configuration of that perspective, in both Church History and Literature, with its application to the Epic of the English language. The task is altogether different than the one set forth in *PARADISE FOUND*.

Harrison, A. W. *The Beginnings of Arminianism*. London: University of London Press, 1926, pp. 408.

A scholarly work on Arminianism from its beginnings to the Synod of Dort.

Hodge, Archibald Alexander. *A Commentary on the Confession of Faith*. Philadelphia: Presbyterian Board of Publication, 1923, pp. 559.

A statement and interpretation of the Westminster Confession.

Hough, Lynn Harold. *The Christian Criticism of Life*. New York: Abingdon-Cokesbury Press, 1941, pp. 312.

This book has been of basic value in the Christian interpretation of Milton's humanism. It presents a dominant appeal for that humanism which has come to its lofty climax in evangelism. In one respect alone is there a similarity between Milton and Paul Elmer More. Both were humanists with the theistic reference, and of the Platonic variety. Intellectualist that he was, More yet saw the necessity of the Cross and accepted the glorious fact of Christian grace. With the spiritual transformation that followed, More declared, "If I were young I would preach." Milton remained the intellectualist without such an acceptance of Christian grace. This may have been the reason why he (Milton) never actually entered the pulpit for which he was trained, and in later years remained outside the Church itself.

Lewis, Edwin. *A Christian Manifesto*. New York: The Abingdon Press, 1934, pp. 245.

A re-statement of the orthodox position in theology, made under the urgency to preserve the Christian Faith against the inroads of sterile humanism. This is a modern affirmation of the importance of the supernatural. There is a directness here that speaks of an inner and contemporary personal glow of a soul set on fire by Christ.

———, *God and Ourselves*. New York: The Abingdon Press, 1931, pp. 311.

This work draws the issue between the uncertainty respecting God, and the God who in Christ is not only real, but adequate and available as well. It is a valid challenge to non-theistic humanism and to the quasitheist. In a day of liberal thinking concerning God, this constitutes a manifesto of faith made without equivocation, in declarations of boldness and lucidity. Surrounded by contemporary doubt concerning God, this serves as

255

a proclamation of the great Christian truths.

————, *A Philosophy of the Christian Revelation.* New York: Harper Brothers, 1940, pp. 356.

This is a solid treatment that focusses upon the centrality of the Christian Revelation, with the consequent importance of the supernatural reference as the Christian claim. The thesis moves through a critical analysis of the problems confronted in respect to the claim, and then comes to a fitting climax in the preservation given Revelation by the Divine Spirit. This book formed the background for much of the theological interpretation for the position developed in the present work.

————, *A New Heaven and a New Earth.* New York: Abingdon-Cokesbury Press, 1941, pp. 248.

These are the Quillan lectures for 1941, delivered at Emory University. The thesis is that the ideal controls the actual. It is in this sense the author uses the word "heaven." Of particular interest is the interpretation of the Trinity as the metaphysical basis for the realization of the Brotherhood of Man on Earth.

Mackintosh, H. R. *The Christian Apprehension of God.* London: Student Christian Movement Press, 1929, pp. 231.

A singular volume especially in respect to the treatment of "The Idea of Revelation" (chapter 3) and "The Sovereign Purpose of God" (chapter 8). God's omnipotence means that God can do everything that He wills. However, what God wills must be in keeping with his character. The nature and quality of that will we learn in Jesus Christ.

Mansel, Henry L. *The Limits of Religious Thought.* Boston: Gould and Lincoln, 1859, pp. 364.

This contains eight lectures delivered before the University of Oxford on the Bampton Foundation. The work comes to a focus in the conclusion that God cannot be apprehended positively in any mode of the human consciousness. There is then no such thing as a positive science of Speculative Theology.

Pringle-Pattison, A. Seth. *The Idea of God.* New York: Oxford University Press, 1920, pp. 443.

These are the Gifford lectures of 1912-1913 in which the author surveys the idea of God in the light of recent philosophy beginning with David Hume.

Schaff, Philip. *The Creeds of Christendom.* 3 Volumes. New York: Harper and Brothers, 1877.

Volume I contains a history of the Creeds. Volume II contains the Greek and Latin creeds with an English parallel translation. Volume III contains the creeds of the Evangelical faiths.

These volumes are a compendium of source material.

Strong, Augustus H. *The Great Poets and Their Theology*. Philadelphia: American Baptist Publication Society, 1897, pp. 531.

In pages 221-277, the author deals with Milton as "The Poet of the Protestant Reformation." While Strong takes into account the heresy of Milton in *De Doctrina Christiana*, he yet exalts him as the poet of Protestant Reformation, indicating his work as "in the cause of truth and righteousness." We cannot agree with this position. Apparently Strong did not make a close study of the parallelism of theology in *De Doctrina* . . . and *Paradise Lost*, particularly the heretical content he admits finding in the treatise.

FOOTNOTES

1. Manuel, Frank E., *Utopias and Utopian Thought,* page 27, 1965, (Houghton Mifflin Company, New York, New York). On page 44 of this work, there is the statement: "Of the famous utopias, the one which shows pastoral influence most consistently is William Morris' *News from Nowhere.*" That there can be news from nowhere becomes sigficant, unless the state "nowhere" ceases, and becomes real!

2. Jowett, Benjamin, *The Dialogues of Plato,* Volume Two, pages 77, 78. Paragraph 114, *The Critias.*

3. Paragraph 114, *The Critias.*

4. Paragraph 114, *The Critias.*

5. Paragraph 114, *The Critias.*

6. Paragraph 114, *The Critias.*

7. Paragraph 114, *The Critias.*

8. Paragraph 114, *The Critias.*

9. Paragraph 114, *The Critias.*

10. Paragraph 116, *The Critias.*

11. Paragraph 120, *The Critias.*

12. Paragraph 121, *The Critias*

13. Paragraph 121, *The Critias.*

14. Paragraph 121, *The Critias.*

15. Paragraph 121, *The Critias.*

16. Paragraph 121, *The Critias.*

17. Paragraph 121, *The Critias.*

18. Paragraph 121, *The Critias.*

19. Paragraph 121, *The Critias.*

20. Page 28, Frank E. Manuel, *Op. Cit.*

21. Henry David Thoreau was a graduate of Harvard University, a scholar, a woodsman: given to the simple life. He did not marry. He lived alone. He never voted. He was a naturalist, never using trap or gun. He followed the simple life in reading great books, thinking, and writing. He is known as "The Sage of Walden Pond."

22. Page 47, Frank E. Manuel, *Op. Cit.*

23. London, Macmillan and Company, published 1881-1894.

24. Plato, *The Republic,* Book I, Paragraph 328, Jowett, Benjamin, *Op. Cit.*

25. Plato, *The Republic,* Book IX, Paragraph 592, *Op. Cit.*

26. G. B. Tatham, *The Puritans in Power* (Cambridge: University Press, 1913), p. 2.

27. David Masson, *The Life of John Milton* . . . (London: Macmillan and Company, 1881-1894), Vol. I, p. 424.

28. *Ibid.,* Vol. I, p. 341.

29. *Ibid.,* Vol. I, pp. 355-366; 395-407.

30. L. M. Larson, *History of England and the British Commonwealth,* (N. Y.: Henry Holt and Company, 1924), p. 373.

31. Masson, *Op. Cit.,* Vol. II. pp. 336-345.

32. Williston Walker, *A History of the Christian Church,* (N. Y.: C. Scribner's Sons, 1944) p. 472.

33. John Milton, *The Works of* . . . (N. Y.: Columbia University Press, 1931), Vol. I, Part I, p. 71.

34. Masson, *Op. Cit.,* Vol. IV, p. 77.

35. Don M. Wolfe, *Milton in the Puritan Revolution,* (N. Y.: Thomas Nelson and Sons, 1941), p. 342.

36. Walker, *Op. Cit.,* p. 415; Wolfe, *Op. Cit.,* pp. 41, 246, 252.

37. Matthew 20: 26, 27.

38. Milton, *Op. Cit.,* Vol VI, p. 120.

39. Wolfe, *Op. Cit.,* p. 242.

40. J. R. Green, *A Short History of the English People,* (N. Y.: A. L. Burt Company, 1886), p. 186.

41. Francis J. McConnell, in *John Wesley,* (N. Y. Abingdon Press, 1939), p. 205 says: "Much of Methodism was an inheritance from Puritanism, and Puritanism of those days, important and necessary as it was, was too solemn to suggest the perfect life. The Puritan ideal has to be supplemented with something else if it is to be held as a Christian aim through-out a lifetime."

42. Douglas Campbell, *The Puritan in Holland, England, and America,* (N. Y.: Harper and Brothers, 1892), Vol. II, p. 127.

43. Emil Legouis, *A History of English Literature,* (N. Y.: The Macmillan Company, 1927), p. 280.

44. George Saintsbury, *A History of English Criticism,* (N. Y.: Dodd, Mead, and Company, 1911), p. 91.

45. Sir Egerton Brydges, *Paradise Lost* . . . (Philadelphia, G. S. Appleton, 1851), p. xv.

46. Milton, *Op. Cit.,* Vol. XVIII, p. 207.

47. Alwin Thaler, *Shakspere's Silences,* (Cambridge: Harvard University Press, 1929), p. 210.

48. Milton, *Op. Cit.,* Vol. III, Part I, p. 239.

49. *Ibid.*, Vol. III, Part I, p. 300.

50. J. R. Green, *History Of The English People,* (N. Y.: Harper and Brothers, n. d.) Vol. III, pp. 9-11.

51. Richard Hooker was an exception to this. "Richard Hooker, an Anglican minister, the author of *Ecclesiastical Polity* (1594) was not only the first religious or philosophical writer of any importance in England, but one of the first good English prose writers. A disciple of the Greeks as well as of the Bible, he gives to his defence of Anglicanism a remarkable steadiness and force of expression." Paul Van Tieghem, *Outline Of The Literary History Of Europe Since The Renaissance,* (N. Y.: The Century Company, 1930), p. 79.

52. Sir Francis Bacon, *The Works of . . .,* (N. Y.: Hurd and Houghton, 1877), p. 438.

53. George Saintsbury, "Milton," *Cambridge History of English Literature,* Vol. VII (N. Y.: G. P. Putnam's Sons, 1911), pp. 134-135.

54. Masson, *Op. Cit.,* Vol. I, pp. 50-54.

55. Milton, *Op. Cit.,* Vol. VIII, p. 121.

56. *Ibid.,* Vol. VIII, p. 119.

57. *Ibid.,* Vol. XII, p. 27.

58. *Ibid.,* Vol. III, Part I, p. 235.

59. Masson, *Op. Cit.,* Vol. II, p. 506.

60. Mark Pattison, *Milton,* (N. Y.: Harper and Brothers, 1899), p. 69.

61. Milton, *Op. Cit.,* Vol. III, Part I, p. 5.

62. *Ibid.,* Vol. III, Part I, p. 79.

63. *Ibid.,* Vol. VIII, p. 129.

64. *Ibid.,* Vol. III, Part I, p. 242.

65. Pattison, *Op. Cit.,* pp. 56, 57.

66. Milton, *Op. Cit.,* Vol. III, Part I, p. 232.

67. Masson, *Op. Cit.,* Vol. III, p. 305.

68. Milton, *Op. Cit.,* Vol. II, Part II, p. 337.

69. *Ibid.,* Vol. II, Part II, p. 338.

70. Masson, *Op. Cit.,* Vol. III, p. 718.

71. Milton, *Op. Cit.,* Vol. V, p. 25.

72. Pattison, *Op. Cit.,* p. 103.

73. Samuel R. Gardiner, *History of The Commonwealth and Protectorate,* 1649-1656. London: Longmans, Green and Company, 1903, Vol. II, p. 17.

74. Milton, *Op. Cit.,* Vol. VII, p. 551.

75. *Ibid.,* Vol. VIII, p. 61.

76. Masson, *Op. Cit.,* Vol. V, pp. 581-587.

77. Wolfe, *Op. Cit.,* p. 273.

78. Hilaire Belloc, *Milton* (Philadelphia: J. B. Lippincott Company, 1935), p. 242.

79. Masson, *Op. Cit.,* Vol. V, pp. 658-659.

80. Milton, *Op. Cit.,* Vol. II, Part I, p. 179.

81. *Ibid.,* Vol. I, Part I, p. 19.

82. *Ibid.,* Vol. I, Part I, p. 21.

83. *Ibid.,* Vol. I, Part I, p. 19.

84. *Ibid.,* Vol. I, Part I, pp. 211, 213.

85. *Ibid.,* Vol. III, Part I, pp. 303-304.

86. *Ibid.,* Vol. I, Part I, p. 25.

87. *Ibid.,* Vol. I, Part I, p. 60.

88. Pattison, *Op. Cit.,* p. 13.

89. T. B. Macaulay, *The Works of* . . . (N. Y.: Longmans, Green and Company, 1897), Vol. V, Essay on *Milton,* pp. 22, 23.

90. Milton, *Op. Cit.,* Vol. I, Part I, p. 293.

91. E. M. W. Tillyard, *Milton,* (London: Chatto and Windus, 1930), p. 90.

92. Belloc, *Op. Cit.,* p. 16.

93. Paul Elmer More, *Shelburne Essays.* Fourth Series. (Boston: Houghton Mifflin Company, 1906), p. 239.

94. Oliver Elton, *The English Muse,* (London: G. Bell and Sons, 1936), p. 238.

95. More, *Op. Cit.,* p. 243.

96. G. R. Elliott, *The Cycle of Modern Poetry,* (Princeton: University Press, 1929), p. 182.

97. Plato, *The Republic,* Book IX, Paragraph 592, *Op. Cit.* See parallels and discussion above, pages xvi and xvii.

98. Milton, *Op. Cit.,* Vol. II, Part II, p. 399.

99. Belloc, *Op. Cit.,* p. 260.

100. Tillyard, *Op. Cit.,* p. 237.

101. C. S. Lewis, *A Preface to Paradise Lost* (Oxford: University Press, 1943) particularly Chapter II, "Is Criticism Possible?"

102. Tillyard, *Op. Cit.,* p. 237.

103. Tillyard, *Op. Cit.,* p. 239.

104. Tillyard, *Op. Cit.,* p. 297.

105. J. H. Hanford, *A Milton Handbook,* (N. Y.: F. S. Crofts and Company, 1936), p. 243.

106. Milton, *Op. Cit.,* Vol. III, Part I, p. 237.

107. *Ibid.,* Vol. II, Part II, p. 405.

108. *Loc. Cit.*

109. Tillyard, *Op. Cit.,* p. 323.

110. Milton, *Op. Cit.,* Vol. II, Part II, p. 477.

111. Masson, *Op. Cit.,* Vol. VI, p. 664.

112. *Ibid.,* Vol. VI, p. 670.
113. Milton, *Op. Cit.,* Vol. I, Part II, pp. 339, 340.
114. *Ibid.,* Vol. I, Part II. p. 350.
115. Milton, *Op. Cit.,* Vol. XVII, p. 427.
116. *Ibid.,* Vol. XIV, pp. 5-7.
117. Tillyard, *Op. Cit.,* p. 213.
118. Hanford, *Op. Cit.,* p. 106.
119. Belloc, *Op. Cit.,* p. 307.
120. Milton *Op. Cit.,* Vol. XIV, p. 7.
121. Milton, *Op. Cit.,* Vol. XIV, pp. 16, 17.
122. *Ibid.,* Vol. XIV, p. 25.
123. *Ibid.,* Vol. XIV, pp. 26, 27.
124. *Ibid.,* Vol. II, Part I, p. 217.
125. *Ibid.,* Vol. XIV, pp. 26-29.
126. *Ibid.,* Vol. II, Part I, pp. 160, 161.
127. *Ibid.,* Vol. II, Part I, pp. 81, 82.
128. *Ibid.,* Vol. II, Part I, p. 81.
129. See discussion above, pages 55 and 56.
130. *Ibid.,* Vol. II, Part II, pp. 381, 382.
131. *Ibid.,* Vol. XIV, pp. 64, 65.
132. *Ibid.,* Vol. II, Part I, p. 80.
133. *Ibid.,* Vol. II, Part I, pp. 81, 82.
134. *Ibid.,* Vol. II, Part II, p. 304.
135. *Ibid.,* Vol. XIV, p. 84, 85.
136. *Ibid.,* Vol. II, Part I, pp, 83, 84.
137. *Ibid.,* Vol. XIV, pp. 116, 117.
138. *Ibid.,* Vol. II, Part II, p. 397.
139. *Ibid.,* Vol. XIV, pp. 104, 105.
140. *Ibid.,* Vol. II, Part I, pp. 85, 86.
141. *Ibid.,* Vol. XIV, pp. 134, 135.
142. *Ibid.,* Vol. XIV, pp. 140, 141.
143. *Ibid.,* Vol. II, Part II, p. 272.
144. John, XIV, 10.
145. John, XVII, 21.
146. Milton, *Op. Cit.,* Vol. II, Part I, p. 165.
147. *Ibid.,* Vol. II, Part I, p. 173.
148. *Ibid.,* Vol. II, Part I, p. 173.
149. *Ibid.,* Vol. II, Part I, p. 202.
150. *Ibid.,* Vol. II, Part I, p. 209.
151. *Ibid.,* Vol. XIV, pp. 180, 181.
152. *Ibid.,* Vol. II, Part I, p. 91.
153. *Ibid.,* Vol. XIV, pp. 186, 187.
154. *Ibid.,* Vol. XIV, pp. 184, 185.

155. *Ibid.*, Vol. II, Part, I, p. 217.
156. *Ibid.*, Vol. II, Part I, p. 250.
157. *Ibid.*, Vol. XIV, pp. 210, 211.
158. *Ibid.*, Vol. XIV, pp. 212, 213.
159. *Ibid.*, Vol. II, Part II, p. 347.
160. *Ibid.*, Vol. II, Part II, p. 306.
161. *Ibid.*, Vol. XIV, pp. 188, 189.
162. *Ibid.*, Vol. II, Part I, p. 165.
163. *Ibid.*, Vol. XIV, pp. 228-231.
164. *Milton, Op. Cit.*, Vol. XIV, pp. 230, 231.
165. *Ibid.*, Vol. II, Part I, pp. 203, 204.
166. *Ibid.*, Vol. XIV, pp. 226, 227.
167. *Ibid.*, Vol. II, Part I, p. 204.
168. *Ibid.*, Vol. II, Part I, p. 168.
169. *Ibid.*, Vol. II, Part I, p. 202.
170. *Ibid.*, Vol. II, Part I, p. 218.
171. *Ibid.*, Vol. II, Part I, p. 88.
172. *Ibid.*, Vol. XIV, pp. 192, 193.
173. *Ibid.*, Vol. II, Part II, pp. 306, 307.
174. *Ibid*, Vol. XIV, pp. 188, 189.
175. *Ibid.*, Vol. II, Part I, p. 165.
176. *Ibid.*, Vol. XIV, pp. 366, 367.
177. *Ibid.*, Vol. II, Part I, p. 91.
178. *Ibid.*, Vol. XIV, pp. 402, 403.
179. *Ibid.*, Vol. XIV, 392-393.
180. *Ibid.*, Vol. XIV, pp. 376-377.
181. *Ibid.*, Vol. XIV, pp. 308-311.
182. *Ibid.*, Vol. II, Part I, p. 250.
183. *Loc. Cit.*
184. Williston Walker, *Op. Cit.*, page 74.
185. *Loc. Cit.*
186. *Loc. Cit.*
187. Milton, *Op. Cit.*, Vol. II, Part II, p. 411.
188. *Ibid.*, Vol. II, Part I, p. 88.
189. Isaiah, XLV, 6, 7. "That they may know from the rising of the sun, and from the west, that there is none beside me: I am Jehovah, and there is none else: I form the light, and create darkness."
190. *Ibid.*, Vol. XV, pp. 4,5.
191. *Ibid.*, Vol. II, Part I, p. 173.
192. *Ibid.*, Vol. XV, pp. 18, 19.
193. *Ibid.*, Vol. XV, pp. 22, 23.
194. *Ibid.*, Vol. II, Part I, p. 160.
195. *Ibid.*, Vol. XV, pp. 36-39.

196. *Ibid.*, Vol. II, Part I, p. 230.
197. *Ibid.*, Vol. XV, pp. 52, 53.
198. *Ibid.*, Vol. II, Part I, p. 246.
199. *Ibid.*, Vol. II, Part I, p. 245.
200. *Ibid.*, Vol. II, Part I, p. 243.
201. *Ibid.*, Vol. XV, pp. 18, 19.
202. *Ibid.*, Vol. XV, pp. 54, 55.
203. *Ibid.*, Vol. II, Part II, p. 398.
204. *Ibid.*, Vol. II, Part II, p. 9.
205. *Ibid.*, Vol. II, Part II, p. 401.
206. *Ibid.*, Vol. XV, pp. 64, 65.
207. *Ibid.*, Vol. II, Part I, pp. 81, 82.
208. *Ibid.*, Vol. XV, pp. 58, 59.
209. *Ibid.*, Vol. II, Part II, pp. 381, 382.
210. *Ibid.*, Vol. XV, pp. 72-75.
211. *Ibid.*, Vol. II, Part II, p. 395.
212. *Ibid.*, Vol. II, Part II, p. 280.
213. *Ibid.*, Vol. II, Part II, p. 396.
214. *Ibid.*, Vol. II, Part II, p. 399.
215. *Ibid.*, Vol. II, Part II, p. 392.
216. *Ibid.*, Vol. II, Part II, p. 401.
217. See the parallels and discussion above. *Treatise*, footnote
210 *Epic*, 211.
218. *Ibid.*, Vol. II, Part II, p. 395.
219. See parallels and discussion above. *Epic*, footnote 215.
220. *Ibid.*, Vol. XV, pp. 100-103.
221. *Ibid.*, Vol. II, Part I, pp. 100, 101.
222. *Ibid.*, Vol. II, Part I, p. 179.
223. *Ibid.*, Vol. II, Part I, p. 102.
224. *Ibid.*, Vol. II, Part I, p. 51.
225. *Ibid.*, Vol. II, Part I, p. 53.
226. *Ibid.*, Vol. II, Part I, p. 106.
227. *Ibid.*, Vol. II, Part I, p. 167.
228. *Ibid.*, Vol. II, Part I, p. 121.
229. *Ibid.*, Vol. II, Part I, p. 114.
230. *Ibid.*, Vol. II, Part I, pp. 233, 234.
231. *Ibid.*, Vol. II, Part I, p. 117.
232. *Ibid.*, Vol. II, Part I, p. 129.
233. *Ibid.*, Vol. II, Part II, p. 356.
234. *Ibid.*, Vol. XV, pp. 154, 155.
235. *Ibid.*, Vol. II, Part I, pp. 132, 133.
236. *Ibid.*, Vol. II, Part I, p. 123.
237. *Ibid.*, Vol. II, Part I, p. 123.

238. *Ibid.*, Vol. II, Part I, p. 114.
239. *Ibid.*, Vol. II, Part II, p. 306.
240. *Ibid.*, Vol. II, Part II, p. 292.
241. *Ibid.*, Vol. II, Part I, p. 84.
242. *Ibid.*, Vol. XV, pp. 180, 181.
243. *Ibid.*, Vol. II, Part I, p. 125.
244. *Ibid.*, Vol. XV, pp. 180, 181.
245. *Ibid.*, Vol. II, Part II, p. 305.
246. *Ibid.*, Vol. II, Part I, p. 124.
247. *Ibid.*, Vol. II, Part I, pp. 124, 125.
248. *Ibid.*, Vol. II, Part II, p. 271
249. *Ibid.*, Vol. II, Part II, p. 292.
250. *Ibid.*, Vol. II, Part II, p. 292.
251. *Ibid.*, Vol. II, Part II, p. 294.
252. *Ibid.*, Vol. II, Part II, pp. 295, 296.
253. *Ibid.*, Vol. II, Part I, p. 258.
254. Glibert Highet, *The Classical Tradition*, (Greek and Roman Influences On Western Literature), 1949, Oxford University Press, page 393.
255. *Ibid.*, Vol. II, Part I, p. 8.
256. *Ibid.*, Vol. II, Part II, p. 308.
257. *Ibid.*, Vol. II, Part II, p. 308.
258. *Ibid.*, Vol. II, Part II, pp. 334, 335.
259. *Ibid.*, Vol. XV, pp. 206, 207.
260. *Ibid.*, Vol. II, Part II, pp. 297, 298.
261. *Ibid.*, Vol. II, Part II, p. 300.
262. *Ibid.*, Vol. XV, pp. 214, 215.
263. *Ibid.*, Vol. II, Part II, p. 332.
264. *Ibid.*, Vol. II, Part II, p. 296.
265. *Ibid.*, Vol. XV, pp. 226-229.
266. *Ibid.*, Vol. II, Part II, p. 332.
267. *Ibid.*, Vol. XV, pp. 218, 219.
268. *Ibid.*, Vol. II, Part II, p. 334.
269. *Ibid.*, Vol. XV, pp. 250, 251.
270. *Ibid.*, Vol. II, Part II, p. 312.
271. *Ibid.*, Vol. XV, pp. 250, 251.
272. *Ibid.*, Vol. II, Part II, pp. 346, 347.
273. *Ibid.*, Vol. XV, pp. 256, 257.
274. *Ibid.*, Vol. II, Part I, p. 87.
275. *Ibid.*, Vol. XV, pp. 258, 259.
276. *Ibid.*, Vol. II, Part II, p. 392.
277. *Ibid.*, Vol. XV, pp. 280, 281.
278. *Ibid.*, Vol. II, Part II, p. 391.

279. *Ibid.,* Vol. XV, pp. 284, 285.
280. *Ibid.,* Vol. II, Part II, p. 306.
281. *Ibid.,* Vol. II, Part I, p. 83.
282. *Ibid.,* Vol. II, Part II, p. 346.
283. *Loc. Cit.*
284. Milton, *Op. Cit.,* Vol. XV, pp. 292, 293.
285. *Ibid.* Vol. II, Part I, pp. 87, 88.
286. *Ibid.,* Vol. XV, pp. 296, 297.
287. *Ibid.,* Vol. II, Part I, p. 88.
288. *Ibid.,* Vol. XV, pp. 300, 301.
289. *Ibid.,* Vol. II, Part I, p. 217.
290. *Ibid.,* Vol. II, Part II, pp. 392, 393.
291. *Ibid.,* Vol. II, Part II, p. 393.
292. *Ibid.,* Vol. II, Part II p. 394.
293. *Ibid.,* Vol. II, Part I, p. 88.
294. *Loc. Cit.*
295. *Ibid.,* Vol. XV, pp. 342, 343.
296. *Ibid.,* Vol. II, Part II, p. 392.
297. *Ibid.,* Vol. XV, pp. 346-349.
298. *Ibid.,* Vol. II, Part II, p. 394.
299. *Ibid.,* Vol. XV, pp. 348-351.
300. *Ibid.,* Vol. II, Part II, pp. 382, 383.
301. *Ibid.,* Vol. II,, Part I, p. 84.
302. *Ibid.,* Vol. XV. pp. 352-355.
303. *Ibid.,* Vol. XV, pp. 364, 365.
304. *Ibid.,* Vol. II, Part II, p. 397.
305. *Ibid.,* Vol. XV, pp. 366, 367.
306. *Ibid.,* Vol. II, Part II. p. 345.
307. *Ibid.,* Vol. II, Part II, p. 389.
308. *Ibid.,* Vol. XV, pp. 376, 377.
309. *Ibid.,* Vol. II, Part II, p. 311.
310. See above, page 141, *Treatise, Ibid.,* Vol. XV, 251 - 283. See above, page 142, *Epic, Ibid.,* Vol. II, Part II, pp. 346, 347.
311. *Ibid.,* Vol. II, Part II, pp. 346, 347.
312. See above, page 150, *Ibid.,* Vol. XV, pp. 366, 367.
313. See above, page 150, *Ibid.,* Vol. XV, pp. 342, 343, and *Epic, Ibid.* Vol. II, Pt. II, p. 392.
314. *Ibid.,* Vol. II, Part II, p. 343, 344.
315. *Ibid.,* Vol. II, Part II, p. 345.
316. *Ibid.,* Vol. XV, pp. 392, 393.
317. *Ibid.,* Vol. II, Part II, p. 351.
318. *Ibid.,* Vol. II, Part II, pp. 395, 396.
319. *Ibid.,* Vol. XV, pp. 406, 407.

267

320. *Ibid.*, Vol. II, Part II, p. 392.
321. *Ibid.*, Vol. II, Part I, pp. 87, 88.
322. *Ibid.*, Vol. II, Part II, p. 396.
323. *Ibid.*, Vol. II, Part II, p. 399.
324. *Ibid.*, Vol. II, Part II, pp. 376, 377.
325. *Ibid.*, Vol. II, Part II, pp. 388, 389.
326. *Ibid.*, Vol. II, Part I, pp. 87, 88.
327. *Ibid.*, Vol. II, Part II, p. 389.
328. *Ibid.*, Vol. II, Part II, p. 394.
329. John, VI. 56.
330. Milton, *Op. Cit.*, Vol. II, Part I, p. 217.
331. *Ibid.*, Vol. II, Part II, p. 393.
332. *Ibid.*, Vol. II, Part II, pp. 370, 371.
333. Genesis, III, 15.
334. I. John, III, 8.
335. Milton, *Op. Cit.*, Vol. II, Part II, p. 345.
336. *Ibid.*, Vol. II, Part II, p. 389.
337. *Ibid.*, Vol. II, Part II, p. 394.
338. *Loc. Cit.*
339. *Ibid.*, Vol. II, Part II, p. 396.
340. *Ibid.*, Vol. XVI, pp. 245-247.
341. *Ibid.*, Vol. II, Part I, p. 88.
342. *Ibid.*, Vol. II, Part II, pp. 396, 397.
343. *Ibid.*, Vol. II, Part II, pp. 396, 397.
344. *Ibid.*, Vol. II, Part II, p. 397.
345. *Ibid.*, Vol. XVI, pp. 326, 327.
346. *Ibid.*, Vol. II, Part II, p. 400.
347. Matthew, XXV, 34.
348. Matthew, XXV, 41.
349. Milton, *Op. Cit.*, Vol. II, Part I, pp. 88, 89.
350. *Ibid.*, Vol. II, Part II, pp. 397, 398.
351. *Ibid.*, Vol. II, Part II, p. 389.
352. *Ibid.*, Vol. II, Part II, p. 346.
353. *Ibid.*, Vol. II, Part II, pp. 345, 346.
354. *Ibid.*, Vol. II, Part II, p. 346.
355. *Ibid.*, Vol. II, Part II, p. 375.
356. *Ibid.*, Vol. II, Part I, p. 50.
357. *Ibid.*, Vol. II, Part I, p. 172.
358. *Ibid.*, Vol. II, Part II, p. 371.
359. *Ibid.*, Vol. II. Part II, p. 382.
360. *Ibid.*, Vol. II, Part II, p. 390.
361. *Ibid.*, Vol. XVII, pp. 212, 213.
362. *Ibid.*, Vol. XVII, pp. 212, 213.

363. *Ibid.*, Vol. II, Part II, p. 364.
364. *Ibid.*, Vol. XVII, pp. 212, 213.
365. *Ibid.*, Vol. II, Part I, p. 160.
366. *Ibid.*, Vol. XVII, pp. 216, 217
367. *Ibid.*, Vol. XVII, pp. 220, 221.
368. *Ibid.*, Vol. II, Part I, p. 253.
369. *Ibid.*, Vol. XVII, pp. 222, 223.
370. *Ibid.*, Vol. II, Part I, p. 257.
371. *Ibid.*, Vol. XVII, pp. 222, 223.
372. *Ibid.*, Vol. II, Part II, p. 339.
373. *Ibid.*, Vol. XVII, pp. 230, 231.
374. *Ibid.*, Vol. II, Part I, p. 155.
375. *Ibid.*, Vol. XVII, pp. 230, 231.
376. *Ibid.*, Vol. II, Part II, p. 311.
377. *Ibid.*, Vol. XVII, pp. 232, 233.
378. *Ibid.*, Vol. II, Part I, p. 248.
379. *Ibid.*, Vol. XVII, pp. 246, 247.
380. *Ibid.*, Vol. II, Part II, pp. 398, 399.
381. *Ibid.*, Vol. XVII, pp. 252, 253.
382. *Ibid.*, Vol. II, Part II, p. 358.
383. *Ibid.*, Vol. XVII, pp. 254, 255.
384. *Ibid.*, Vol. II, Part II, p. 363.
385. *Ibid.*, Vol. XVII, pp. 372, 373.
386. *Ibid.*, Vol. XVII, pp. 382, 383.
387. *Ibid.*, Vol. II, Part I, p. 155.
388. Masson, *Op. Cit.*, Vol. VI, p. 682.
389. George P. Fisher, *The Reformation*, (N. Y.: Charles Scribner's Sons, 1902), p. 460.
390. Romans VII, 19-24.
391. Augustine, *The Confessions of* . . . (N. Y.: E. P. Dutton and Company, 1913) page 144.
392. Walker, *Op. Cit.*, p. 337.
393. John Calvin, *The Institutes of the Christian Religion*, (Philadelphia: Presbyterian Board of Christian Education, 1936), Book II. Chapter I, Section VIII.
394. Archibald Alexander Hodge, *A Commentary on the Confession of Faith*, (Phila.: Presbyterian Board of Publication, 1923), pp. 147-161.
395. Milton, *Op. Cit.*, Vol. II, Part II, p. 399.
396. *Ibid.*, Vol. II, Part II, p. 341.
397. *Ibid.*, Vol. II, Part II, p. 477. Cf. discussion above, p. 61 ff.
398. Genesis II, 7.
399. Matthew X, 28.

400. II Corinthians V.
401. Augustine, *Op. Cit.*, p. 138.
402. Calvin, *Op. Cit.*, Book I, Chapter XV, Section II and III.
403. Hodge, *Op. Cit.*, p. 515.
404. Cf. discussion above, pp. 108, ff.
405. Milton, *Op. Cit.*, Vol. XV, pp. 226-229.
406. *Ibid.*, Vol. II, Part II, p. 332.
407. Calvin, *Op. Cit.*, Book I, Chapter XIII, Section I.
408. Hodge, *Op. Cit.*, p. 70. . .
409. Romans XII, 33.
410. Milton, *Op. Cit.*, Vol. XIV, pp. 30-33, Cf. discussion above. p. 74 ff.
411. Henry L. Mansel, *The Limits of Religious Thought* (Boston: Gould and Lincoln, 1859), pp. 220, 221.
412. Edwin Lewis, *A Philosophy of the Christian Revelation*, (N. Y.: Harper and Brothers, 1940), p. 178.
413. H. R. Mackintosh, *The Christian Apprehension of God*, (London: Student Christian Movement Press, 1929), pp. 204, 205.
414. Paul Tillich, *Religious Experience and Truth*, New York University Press, 1961. Section III, paragraph two.
415. John I, 1, 2.
416. Philippians II, 5, 6.
417. Calvin, *Op. Cit.*, Book I, Chapter XIII, Section VIII.
418. Hodge, *Op. Cit.*, p. 83.
419. Cf. discussion above, pages 84 ff.
420. Milton, *Op. Cit.*, Vol. II, Part II, pp. 306, 307.
421. J. C. Ayer, Jr., *A Source Book for Ancient Church History* (N. Y.: Charles Scribner's Sons, 1913), pp. 458-459. Pelagius wrote: "I am accustomed first of all to call attention to the capacity and character of human nature, and to show what it is able to accomplish; then from this to arouse the feelings of the bearer, that he may strive after different kinds of virtue . . . . just in this freedom in either direction, in this liberty toward either side, is placed the glory of our rational nature. Therein I say, consists the entire honor of our nature. therein its dignity; from this the very good merit praise, from this their reward. For there would be for those who always remain good no virtue if they had not been able to have chosen the evil. For since God wished to present to the rational creature the gift of voluntary goodness and the power of the free will, by planting in man the possibility of turning himself toward either side, He made His special gift the ability to be what he would be in order that he, being capable of good and evil, could do either and could turn his will to either of them."

Philip Schaff, *The Creeds of Christendom*, (N. Y. Harper and Brothers, 1877), Vol. I, p. 930. "Socinianism denies the following ecumenical doctrines: 1. The Trinity; 2. The Incarnation and eternal Divinity of Christ; 3. Original sin and guilt; 4. The vicarious atonement."

422. Milton, *Op. Cit.*, Vol. II, Part I, p. 165.

423. *Ibid.*, Vol. II, Part I, p. 88.

424. Calvin *Op. Cit.*, Book I, Chapter XIII, Section V.

425. Cf. discussion above p. 201.

426. Philip Schaff, *The Creeds of Christendom*, (N. Y. Harper and Brothers, 1896), Vol. II, p. 66.

427. Milton, *Op. Cit.*, Vol. XIV, pp. 402, 403. Cf. discussion above, p. 98.

428. *Ibid.*, Vol. XIV, pp. 376, 377. Cf. discussion above, p. 98 ff.

429. *Ibid.*, Vol. II, Part. I, p. 250. Cf. discussion above, p. 98 ff.

430. *Loc. Cit.*, Cf. discussion above, p. 98 ff.

431. In the work by A. V. Allen, *The Continuity of Christian Thought*, (N. Y.: Houghton Mifflin Company, 1894) there is set forth an important statement respecting the development of thought up to and inclusive of the Athanasian view of Christ's person. The theology of the Greek church had only Christ's person. The theology of the Greek church had only one dogma, that of the incarnation. This dogma was founded not upon any church council, but on reason or the Christian consciousness. Thus it was that Justin (A.D. 166) did not renounce philosophy as an evil thing when he became a Christian.

Christ for Justin was the eternal wisdom become incarnate. Clement of Alexandria (?-c.215) found in the highest exercise of reason the fruit of divine revelation. He made no distinction between what man discovers and what God reveals. Thus in the redemptive work of Christ, Clement saw no need for the restoration of a broken relationship between God and humanity. The relationship always had been there, and was obscured not broken by human ignorance and sin.

In the life and particularly the death of Christ, God gives evidence of his identification with man. The incarnation is for Clement the same as the atonement. Origen (186-254) put forth the doctrine of the eternal generation of the Son, maintaining that from all eternity, God, by a necessary law of His being, communicated himself to the Son. This doctrine allowed for two directions in theology. One maintained the subordination of the Son to the Father. The other asserted the coequality of the three persons of the Godhead. The latter was further developed by Athanasius (296-373), known as "the father of orthodoxy" — and finally adopted by the Council of Nicea as the orthodox position of the church respecting the Trinity.

432. In the work by Emil Brunner, *The Mediator* (N. Y.: The

Macmillan Company, 1934), p. 214, there is this statement: "For this is the difference between the Word and the Idea, that the Word is a real, sensible, and mental concrete event, and therefore is a personal communication. That we can only have fellowship through the Word — and not through spirit directly or through an idea of the Logos — reminds us that we are creatures and not the Creator. The fellowship of the Creator with the creature through the Word of the Creator, the real, spoken Word, the Word which is an actual temporal event; this is the revelation of which the Bible speaks, and of which the religious philosophy of Idealism, whether Greek or modern, does not speak."

433. *Ibid.*, p. 281.

434. *Ibid.*, p. 273, 274.

435, Milton, *Op. Cit.*, Vol. XIV, pp. 180, 181. Cf. discussion above, p. 90.

436. *Ibid.*, Vol. II, Part I, p. 91.

437. *Ibid.*, Vol. XIV, pp. 226-227, Cf. discussion above, p. 94.

438. *Ibid.*, Vol. II, Part I, p. 202, Cf. discussion above, p. 89.

439. Cf. discussion, page 205, footnote 431

440. Cf. discussion above, pages 204, and 205, footnote 431. Also, Williston Walker, *Op. Cit.*, p. 452.

441. Milton, *Op. Cit.*, Vol. II, Part I, pp. 346, 347.

442. Cf. discussion above, p. 202 ff.

443. Cf. discussion above, 205, 206.

444. Milton, *Op. Cit.*, Vol. XIV, pp. 308-311. Cf. discussion above p. 99 ff.

445. *Ibid.*, Vol. II, Part I, p. 250, Cf. discussion above, p. 99 ff.

446. *Loc. Cit.*

447. *Ibid.*, Vol. II, Part I, p. 88.

448. Lewis, *A Philosophy of* . . . p. 287.

449. Milton, *Op. Cit.*, Vol. II, Part I, p. 250.

450. *Ibid.*, Vol. II, Part I, p. 250.

451. Hodge, *Op. Cit.*, p. 190.

452. Brunner, *Op. Cit.*, pp. 490, 491.

453. Milton, *Op. Cit.*, Vol. II, Part II, pp. 346, 347.

454. *Ibid.*, Vol. II, Part II, pp. 381, 382. Cf. discussion above, p. 112.

455. Cf. discussion above, p. 114 ff.

456. Milton, *Op. Cit.*, Vol. II, Part II, pp. 295, 296.

457. *Ibid.*, Vol. II, Part II, p. 292.

458. Edwin Lewis, *A Christian Manifesto*, (N. Y. The Abingdon Press, 1934), p. 154.

459. Milton, *Op. Cit.*, Vol. II, Part II, p. 395.

460. Lewis, *A Christian Manifesto*, pp. 14, 15.

461. John Keats, *Letters* (London: Macmillan and Company, 1921). p. 314. For interpretation of this quotation see Murry, *Heroes of Thought*, (N. Y.: Julian Messner, Inc., 1938), pp. 142-145.

462. Milton, *Op. Cit.*, Vol. XIV, pp. 64, 65.

463. Milton, *Op. Cit.*, Vol. XIV, pp. 64, 65.

464. *Ibid.*, Vol. II, Part I, p. 152.

465. *Ibid.*, Vol. XIV, pp. 90, 91.

466. *Ibid.*, Vol. II, Part II, p. 399. Cf. discussion above, p. 192.

467. Lewis, *A Christian Manifesto* p. 137.

468. Cf. discussion above, p. 64 ff.

469. Milton, *Op. Cit.*, Vol. I, Part II, p. 350.

470. Cf. discussion above. Part. II, pp. 69 ff.

471. Milton, *Op. Cit.*, Vol. II, Part I, p. 81.

472. George Park Fisher, *History of Christian Doctrine* (N. Y.: Charles Scribner's Sons, 1923), p. 366 — "They (Latitudinarians) were appointed under the Long Parliament, and kept in their places by Cromwell. They manifest in its most tangible and effective form *a rising spirit of liberalism,* which was more stimulated than repressed by the work of the Westminster Assembly."

473. Cf. discussion above, pp. 20 ff.

474. *Ibid.*, Vol. II, Part II, p. 399.

475. *Loc. Cit.*

476. *Loc. Cit.*

477. *Loc. Cit.*

478. Frank E. Manuel, *Op. Cit.*, p. 298.

479. *Ibid.*, p. 296, 297.

480. *Loc. Cit.*

481. *Op. Cit.*, p. 262.

482. Mark 4:8.

483. Manuel, *Op. Cit.*, p. 264.

484. Milton, *Op. Cit.*, Vol. II, Part I, pp. 83, 84. Cf. discussion above, p. 114 ff.

485. Manuel *Op. Cit.*, p. 308.